AF841014

China 2020

Chandos
Asian Studies Series:
Contemporary Issues and Trends

Series Editor: Professor Chris Rowley,
Centre for Research on Asian Management, Cass Business School,
City University, UK; HEAD Foundation, Singapore
(email: c.rowley@city.ac.uk)

Chandos Publishing is pleased to publish this major Series of books entitled *Asian Studies: Contemporary Issues and Trends*. The Series Editor is Professor Chris Rowley, Director, Centre for Research on Asian Management, City University, UK and Director, Research and Publications, HEAD Foundation, Singapore.

Asia has clearly undergone some major transformations in recent years and books in the Series examine this transformation from a number of perspectives: economic, management, social, political and cultural. We seek authors from a broad range of areas and disciplinary interests: covering, for example, business/management, political science, social science, history, sociology, gender studies, ethnography, economics and international relations, etc.

Importantly, the Series examines both current developments and possible future trends. The Series is aimed at an international market of academics and professionals working in the area. The books have been specially commissioned from leading authors. The objective is to provide the reader with an authoritative view of current thinking.

New authors: we would be delighted to hear from you if you have an idea for a book. We are interested in both shorter, practically orientated publications (45,000+ words) and longer, theoretical monographs (75,000–100,000 words). Our books can be single, joint or multi author volumes. If you have an idea for a book, please contact the publishers or Professor Chris Rowley, the Series Editor.

Dr Glyn Jones
Chandos Publishing
Email: gjones@chandospublishing.com
www.chandospublishing.com

Professor Chris Rowley
Cass Business School, City University
Email: c.rowley@city.ac.uk
www.cass.city.ac.uk/faculty/c.rowley

Chandos Publishing: Chandos Publishing is an imprint of Woodhead Publishing Limited. The aim of Chandos Publishing is to publish books of the highest possible standard: books that are both intellectually stimulating and innovative.

We are delighted and proud to count our authors from such well known international organisations as the Asian Institute of Technology, Tsinghua University, Kookmin University, Kobe University, Kyoto Sangyo University, London School of Economics, University of Oxford, Michigan State University, Getty Research Library, University of Texas at Austin, University of South Australia, University of Newcastle, Australia, University of Melbourne, ILO, Max-Planck Institute, Duke University and the leading law firm Clifford Chance.

A key feature of Chandos Publishing's activities is the service it offers its authors and customers. Chandos Publishing recognises that its authors are at the core of its publishing ethos, and authors are treated in a friendly, efficient and timely manner. Chandos Publishing's books are marketed on an international basis, via its range of overseas agents and representatives.

Professor Chris Rowley: Dr Rowley, BA, MA (Warwick), DPhil (Nuffield College, Oxford) is Subject Group leader and the inaugural Professor of Human Resource Management at Cass Business School, City University, London, UK, and Director of Research and Publications for the HEAD Foundation, Singapore. He is the founding Director of the multi-disciplinary and internationally networked Centre for Research on Asian Management (http://www.cass.city.ac.uk/cram/index.html) and Editor of the leading journal *Asia Pacific Business Review* (http://www.tandf.co.uk/journals/titles/13602381.asp). He is well known and highly regarded in the area, with visiting appointments at leading Asian universities and top journal Editorial Boards in the UK, Asia and the US. He has given a range of talks and lectures to universities, companies and organisations internationally with research and consultancy experience with unions, business and government, and his previous employment includes varied work in both the public and private sectors. Professor Rowley researches in a range of areas, including international and comparative human resource management and Asia Pacific management and business. He has been awarded grants from the British Academy, an ESRC AIM International Study Fellowship and gained a 5-year RCUK Fellowship in Asian Business and Management. He acts as a reviewer for many funding bodies, as well as for numerous journals and publishers. Professor Rowley publishes extensively, including in leading US and UK journals, with over 370 articles, books, chapters and other contributions.

Bulk orders: some organisations buy a number of copies of our books. If you are interested in doing this, we would be pleased to discuss a discount.
Please email info@chandospublishing.com or telephone +44 (0) 1993 848726.

China 2020

The next decade for the People's Republic of China

EDITED BY
KERRY BROWN

CHANDOS PUBLISHING

Oxford Cambridge Philadelphia New Delhi

Chandos Publishing
TBAC Business Centre
Avenue 4
Station Lane
Witney
Oxford OX28 4BN
UK
Tel: +44 (0) 1993 848726
Email: info@chandospublishing.com
www.chandospublishing.com

Chandos Publishing is an imprint of Woodhead Publishing Limited

Woodhead Publishing Limited
80 High Street
Sawston
Cambridge
CB22 3HJ
UK
Tel: +44(0)1223 499140
Fax: +44(0)1223 832819
www.woodheadpublishing.com

First published in 2010

ISBN:
978-0-08-101740-1
ISBN:
978 0 85709 147 5

British Library Cataloguing-in-Publication Data.
A catalogue record for this book is available from the British Library.

Typeset by RefineCatch Limited, Bungay, Suffolk

Transferred to Digital Printing in 2016

To Kalley

Contents

Foreword

As a relative newcomer to appreciating the importance of China to UK policy I have of necessity required to read a fair number of books on China over the last few years. Inevitably there is somewhat of a variation in the quality of the output. Some are in the style of a business travelogue, others warning of one or other form of impending doom and some others of real merit and utility. This work is one of those last. It not only provides a number of authoritative analyses but also is directed very pointedly at the critical issues that confront policymakers outside of China. What is helpful is the absence of any particular 'line' being advanced and yet there is a coherent appreciation from a number of different angles germane to policy.

As an aid to understanding a highly complex society that has for too long been something of a terra incognita for most UK policymakers, it is invaluable. The insights it offers into the world view of and pressures on the Chinese Communist Party are both thought-provoking and first class in their presentation. The tendency in certain other quarters to see China either as a threatening monolith or alternatively as a society tottering towards internal collapse should not survive a reading of this book. And while policymakers will benefit from a reading of this book, foreign investors, current and potential, will also find a reading repays the time taken. Although many business people appreciate that the state is ever present in China the underlying political imperatives and how they work through are subtly analysed in the early chapters.

Although my acquaintance with matters military is sketchy at best I found the chapter on the People's Liberation Army a balanced instruction and a counterweight to some of the more vivid alarms that are sounded from time to time. Separately the examination of China's policy on the environment explains how more sophisticated policies are in play than the picture of heedless rush for growth sometimes portrayed in climate change debates in the West.

As my personal interest goes beyond the major cities in the east of China I was particularly interested in the analysis of the western regions and their importance to an understanding of the development of the PRC.

The chapter on Rule of Law should be required reading before any attempt to enter into legal relationships and, even more importantly perhaps, any legal proceedings in China. No matter how many times Western lawyers take on board the distinctly different concept of rule of law in China I have frequently encountered a tendency to revert to imposing a Western legal framework on legal questions. This is usually a profound error which this chapter should at least help to dispel.

'Soft power', which the US has perhaps not developed as much as recent proponents of the theory might have anticipated, provides the basis of a chapter which suggests among other points that few political concepts are genuinely new. The discussion of the concept from Confucius forward to the present day informs this debate in an attractive and engaging manner.

Dr Kerry Brown is to be congratulated for assembling a range of contributors who cover most of the critical issues facing today's policymakers, each bringing to bear their own particular assessments of the People's Republic. Policymakers and others will benefit from a reading of this both scholarly and pragmatic work.

Neil Davidson QC, Baron Davidson of Glen Clova
Former Advocate General for Scotland

Preface

Ten years is barely any time at all. In the great sweep of Chinese history, it hardly registers. Why, therefore, have the hubris to present essays on where China will be in a mere ten years' time? After all, governments and academics are already working out their scenarios for 2030, or 2040. To them, 2020 is old news.

The scale of what the Chinese are going to do, and the rate at which they are trying to do it, are two very good reasons why a ten-year window into the future is reasonable. In many ways, what is going to happen in China needs to be tracked year by year, rather than decade by decade. Even a book on China in 2015 would be looking at a place with, on current trajectories, a huge increase in GDP, further significant urbanisation, and great international integration. No country in the world at the moment is undergoing a more dynamic process of reinvention, rebalancing and reform.

In 2000, Chatham House produced a report called 'The Winds of Change' in which a group of policymakers, business people and military officials tried to set out what would be happening in the next 20 years. Needless to say, no one foresaw September 11th, or the further wars in the Middle East or Afghanistan. There was already some inkling of the profound impact of the Internet on global society and the economy. But there was no sense that by 2008 the wheels would come off the global economy and that the economies which were thriving in 2000, and lecturing Asian countries just emerging from the regional recession from 1998, would themselves be saddled by public debt and just limping out of the worst recession since the 1930s.

The case of China is the most challenging of all. In 2000, it had still not joined the World Trade Organization (WTO). The succession of leaders after Jiang Zemin and Zhu Rongji was still not entirely clear, nor was there complete confidence that the transition process would be smooth. The impact of vast lay-offs from the State Owned Enterprise (SOE) sector were still being absorbed in society, with real fears that there might be greater unrest. In 1998, the late Gerald Segal could write his celebrated and widely debated essay, 'Does China Matter', wondering aloud whether, like Brazil, the People's Republic of China (PRC) had a great potential, and always would. He famously declared that the Chinese market was no greater than Belgium's.[1]

China's entry to the WTO, in fact, is a good case study of how pessimistic many were about the country's ability to weather the coming competition from multinational companies and global economic forces which were about to finally get access to many of China's key markets. *The Economist* magazine gave a dystopic view of how well China would fare, predicting that it was in line for some tough days ahead. Nicholas Lardy, the American economist, focused on the huge problems in China's banking sector in his *China's Unfinished Economic Revolution*, looking in particular at bad debts that the banks were still carrying, and the huge problems within the financial sector.[2] As if to prove everyone's pessimism, in late 1999 one of the major state investment corporations in Guangzhou collapsed.

Many of the essays in this collection set out exactly where China is today before looking into the future. They make clear that, for all the challenges the country has faced since 2000, few would have seen how strongly it would stand in a mere decade. It is now the world's second largest economy, the world's largest exporter, the world's largest holder of foreign currency reserves, the second largest destination for inward investment, and the largest emitter of greenhouse gases. There are dozens of other first places it holds, in terms of its use of energy, natural metals and minerals, and growth rates. The bellicose attitude towards Taiwan under the late Jiang Zemin presidency has been replaced by the signature, in June 2010, of a huge Economic Cooperation Framework Agreement between the two. China has held a successful Olympics in 2008, a six-month Expo in Shanghai in 2010, and has continued to integrate into the global economy, with over half a billion mobile phone users, and 350 million on the Internet. A million of its young have studied abroad, and unlike in 2000, they are returning to China rather than staying away. Millions of Chinese travel, and many are starting to invest outside of China. Chinese consumption, in 2010, is seen as being one of the most important areas of potential growth in a world which has seen little but stagnation elsewhere.

Bold predictions of China's imminent collapse, by commentators like Gordon Chang, have so far proved wrong.[3] So too have worrying fears for China's desire to start flexing its military muscle in the region. On the whole, as some of the essays will show, it has been keen to be a cooperative member of the international community. Those who wondered if the

Chinese Communist Party (CCP) might, under Hu Jintao, usher in major new reforms and allow more political opposition have seen, in fact, perhaps an ever more repressive environment. As of 2010, the Communist Party remains master of all it surveys, and has never looked in better health. The huge enigma of an economy which embraces the market, and often acts as if wild capitalism rules, and yet maintains its highly controlled political system where one party enjoys a monopoly on power, remains. It is this that gives China its ability to fascinate and infuriate, simply because it does not obey the rules.

There are already many thousands of books on China, so anything new needs to contain a justification for why it has been written, and what if offers. In this collection I have tried to achieve two things. One is simply to bring the perspectives of relatively new writers to a wider audience. Most of the authors of this collection are here in print for the first time. They come from backgrounds as diplomats, lawyers, journalists or students. Along with my own contributions, three of the chapters that follow have been written by former members of the British Foreign and Commonwealth Office (FCO). Peter Wood served several times in Beijing, in the 1980s and 2000s. Kate Westgarth is currently on sabbatical from the FCO, but has a background in China reaching back to the mid 1980s. Tim Summers served in Hong Kong, and then as Consul General in Chongqing. They therefore bring unique experiences in framing their study and understanding of contemporary China, and these have quite obviously informed what they write.

My second objective in this book, building on the unique background of the authors, is to approach each aspect of modern China and its next ten years from the standpoint of a policymaker. The overriding question hovering behind all these various treatments is simply how can policymakers, in the EU, the US, or any other country for that matter, factor China and the risks and opportunities it presents into their own bilateral and multilateral thinking. This book has therefore a strongly practical bent. It is written not as an academic exercise, but by people who have had to deal with China as real policymakers in the real world, and therefore know how to give what they write about the country a major reality check.

I am glad that the other contributors also have very specific experiences within which to frame their approach to China. Elizabeth Corrin has worked for a top UK law firm in China, and brings this experience to her analysis of its current challenges of creating a rule of law, in a society where in fact many assumptions are to place politics above law. Victoria Tuke is a student looking at the issue of China's 'soft power', and its increasing role in the modern world, largely through huge investments into Confucian Institutes which have started to appear across the globe. Not surprisingly, the Beijing Olympics in 2008 figures prominently in her analysis, with all of the ambiguity and mixed messages that it conveyed. Gary Li of the International Institute of Strategic Studies takes a long, hard look at the role of the military in contemporary China, and shows the areas in which China's hard power has grown strong, along with the real challenges it faces in the years ahead in order to meet its key strategic needs. Jonathan Watts, based in Beijing for a number of years as the correspondent for *The Guardian*, sets out a powerful, disturbing vision of how China's green agenda and its success or failure will have a massive impact on the world in the next decade. China's battle with sustainability is going to be a key global story up to 2020, and one of the main areas where the world and China will need to work together.

None of these essays has aimed to be either pessimistic or optimistic, but to look realistically at what exists now, and what is likeliest to happen in the coming decade. In the space of only ten years, China will be hitting some major milestones. Demographically, it will be ageing, and its gender imbalance will be getting more dramatic. It will continue to be a country undergoing huge processes of urbanisation. Its energy use will soar, remaining predominantly reliant on fossil fuels, and that means its environmental problems will also grow graver. Its economy is likely to grow, but needs to achieve increasingly complex outcomes – and its political system will have to undergo at least one major power transition in 2012, and then some huge readjustment as it tries to maintain consensus and stability over an increasingly complex, unequal and contentious society.

Policymakers and those engaged in China (and, in many ways, that means all of us) are going to have to be well informed, and get our framework right, as we seek to engage with this immense new global force. All the varied perspectives here agree perhaps on one thing above all others – that China's importance is going to increase, and that the only policy which is not going to work is one which ignores, or underestimates, China's impact. We hope that at least some of the insights and ideas here can help in the complex challenge of getting China right in the decade ahead, so that in ten years' time, when we might reassemble to write *China 2030*, our task will be much easier!

Kerry Brown
Charing, Kent
July 2010

Notes

1. Gerald Segal, *Foreign Affairs*, September/October 1999.
2. Nicholas R. Lardy, *China's Unfinished Economic Revolution*, Brookings Institute Press, Washington, DC, 1998.
3. Gordon C. Chang, *The Coming Collapse of China*, Random House, New York, 2001.

Acknowledgements

I would like to thank John Everard and Stanley Crossick for detailed comments on earlier drafts of this work. I would also like to thank Glyn Jones and his team at Chandos for commissioning and then steering this work to its conclusion.

List of abbreviations

AD	Air Defence
ALL	Administrative Litigation Law
APC	Armoured Personnel Carrier
ASAT	Anti-Satellite Weapon
ASBM	Anti-Ship Ballistic Missile
ASEAN	Association of South East Asian Nations
ASW	Anti-Submarine Warfare
AWACS	Air Warning and Control System
BMD	Ballistic Missile Defence
BRIC	Brazil, Russia, India and China
C4ISR	Command, Control, Communications, Computers, Intelligence, Surveillance and Reconnaissance
CCP	Chinese Communist Party
CDIC	Central Discipline Inspection Commission
CMC	Central Military Commission
CNO	Computer Network Operations
COO	Country of origin
CYL	Communist Youth League
DPP	Democratic People's Party (Taiwan)
DPRK	Democratic People's Republic of Korea
ELINT	Electronic Signals Intelligence
ERA	Explosive Reactive Armour
EU	European Union
EW	Electronic Warfare
FCO	Foreign and Commonwealth Office
GA	Group Army
GDP	Gross Domestic Product
GSD	General Staff Department
HDI	Human Development Index
ICBM	Intercontinental Ballistic Missile
IFV	Infantry Fighting Vehicle
ILD	International Liaison Department

IRBM	Intermediate Range Ballistic Missile
KMT	Kuomintang (Chinese Nationalist Party) (Taiwan)
LACM	Land Attack Cruise Missile
MBT	Main Battle Tank
MD	Military District
MLR	Multiple Rocket Launcher
MOOTW	Military Operations Other Than War
MR	Military Region
MRBM	Medium Range Ballistic Missile
NCO	Non-Commissioned Officer
NDRC	National Development and Reform Commission
NGO	Non-Government Organization
NPC	National People's Congress
ODI	Overseas Direct Investment
OSINT	Open Source Intelligence
PACOM	Pacific Command (US)
PAP	People's Armed Police
PBSC	Politburo Standing Committee
PLA	People's Liberation Army
PLAAF	People's Liberation Army Air Force
PLAN	People's Liberation Army Navy
PLANAF	People's Liberation Army Naval Air Force
PRC	People's Republic of China
RRU	Rapid Reaction Unit
SAC	Second Artillery Corps
SAFE	State Administration for Foreign Exchanges
SAM	Surface to Air Missile
SASAC	State-owned Assets Supervision and Administration Commission
SCO	Shanghai Cooperation Organisation
SFA	State Forestry Administration
SIGINT	Signals Intelligence
SLBM	Submarine-launched Ballistic Missile
SLOC	Sea Lines of Communication
SOE	State-Owned Enterprise
SRBM	Short Range Ballistic Missile
SSBN	Ballistic Missile Submarine
WTO	World Trade Organization
WZC	War Zone Campaign

About the authors

Kerry Brown is Senior Fellow on the Asia Programme at Chatham House. He previously worked as a diplomat for the FCO, serving in London and Beijing. He is the author of *The Purge of the Inner Mongolian People's Party in the Cultural Revolution in China 1967–1969* (Global Oriental), *Struggling Giant: China in the 21st Century* (Anthem), *The Rise of the Dragon: Chinese Inward and Outward Investment Flows in the Reform Period* (Chandos), *Friends and Enemies: The Past, Present and Future of the Communist Party of China* (Anthem) and *Ballot Box China* (Zed). He is currently working on a biography of Hu Jintao.

Elizabeth Corrin works as a solicitor with a leading UK law firm and has worked for law firms in both Beijing and London. She is a graduate of Cambridge University and read Chinese Law at the University of Inner Mongolia.

Gary Li is a Research Analyst based at the International Institute for Strategic Studies (IISS). He has also previously worked at the Royal United Services Institute (RUSI) as well as being an associate of King's College London. He has an MSc from the LSE as well as an MA from the University of Glasgow. He has worked extensively on Chinese security issues and has been responsible for the research of the *IISS Military Balance* as well as contributing to the IISS journal *Survival*. He has published numerous articles on the PLA as well as broader China-related issues, such as the traditional and non-traditional security implications of the continued rise of the Chinese economy. He is currently focusing his research on the escalating territorial disputes in the South China Sea.

Tim Summers was British Consul-General in Chongqing (south-west China) from 2004 to 2007. He is now based in Hong Kong, where he engages in research, teaching and consultancy on China. His PhD thesis examined the regional and national relationships of the south-western province of Yunnan.

Victoria Tuke is a PhD student at the University of Warwick. For her Masters in International Relations (Warwick), awarded in 2008, her dissertation looked at China's soft power strategy during the countdown to the Beijing Olympics, a subject on which she continues to write. Her current doctoral thesis analyses Japanese foreign policy towards India in the Department for Politics and International Studies. She lives in London.

Jonathan Watts is environment correspondent for *The Guardian* and has been based in Beijing since 2003. He is the author of *When a Billion Chinese Jump* (Faber).

Kate Westgarth previously worked in the British Foreign Office in a number of positions related to China. She is currently on sabbatical, and based at the Chinese Academy of Social Sciences.

Peter Wood is an independent analyst and consultant based in Hong Kong. He previously worked for the British Foreign Office, serving as political counsellor in Beijing, before joining HSBC.

The contributers may be contacted via the publishers.

RUSSIA
KAZAKHSTAN
MONGOLIA
KYRGYSTAN
PAKISTAN
CHINA
Heilongjiang
Qiqihar
Harbin
Jixi
Jilin
Changchung
Jilin
Nei Mongol
Fuxin
Sheinyang
Liaoning
NORTH KOREA
SOUTH KOREA
Sea of Japan
JAPAN
Karamay
Urumqi
Korla
Hami
Kashi
Xinjiang
Hotan
Qiemo
Yumen
Hohhot
Baolou
Beijing
Beijing*
Tianin
Tianjin
Dalian
Hebei
Shijlazhuang
Taiyuan
Shanxi
Yinchuan
Ningxia
Golmud
Dinghai
Xining
Gansu
Jinan
Taian
Shandong
Qingdao
Yellow Sea
Zhengzhou
Kaifeng
Henan
Xian
Shaanxi
Jiangsu
Nanjing
Hefei
Anhui
Shanghai
Shanghai
Xizang
Mianyang
Chengdu
Sichuan
Chongqing
Zigong
Hubei
Wuhan
Hangzhou
Ningbo
East China Sea
NEPAL
Lhasa
BHUTAN
Yueyang
Changsha
Nanchang
Zhejiang
Wenzhou
Jiangxi
Hunam
Guizhou
Dukou
Guiyang
Fuzhou
Fujian
Taipei
T'ai-chung
Taiwan
T'ai-nan
Kao-Hsiung
INDIA
BANGLA-DESH
Kunming
Yunnan
Guangxi
Guangdong
Xiamen
Shantou
Guangzhou
Nanning
Hong Kong
Bay of Bengal
MYANMAR
VIETNAM
LAOS
THAILAND
Haikou
Hainan
South China Sea

China in 2020: the leadership and the Party

Kate Westgarth[1]

To attempt to discuss how the Chinese Communist Party (CCP) and the Chinese leadership might look in 2020 seems courageous, if not foolhardy. After all, Western predictions about China's future are notable for their inaccuracy. In the aftermath of the Tiananmen protests in 1989 there was a general consensus in the first place that the regime could not survive long, and, when that proved to be inaccurate, that the cost of perceived repression would be economic growth and modernisation. Western and Western-based Chinese pundits have been foretelling China's imminent collapse for the 20-odd ensuing years – but, so far at least, the PRC has confounded them all. So, in a departure from tradition, this chapter will not consider the future of the Party through a Western prism but through what Chinese Party members – in particular the current Chinese leadership – are saying about their own plans, fears, ideals and predictions for the future. It is also written on the assumption that Party rule will persist in 2020: to assume otherwise would suggest that consultation of a crystal ball is more appropriate than seeking truth from fact. Given the slow, cautious and incremental nature of reform and change in the Chinese system thus far, it also seems safe to say that moves proposed now are likely to take us well on the way to 2020 before we see their full implementation, or can judge their impact and assess their success. To put it another way, 2003 saw the first serious mention of what became Hu Jintao's theories of Harmonious Society and the Outlook on Scientific Development. Seven years later, they are both still very much with us.

The background

Despite the CCP's reputation for opacity, the Chinese leadership has recently shown a remarkable willingness to discuss the Party's future. Indeed, a few days after the road map for Party building and ideology for the early twenty-first century was explicitly set out by Hu Jintao in his speech to the Fourth Plenum of the 17th Party Congress in September 2009, the CCP International Liaison Department (ILD) held an unprecedented briefing for foreign journalists and diplomats. Perhaps disappointingly for the hosts – who had taken the trouble to field Professor Wang Changjiang, a top Party building expert from the Central Party School – interest from the invited foreigners reportedly focused on the non-appointment of Vice-President Xi Jinping to the Central Military Commission rather than on the nitty-gritty of Party building (*Ta Kung Pao, 23 September 2009*), but the message was nevertheless clear. The 'Decision on a Number of Issues in Strengthening and Improving Party-building in the New Situation' was intended to be highly significant.

So what exactly went on at the Fourth Plenum? Although the full speeches made by Hu and Xi have not been published (extracts from Hu's appeared in a Xinhua report of 18 September 2009), we know that only those two made significant speeches. Hu first read out most of the Decision and was immediately followed by Xi, who provided the customary explanation of how the decision was drafted. This was significant in two respects, firstly in underlining the importance of Xi's position as responsible for Party internal affairs as head of the Secretariat and secondly, by extension, as secure in his position as heir apparent to the position of General Secretary of the CCP. The issues surrounding leadership succession will be considered later. For now, let's concentrate on the contents of the 'Decision', the circumstances that led to its adoption and the blueprint for the Party's immediate future that emerged from the Plenum.

A learning-oriented Marxist party

In his speech, Hu Juntao was explicit that the CCP's goal in the twenty-first century should be on the one hand the continued 'sinicisation of Marxism' (a concept first identified by Mao in the 1930s) and on the other 'rendering Marxism timely and popular.'[2] In an interview with the *New York Times* two days later, Central Party School political scientist Gao Xinmin characterised Hu's stated aim of popularising Marxism as a 'theoretical breakthrough' and described the CCP's intent to construct a 'learning-oriented Marxist political party'. There is a tendency among many Western analysts to pass rapidly (and cynically) over any discussion of CCP Marxist theory as irrelevant or essentially retrospective and conservative, and, as Cheng Li has noted, to consider the concept of intra-Party democracy to be little more than expedient rhetoric, with little real substance.[3] Yet the evident importance placed on these concepts by the leadership strongly suggests a real rather than a merely rhetorical value, which we should consider seriously.

On the theoretical front, the most important new thinking to come out of the Plenum is the new political campaign, which looks set to influence the inner life of the Party at least up to 2020 – the construction of a learning-oriented Marxist party (*jianshe xuexi xing zhengdang*). Since the Plenum, the senior leadership has busied itself with promoting the new concept. For example, Xi Jinping spoke on the subject at a CPS conference 'to actively encourage the building of a learning-oriented Marxist party', recommending the study of socialist theory with Chinese characteristics and applying the core values of socialism;[4] Li Changchun further expounded on it when he launched the publication of new versions of *The Works of Marx and Engels* and *The Specialised Works of Lenin*;[5] the CCP General Office issued its 'Opinions on Promoting the Building of Learning-Oriented Party Organisations' in February 2010, combined with a circular containing detailed implementation instructions;[6] and *Qiushi* on 16 March 2010 commented on 'A Major and Urgent Strategic Task – On Efforts to Build a Learning-oriented Marxist party'.

The last document provides some insight into the problems the campaign is intended to address, commenting that, while overall the Party is up to the task of governance, there remain some serious unresolved issues:

> Some leading groups don't make enough effort to promote Scientific Development, or don't have the ability to deal with complex issues, and some grassroots organisations are weak and lazy. Some cadres do not have firm ideals and beliefs; some are content with the status quo, lead a vain and unchallenging life and lack a pioneering and creative attitude; some have a weak sense of purpose, show strong signs of individualism, and display formalism and bureaucracy; a small number abuse power for personal gain and are corrupt.

Part of the solution to these problems is a return to the classroom, although the author is well aware that there may be some resistance:

> Some cadres lack a sense of urgency and a sense of responsibility. Some rely on old skills, and don't care that they don't have enough ability to cope with rapidly developing and increasingly difficult tasks; some set work against learning, separate learning from work, and regard learning as an imposition; some are flighty, impetuous and restless, cannot concentrate on study, and are not interested in it; some focus on paperwork in office hours and parties after work, then claim they have no time to study.

But a return to the Marxist classics, Mao Zedong thought, Deng Xiaoping theory, the Three Represents and (particularly) Scientific Development theory is only a partial answer. Textbook learning, and analysis of how Marxist theory can be adapted to fit contemporary circumstances are essential, but the campaign has another facet. Li Changchun made it clear that enthusing the public about contemporary Chinese Marxism is also part of the deal:

> We must stick to being grounded in the masses, satisfy the demands of the public, respond to the concerns of the public, and solve the problems that vex the public, speak clearly about profound theory using plain and real language, explain deep truths in ways that the masses are willing to accept and do a better job of getting scientific theory to the people and into their hearts.

The points about clear speech, plain and real language and accessible presentation have been the focus of another speech by Xi Jinping, again to the Central Party School, extracts from which were published in the *People's Daily* (*Renmin Ribao*) on 14 May 2010. Once again, cadres were directed both to look back to the classics – ancient Chinese literature in this case – in order to make their communications simple and concise, and to learn 'colloquial wisdom' from the public in order to make their speeches and articles more accessible. If current rhetorical styles continued to proliferate, they were warned, the Party's authority would be undermined and its officials would be increasingly isolated from the public. Xi also suggested some reasons for the failings of cadres in this area:

- Some lacked knowledge, experience and skill, and were unable to say anything useful or new.
- Some were lazy, failed to undertake independent research and cribbed from existing documents.

- Some tried to demonstrate alignment with the Centre by slavishly copying official documents.
- Some thought long speeches were a sign of devotion to their work, or that long speeches showed respect to their audience.
- Some were irresponsible and read out what their speech writers provided without engaging their brains.
- And some thought empty words, clichés and flattery were safest because they couldn't be wrong.

Li Jingtian, executive vice-president of the Central Party School, had further suggestions to improve cadres' work style which one imagines will prove popular if adopted, in particular fewer meetings, unscripted speeches, limits on speech time, and a more tolerant work environment to enable officials to improve their performance. Less popular could be his proposal that evaluation of officials' drafting and speechmaking performance should be included in their annual Party appraisals.

But all of the above points to the conclusion that the Party is painfully aware that its traditional behaviours, presentation, communication style and work methods are no longer fit for purpose. It recognises that a major task for the first years of this century is to bring the Party into the modern world, while maintaining an awareness of, and close connection to, its history, its roots and its ideological background. The experience of the Eastern European communist parties continues to ring alarm bells for the CCP. As the *Qiushi* article has it: 'Some experienced parties which were once powerful and led states over a long period of time became stale and no longer of interest, and an important reason for this is that they stuck to old ways, stood still and refused to make progress, and were conservative and rigid.' The General Office 'Opinion' is open about the fact that 'there are a lot of things we are not familiar with, still do not understand and still do not know'. In this document, a new urgency is accorded to the customary exhortations to 'keep abreast of the times'. The Party is aware that the speed with which circumstances can change in a globalised world requires a new dynamic and better-informed officials, competent to deal with issues arising in 'the modern market economy, contemporary international relations, contemporary social management and contemporary information technology'. China is in danger of being left behind by 'the rapid progress of science and technology and the rapid pace of knowledge creation and innovation'. Creativity and innovation are recognised increasingly to be 'the core of a country's comprehensive national power and international competitive power'. Should China fail to rise to the challenge, it will 'inevitably lag behind'.

Another focus of the Opinion is the need for better conflict resolution, particularly over issues 'most directly related to the most direct interests of the people' and where the Party and the masses are in conflict. This aspect of the campaign was highlighted in interviews with senior Party officials in Beijing in June 2010 as being one of its key points, one which had been flagged up by a series of provincial inspection tours by central Party officials over the last 18 months. Special mention is made of issues arising from the impact of the global financial crisis, and of the 'bureaucratic and formalistic work styles which arouse strong resentment among the masses'. But despite the problems in Tibet and Xinjiang over the last two years, no particular emphasis is laid on ethnic or religious conflicts.

It seems likely, therefore, that over the next ten years learning-oriented cadres will rise within the ranks of the party. An item in the CCP news section of *People's Daily* online on 26 May 2010 defined such cadres as having 'a relatively higher self-awareness of learning' and, interestingly, 'a relatively higher learning capacity', suggesting that innate ability as well as attitude will be rewarded. Learning in this sense is defined as Marxist theory and CCP policies and guidelines, along with national laws and regulations, theoretical accomplishment and policy understanding. Such cadres are also expected to read a variety of work-related professional books, and to 'strengthen their personal self-cultivation'. The news item is quite clear that such cadres will be 'valued and promoted'. The implication is that knowledge and familiarity with an area of work as well as Marxist theoretical knowledge will become an important determinant for appointment and promotion.

Intra-Party democracy

Fourth Plenums since the 13th Party Congress have more often than not addressed both Party building and personnel changes at a senior leadership level. As mentioned above, at the Fourth Plenum of the 17th Party Congress (2005) no personnel changes were announced, or were even, according to Wang Changjiang, on the agenda. The decision instead focused on intra-Party democracy, making proposals that, while expanding on some of the ideas expressed in Hu Jintao's speech to the 17th Party Congress, were still not detailed or precise enough for some Western commentators or indeed some more liberal Party members. So how should we view the new proposals and the commitment of the leadership to their implementation? Are they, as some have suggested, a prelude to a new system of choosing the top leadership in 2012? Are they hostage to fortune and factional pressures? And what is their influence likely to be over the next ten years?

Hu Jintao has been closely identified with moves towards Party building and intra-Party democracy since calling in his speech to the 17th Party Congress for 'an organic integration of the CCP leadership, the position of the people as masters of the country, and the rule of law', supporting recommendations for candidates for leading positions in grassroots Party organisations from both Party members and the general public, and calling for the extension of direct elections of grassroots Party leaders by the local membership to more areas. The Fourth Plenum was thus widely expected to outline more concrete moves towards intra-Party democracy, and some liberal scholars expressed publicly their wish for bold decisions.

The Fourth Plenum was prefigured by the Politburo's 14th collective study session on 29 June 2009, which also took promoting intra-Party democracy as its theme. Hu Jintao used the opportunity to underline again that 'under the new conditions, we must attach great importance to and actively promote intra-Party democracy'.[7] The study session was followed the next day by a press conference under the auspices of the State Council Information Office given by Li Zhongjie, deputy director of the Central Party History Research Centre, at which he provided some background to the 'Opinions for Establishing a Mechanism for Evaluating Leadership Groups and Leading Cadres of the Party in Government to Accelerate Scientific Development' which the Politburo study session had just ratified. Li revealed that the system had been designed in the Organisation Department as early as 2004 as a general cadre evaluation method, and had been piloted. In the run-up to the 17th Party Congress it was extended to act as an evaluation and appraisal system for judging Central Committee members and leadership groups in provinces, autonomous regions and municipalities directly under the central government on their success in implementing the scientific development concept – or, as some have described it, a tool for imposing orthodoxy. Following further adjustments and improvements, the Politburo had felt able to adopt it formally.

Li emphasised that the whole evaluation process is designed to present a true picture of the behaviour and track record of cadres, rating not merely their achievements in promoting economic development, but also in social development, environmental protection and sustainable development. And, importantly, 'it pays great attention to public credibility, making the evaluation more accurate and scientific, and making sure that the broad masses feel the results of the evaluation are a true reflection of the characteristics, strengths and weaknesses of the person being assessed'. Public recognition should be an important factor in promotions and appointments, which should occur on the basis of 'democratic recommendation, appraisal and observation'.[8] The Party had clearly taken on board the findings of a 2008 Organisation Department survey which had discovered that a third of those polled were unhappy with the system of cadre appointments, and a third unhappy with the performance of the CCP's senior leadership.

The stage was thus set for the Fourth Plenum to produce some major thinking and proposals to promote further reform. And in the language of the Decision which emerged from the Fourth Plenum there is no doubt about the importance the CCP leadership attaches to the question. Intra-Party democracy is 'the life blood of the Party', without which the CCP will be hard pressed to maintain its primacy and legitimacy. The need for the Party to demonstrate vigorous as well as rigorous self-governance is now 'more urgent than at any time in PRC history'. But those who hoped for bold moves to increase public confidence in the Party were disappointed. Instead, the Decision focuses on five wide-ranging areas and outlines some fairly cautious and incremental moves towards better governance. They are:

More contested elections to choose CCP officials

It has often been acknowledged by the top leadership and by Chinese academics and think-tankers that the key to the credibility of intra-Party democracy lies in the expansion of elections, both in terms of the number of candidates competing for a post, and in the number of elections held under such circumstances.

Perhaps the most interesting factor here when considering the prospects for China in 2020 – as Cheng Li notes – is the close involvement of at least two of the contenders for a Politburo Standing Committee (PBSC) position in 2012 in such pilot schemes. Li Yuanchao, now head of the Organisation Department and a possible contender to replace He Guoqiang in 2012, was Jiangsu Party Secretary from 2002 to 2007, during which period there were a number of trial contested elections for heads of counties or urban districts, particularly in Nanjing. Shenzhen, under the leadership of Guangdong Party Secretary Wang Yang, has also experimented with multi-candidate direct elections involving public debates and statements of intent. There is now talk – and explicit mention in Hu Jintao's speech to mark the 30th anniversary of Shenzhen as a special economic zone in September 2010 – of extending this electoral process to the civic positions of Shenzhen mayor and vice-mayor.

The introduction of a more consensus-based decision-making process

These measures are designed in part to reduce the personal influence of individual Party secretaries by ensuring that all major decisions are dependent on a voting process during Party committee or standing committee meetings. Decisions on large-scale construction projects, major expenditure and senior appointments will all be made by the new method, which requires attendance by two-thirds of the Committee's members. Appointments will require approval from two-thirds of the members present. They also stipulate soliciting a greater range of opinion from think tanks, other political parties as well as from public hearings in order that major decisions are made on a basis of broad consensus.

More rules to regulate the tenure, transfer and regional postings of high-ranking officials

This point seeks to reaffirm the current rules governing cadre deployment, including both regulations and informal but established practices designed to stop various forms of improper extension or abuse of power. Length of tenure, enforced retirement age, cadre rotation and the appointment of non-natives to supervisory positions in a province all fall into this category. Should the Decision immediately extend to the Politburo Standing Committee, it will of course impact on senior appointments in 2012 by formalising the retirement age imposed by Hu Jintao at the 17th Party Congress (68 years of age).

Such rules serve two purposes. On the one hand they bolster public confidence in the fairness and even-handedness of the appointments and promotions system. On the other, frequent rotation of personnel, limited tenure and the non-appointment of cadres to senior positions in their home provinces all act against factionalism, position-based individual power and *guanxi* (personal relationship) networks and the domination of particular geographical areas and ensure that the centre is the hub of power.

New supervisory measures to prevent corruption

It has not escaped the notice of the top leadership that corrupt officials have seriously undermined the reputation and legitimacy of the CCP. The Decision offered four new methods of supervision to tackle corruption and other abuses of power: an ombudsman to supervise anti-corruption work; public hotlines to report corrupt official behaviour; the separation of Party functions into policy formulation, policy implementation and supervision; and an obligation on cadres to declare their property/business interests as well as those of their immediate family.

Personal corruption among cadres, in particular senior leaders and their families, is of course a perennial source of discontent among the general public in China. The initial measures announced in the Decision required high-ranking cadres to report the incomes, business interests, investments and property of their spouses and children, including those that live and/or work, or the assets that are held, overseas. Public disclosure was not, however, required: declaration needed only to be made to the Central Discipline Inspection Commission (CDIC) at the appropriate level. This stipulation was initially widely considered to be disappointingly weak and unlikely to be implemented effectively. However, it was followed in February 2010 by a much more explicit and detailed revision of the CCP Code of Ethics for cadres issued by the CDIC. The Code stipulates 52 unacceptable practices, and warns that those found to be in violation of its provisions face severe disciplinary measures and can also be charged under criminal law.

The practices banned by the Code provide an interesting, if not unexpected, insight into bad behaviour by cadres. Accepting gifts of cash or financial instruments as gifts, using their influence to benefit their spouses, children or 'special concerned persons' with regard to employment, stock trading or business interests are all banned. Nor should cadres use their position to make illicit gains, accept money or gifts under assumed names, or to appropriate public funds or properties. They are barred from spending inappropriately large sums of public money on purchasing vehicles, constructing office buildings, expensive recreational activities and overseas tours. For-profit activity is also out: leading cadres may not establish enterprises, register off-shore companies, own stocks or bonds of non-listed companies, or take part-time jobs in enterprises or social organisations. They are strictly prohibited from meddling in economic activities against the relevant regulations, particularly with respect to construction projects, land transfer, government purchases, real estate development and operation, mineral resources exploration and utilisation, intermediary services and enterprise restructuring.[9]

The cynical, while applauding the thought behind the new Code, will of course doubt that there is any possibility of effective implementation, particularly with regard to the business activities of the children of top leaders. Despite the fact that mention of such activities in the media is routinely censored in China, some knowledge and much resentment of the alleged corrupt activities of, for instance, Wen Jiabao's son Winston Wen Yunsong or Hu Jintao's son Hu Haifeng, are widespread, probably due to the somewhat lurid accounts which circulate from time to time in the Hong Kong press and on the Internet. We will consider further what implications allegations of, or investigations into, personal corruption may have on the prospects of aspirant members of the Fifth generation leadership later.

A new emphasis on transparency in Party matters

The Party has also committed itself to a range of measures designed to increase transparency, from the appointment of official spokesmen for higher level Party committees to a possible greater role for delegates to the Party Congress, whose function is limited at present to electing the members of the Central Committee every five years. A greater degree of consultation between high-level and grassroots party members is also promised, again emphasising the CCP's wish to be perceived as a more responsive 'listening Party'.

So, the rhetoric of CCP perceptions of its state in 2010, the fair degree of self-criticism it is content to articulate, the broad way in which it plans to address these issues and its commitment to promoting a greater degree of intra-Party democracy are all clear. The devil, as ever in China, will be in the detail of implementation. The Hu Jintao administration has two years to run before the transition of power to the next generation of leaders in 2012. It is unlikely that all the ideas and concepts in the Decision and in the drive to establish a learning-oriented Marxist Party will have been worked through, piloted, assessed and implemented by that time. The Fifth Generation will thus inherit, along with the ever-increasing litany of guiding thought in the Party constitution, a raft of incomplete and partially implemented Party work, which is likely to take up much of its time until at least midway through its first term.

The transition

Despite the smooth transition of power from the Third to the Fourth Generation of Chinese leaders in 2002, generational change was previously fraught in PRC history. Mao's three designated successors – Liu Shaoqi (1967), Lin Biao (1971) and Hua Guofeng (1981) – failed to take up the reins of power successfully. Deng Xiaoping's choices of Zhao Ziyang and Hu Yaobang in the 1980s fell victim to political struggle. Many were therefore expecting trouble when Hu Jintao – himself picked by Deng Xiaoping as a future leader – came to take over from Jiang Zemin, who had been an unexpected choice for General Secretary in the political turmoil following the Tiananmen demonstrations in 1989. In the event these fears proved unfounded. Power was transferred smoothly. Hu moved rapidly to consolidate his position, having his concept of Scientific Development written into the Party Constitution more swiftly than either Deng or Jiang's theoretical contributions, and promoting cadres who were either known to him personally from his days at the Communist Youth League (CYL), or shared his work style. Jiang Zemin continues to take the number two protocol position on major state or Party occasions and to be consulted as a Party elder. Anecdotal evidence suggests that, like many retired leaders worldwide, he continues to take an interest in politics that some might construe as interference, but there is little evidence that Hu Jintao is not in a commanding position within the Party. (Nor indeed to back the sensational allegations in elements of the Hong Kong press that Jiang was plotting a coup during the opening of the Shanghai Expo . . .)

Hu has, of course, to combine his own agenda with the task of balancing competing views and interests within the Party, but thus far his success in promoting Scientific Development, his ability in the face of deep internal divisions within the Party to reiterate and drive forward the reform and opening policy and his achievements in codifying Party personnel appointments and rotations suggest that he is unlikely to be sidelined or out-manoeuvred when power transfers to the Fifth Generation. Jiang Zemin may be demonised in some media circles largely because of his involvements in the events of 1989, but it is quite conceivable that in 2020 commentators contemplating the next generational change will be attributing all kinds of machinations and power plays to the retired Hu Jintao.

The previous paragraph referred to Hu Jintao's need to balance the various interest groups within the Party. The shorthand term 'factions' is often used to describe these groups, almost as though China mirrored the

West in terms of party politics. Elite politics are polarised into, for example, Hu Jintao's CYL faction versus the 'princelings' (children of former senior leaders), or the rump of former President Jiang Zemin's Shanghai gang, and various other groupings are posited – technocrats, the Qinghua University group, the Shandong faction to name but three. While there is some truth in this analysis, it is an incomplete picture and can lead the general reader into believing that factions are drawn up on largely ideological lines akin to western political parties. The important thing to emphasise is that these groupings in China are neither exclusive – Politburo member Liu Yandong, for example, can be reckoned a princeling, a member of the CYL faction and part of the Qinghua group – nor mandatory – Wu Bangguo, despite his Shanghai background, is not normally reckoned part of the Shanghai gang or any other grouping. They are based to a considerable extent on shared experience (for instance in the CYL or one's alma mater), loyalty groups (patronage networks) and family ties (many of the princelings have known each other since they were children). The princeling grouping in particular seems a little tenuous, often indicating those resented in the popular imagination of being where they are merely through nepotism or genetics. Despite his close association with Zhu Rongji and the economic technocrats, Wang Qishan is normally considered part of this group – though his only historical leadership ties are by marriage to former President Yao Yilin's daughter. As Alice Miller has pointed out, an equivalent analysis of US princelings would have put Al Gore and George W. Bush on the same side in 2000.

But however one defines factions in China, there is currently nothing to suggest that there will be a significant public outbreak of factional infighting, as opposed to private jockeying for position, before the 18th Party Congress. And in political terms such a display would send all the wrong messages, destroying the unity and consensus the Party has tried so hard to display on major showcase occasions like the Beijing Olympics, 60th anniversary celebrations and the Shanghai Expo, and to build in the face of the global economic downturn, the Wenchuan earthquake and the ethnic disturbances in Tibet and Xinjiang in 2008 and 2009 respectively. The role model of the assiduous, clean and self-sacrificing leader is promoted in Party propaganda and sanctioned by the leadership, making naked ambition or overt advocacy for one's protégés far more difficult. This perception has led many admirers of Bo Xilai's performance in tackling organised crime and promoting social development as Party Secretary in Chongqing to fear that his charisma and flamboyant style will hinder rather than help his chances of promotion.

The posts

Whatever their factional allegiances, there seems already to be a broad consensus on the pool of contenders for the Politburo Standing Committee in 2012 – the Fifth Generation leaders who (assuming the current system survives) will take us through to the 20th Party Congress in 2022. There is also some concern about their ability to run the country. The older generation in particular is concerned that those born in the 1950s are a damaged generation, their education interrupted by the chaos of the Cultural Revolution, and many of them deeply marked by their experience as adolescents at the time. Some possible candidates for leadership positions are known to have been active members of Red Guard factions, many saw their parents imprisoned, and almost all were sent down to the countryside to learn from the peasants. Some Party academics believe that it is in some part the fears about the competence of this generation that have informed the drive to regulate, codify and supervise Party procedures.

The temptation to speculate at this stage about which individuals (with the exceptions of Xi Jinping and Li Keqiang) will be holding which Standing Committee posts in 2020 is probably best resisted or at least minimised. A broad consensus does seem to have been established about the pool of leading candidates for the Fifth Generation, and some identifications have been made of promising Sixth Generation candidates. But a structural consideration of the composition of previous Politburo Standing Committees can also be revealing, as shown in Table 1.1.

Several points are immediately apparent.

- The responsibilities of the nine positions (the Standing Committee was expanded from seven posts to nine in 2002) are clearly defined and do not change, although their ranking varies. It is hard to imagine that there will be any contraction of the number of Standing Committee members in 2012, particularly in light of the burden of supervisory activity which falls to each role.
- A retirement age of 68 was imposed at the 17th Party Congress in 2007, following the precedent set at the 16th Party Congress. There are no binding rules governing retirement ages, and at both the 15th and 16th Party Congresses the imposition of one was interpreted as a power play in order to remove older leaders at odds with the incumbent General Secretary. Jiang Zemin set retirement at 70 in 1997 in order to force Qiao Shi to retire, and lowered it again to 68 in 2002 to remove Li Ruihuan. Hu Jintao kept the retirement age at 68 in 2007, which some interpreted as a move designed to precipitate the departure of

Table 1.1

Elected at the 16th Party Congress, 2002			Elected at the 17th Party Congress, 2007		
	DOB	**Position/ portfolio**		**DOB**	**Position/ portfolio**
Hu Jintao	1942	General Secretary	Hu Jintao	1942	General Secretary
Wu Bangguo	1941	NPC	Wu Bangguo	1941	NPC
Wen Jiabao	1942	Premier	Wen Jiabao	1942	Premier
Jia Qinglin	1940	CPPCC	Jia Qinglin	1940	CPPCC
Zeng Qinghong	1939	Secretariat	Li Changchun	1944	Propaganda
Huang Ju	1938	Vice-premier/ economic	Xi Jinping	1953	Secretariat
Wu Guanzheng	1938	CDIC	Li Keqiang	1955	Vice-premier/ economic
Li Changchun	1944	Propaganda	He Guoqiang	1943	CDIC
Luo Gan	1935	Pol.–Legal Affairs/ Security	Zhou Yongkang	1942	Pol.–Legal Affairs/ Security

Zeng Qinghong, a powerful figure closely aligned to Jiang Zemin and seen by many as a challenge to Hu's authority. However, it is also possible that Hu was following precedent in order to codify personnel arrangements for the PBSC, in keeping with his other moves towards transparency and regulation of personnel affairs. If, as seems likely, a retirement age of 68 is also applied to the 18th Party Congress, all members of the current Standing Committee except Xi Jinping and Li Keqiang will stand down.

- Two positions – the no. 6 and no. 7 slots – were given to the two representatives of the Fifth Generation leadership widely predicted to succeed Hu Jintao and Wen Jiabao, respectively Xi Jinping and Li Keqiang. The obvious assumption is that this was to groom them for their future roles by giving them relevant hands-on experience. Xi's position at the head of the Secretariat, and thus at the centre of Party affairs, was held by Hu Jintao at the same stage in his career. Li's, as vice-premier in charge of the economic portfolio, is giving him direct experience of the functions he is expected to fulfil as Premier. It follows that at the 19th Party Conference in 2017, the two leading Sixth Generation candidates destined for top office in 2022 will in turn take their places on the Standing Committee. It follows then that at least two of those appointed in 2012 will be for one term only, retiring in 2017 to make room for the heirs apparent. This also allows for the appointment of some slightly more senior candidates to the Standing Committee, which will otherwise lack experience. It seems likely that they will take over the slots that Xi and Li vacate, on the basis that these will be the training slots for the Sixth Generation in 2017. And particularly in the case of the Secretariat job, it suggests Hu Jintao can seek to appoint a candidate he trusts to carry through the unfinished work from his last term.

Looking at the responsibilities of the Standing Committee positions, one of the most sensitive is the CDIC slot heading the internal Party body which investigates corruption and allegations of malfeasance among Party members. Official corruption pervades government circles, and is at the top of the list of most ordinary citizens' complaints against the Party. The Party itself is well aware of this, as previous discussion highlighted, and Hu Jintao has been closely associated with the battle against it. Yet, although it is true that the former Party Secretary of Shanghai, Chen Liangyu, was dismissed and subsequently successfully prosecuted on corruption charges in 2006–7, the Standing Committee and Politburo still contain members against whom anecdotal evidence at least is fairly compelling. Jia Qinglin is widely considered to have been complicit in the Yuanhua scandal of 1999, and Wang Lequan to have corrupt business interests in Shandong. There have been numerous allegations of corruption against Wen Jiabao's wife and son, some of which, according to the Hong Kong media, have been officially investigated. Despite Bo Xilai's high-profile campaign against organised crime in Chongqing, questions have been asked about his family finances. And a corruption scandal in Africa in 2009 led to the suggestion that Hu Jintao's son Hu Haifeng might be called as a witness through his association with the Qinghua University-backed company Nuctech. Most serious for the Fifth Generation leadership, rumours surfaced in Hong Kong in mid-2009 that two of Li Keqiang's personal secretaries whom he had brought with him to Zhongnanhai had been caught taking backhanders. The corruption question will have implications for the reputation and legitimacy of the Party well past 2020, and for this reason it seems unfeasible to appoint anyone who is suspected of serious corruption to this position.

The propaganda apparatus is widely considered to be one of the most, if not the most, powerful parts of the Chinese political machine, with a reputation for hard-line conservatism as well as the responsibility for censorship. The Standing Committee member with overall responsibility for it thus wields considerable influence in terms of persuasion, coercion and, since China began to develop its soft power profile, budget. The next ten years are likely to see a shift away from more traditional forms of mass media propaganda to new media, a corresponding focus on the technological side of media management and continued engagement with spreading the message to the outside world as well as domestically, which may argue for the appointment of a figure with at least some understanding of and credibility in the world outside China.

The role least understood in the West is probably the no. 2 slot in the Party hierarchy, currently held by Wu Bangguo, as Chairman of the National People's Congress (NPC). The NPC is often dismissed – both inside China and in the outside world – as a mere rubber stamp organisation, devoid of real power and serving only to provide the Party with a fig leaf of democratic respectability. Yet the importance of the position in Party terms is clear. Wu himself is also an enigmatic figure, regarded as personality-free by some Chinese commentators but as a conservative hardliner whose job is to balance the divergent opinions within the PBSC by others. His attempts to control the flow of information emerging from NPC sessions in recent years have certainly not endeared him to more liberal delegates at a central level. The question for 2012 – and thus for the leadership in 2020 – is whether to continue the conservative tradition by appointing another no. 2 in the Wu Bangguo mould, or to give a cautious push to the reformist agenda by appointing a figure to develop the role and enhance the powers of the NPC.

But regardless which individuals are leading China in 2020, the overarching concern for the Party will remain its legitimacy, and its ability to manage the complex nexus of domestic issues adequately. Scientific Development Theory has already identified the main issues China faces: the urban rural divide, income disparity, degradation of the natural environment and the need to continue economic development in a sustained and balanced manner, along with the need to respond more effectively and rapidly to change. Consensus has been articulated that the Dengist policy of reform and opening has been successful and will continue. (This, incidentally, has been and remains a far more contentious ideological issue than many in the West realise.) At present there appears to be no likely alternative to continued Party rule for the next ten years, although we may well see an increase in the number of non-Party members appointed to senior-level positions in the state apparatus (at present there are but two non-Party Ministers). If policymakers in the West are to establish a constructive dialogue with the Chinese leadership they will need to acquire a greater understanding of the domestic pressures China faces, and to move towards a better understanding of consensus-led decision making. If they can cut through the ideology-based discourse of Chinese politics to focus on the substance of policies and approaches they may well find greater commonalities across administrations than they had anticipated.

Notes

1. Opinions expressed in this chapter are the personal views of the author, and are not expressions of official British government policy.
2. *People's Daily*, 19 September 2009.
3. 'Intra-Party democracy in China – should we take it seriously?' *CDM*, Fall 2009.
4. *Xinhua*, 14 November 2009.
5. *Renmin Ribao*, 31 December 2009.
6. *Xinhua*, 8 February 2010.
7. *Ta Kung Pao*, 5 September 2009.
8. *Xinhua*, 30 June 2009.
9. *Xinhua: China Focus*, 23 February 2010.

2

China 2020: international relations

Kerry Brown[1]

In the coming decade, China will continue to wrestle with the quandary of being a reluctant global power, while still maintaining its own development. This is likely to be a difficult, and at times rocky, process. China will tell the world that it is focused on its own internal issues, as outlined by Kate Westgarth in the first chapter, trying to shy away from leadership on issues that do not directly relate to it. However, there will be rising expectations that it will need to play a bigger role internationally. It will have increasing assets abroad which will demand its protection and involvement, along with large numbers of Chinese citizens working and travelling outside the borders of their home country. It has a wide network of diplomatic partners in both the developed and developing world. It will be torn between representing the interests of the developing world, as it has tended to do historically, and also being a fully paid-up member of the most powerful nation group. Its own internal governance and stability will become critical international issues. By 2020, China and the US will be the key actors in global affairs, and will need to deal with sharper potential conflicts. China must articulate its own vision of its global role, and be led by politicians who are more visible, better communicators outside of the country, and have an international perspective – leaders quite different to the ones currently at the head of the Fourth Generation. China will no longer be able to hide itself behind the mantra of being a poor, developing nation, when it has the world's second largest economy, and be well on its way to matching the United States. And it will need to have a positive vision of dealing with the issue of Taiwan, and of regional problems like North Korea and Iraq. It will also have to handle potentially difficult clashes of interests with other regional partners like India and Russia, and avoid nationalists within China dominating the policy agenda and creating conflict with Japan, or other major partners.

The current parameters of China's foreign policy

Since its foundation in 1949, the People's Republic of China (PRC) has been dominated by two great relationships. From 1949 to 1968, the focus of its international relations was on the USSR. This period divides into the first ten years, when relations between the two countries were positive, and the USSR, building on strong political links, supplied the PRC with a great deal of technical aid and help, to the final decade, when relations soured to such an extent that from the early 1960s tens of thousands of Russian experts were withdrawn from the PRC, and the Soviet Union became one of the key targets of hatred and anger during the Cultural Revolution from 1966 onwards. This era of decline was set off by Khrushchev's secret denunciation of Stalin in 1956 at the Twentieth Congress of the Soviet Union Communist Party. Mao Zedong strongly disagreed with this policy, and started to place increasing distance between himself and the new Russian leadership. The absolute nadir of their relationship came when both sides clashed in 1969 on the Sino-Soviet border, leading to hundreds of casualties.

From 1969, officials in China were asked to think through how, and when, a rapprochement might be made with the United States.[2] Their recommendation was that low-level, secret discussions be started via their embassy in Warsaw, where there was also a US diplomatic presence. The outcome of these was to eventually be the visit by Nixon to the PRC in 1972. From this period, the PRC, despite its profound ideological and political differences with the US, kept increasingly close to it. The US and China formalised full diplomatic relations in 1978, only months before the first signs of the profound economic reforms came out, in December 1978, which were to radically transform Chinese society and the role that China plays in the world.

Maintaining this closeness to the US has been one of the striking features of China's economic and diplomatic activity in the last three decades. According to Robert Ross, 'Pax Americana establishes its rule and imposes order in East Asia in the twenty-first century in just the same way that Pax Britannica established its rule in the nineteenth century – through sea power.'[3] China remains a land power, and one which has exerted great efforts in the last four decades in resolving its border disputes (of 23 such land and sea border issues in 1949, 17 have now been resolved; none of them by force, all by negotiation).[4] Its sea capacity is still limited. It has, for instance, no modern aircraft carrier.[5] Positive relations with the US supplied much of the economic stimulus in the 1980s and 1990s, through which China was able to build up its industrial capacity. The crowning moment of this was in 2001 when, after 14 years of painstaking negotiations, the PRC joined the World Trade Organisation (WTO) and opened its own markets to inward and outward trade flows and investment far more profoundly than ever before. The results of this, by 2010, are clear: the world's largest exporter, largest car maker, largest holder of foreign reserves, and second largest economy.

China's relations with the US will dominate the next decade. They are likely to be the pivotal relationship of the twenty-first century. And yet where once there existed a very asymmetrical arrangement, where a mighty US faced a developing, and in many ways weakened China, there are already clear signs that this phase of the story is drawing to an end. According to an article in the *Financial Times* on 29 March 2010, 'Beijing no longer believes American power is indispensible to Chinese economic expansion and the Communist Party's political survival.'[6] For thirty years, the key mantra for Chinese international affairs, particularly as it related to the US, was the '24-character phrase' imputed to Deng Xiaoping: 'Bide our time and build up our capabilities (*tao guang yang hui*).' But now there are increasing signs within China that many policymakers and opinion formers want a higher profile, something more appropriate to China's current situation, and more focused on its national interests and needs. This need is likely to grow more intense in the coming decade, and will be one of the most difficult issues to control and balance for China's leaders. Public expectations of China being a true global power have risen since the mid 2000s. This was built on Chinese leaders and elites' desire to construct a great power identity for China which began from the early 1990s, if not earlier.[7] How the world responds to a China that is more assertive, and in some areas may well come into clear conflict with other countries, is another key dimension of this new dynamic.

A China that can say no but is still unhappy

In 2010, and for the ensuing decade, China's international relations cannot be decoupled from its own internal dynamics. By 2020, it aims to be a middle-income country. What sort of China do its own increasingly affluent people want? And how does this impact on government policymaking?

There has been a small but vociferous group within China for some years who have demanded the PRC be more assertive, and that it aim to resolve some of its historic grievances. This fight for the soul of the new, rising China is only likely to grow fiercer in the next decade. William Callahan calls this the 'pessoptimist' streak of modern Chinese nationalism. 'To understand the success of China's current rise, we need to understand the failures of China's 'Century of humiliation.'[8] He continues, 'To understand China's dreams, we also need to understand its nightmares.'[9] Campaigns in the last three decades to reawaken resentments over historic atrocities like the Nanjing Massacre of 1937 have been framed in patriotic movements, through which a generation of younger Chinese have more focused anger than their parents. Wang Xiaodong, one of the authors of the 1998 *The China That Can Say No* has become one of China's most successful bloggers, with a following of over two million. In *China is not Happy (Zhongguo Bu Gaoxing)*, published in 2009, Wang and his fellow authors state that despite the fact that there are 'good things from the west',[10] the power structures of the old world are breaking apart. They see this as causing resentment on the part of the West, which is paradoxical: 'We acknowledge we need your acceptance, but do you want to strive to have ours?'[11] Asking what modern China's great objective might be, they blame the post-Second World War settlement for creating a situation in which the PRC's elites have allowed it to become the sweatshop of the world, making over-consuming westerners even greedier and more selfish. Dismissing neo-Confucianism as a belief system that will only support more power-hungry elites, they see Western-led (and in particular US-led) schemes to dilute the PRC's new hard-won power by creating potential conflict between it and either Russia or Japan.[12] The options they see in the future are stark: either to continue being the world's factory, to support the western economic model, or to have out-and-out conflict.[13] 'We were wrong', they state, 'to have studied the US.'[14] Laying aside any talk of soft power being the key area to build up China's international stability and influence, they demand that their elites instead focus on traditional hard power – and in particular, aircraft carriers. Having won the battle of the market, now, they say, it is time to fight the battle of the army.[15]

The elephant in the room: the US will always be number one

Awareness of China's struggles with how it needs to present itself and where it fits into the global system has existed for the last two decades.

As Ross argues, the US, 'despite its superior strategic and economic position in the post cold-war world made a succession of compromises in the face of initial Chinese intransigence' after the shock of the Tiananmen Square incident in 1989.[16] It managed to avoid the possibility of China being locked out of the international system, meaning that Deng Xiaoping was able to face down the hardliners in his own government, and, in 1992, start moving on to a more constructive role in international affairs. Even so, China's economic growth in the last 15 years, and in particular since 2001 and entry to WTO, has posed issues both for those looking at the right framework within which to fit China (a threat, an opportunity, engagement, disengagement) and those within China, from the moderates who want to stay within the traditional parameters of Deng's pragmatic foreign policy and those who are now moving more towards demanding the country has a more assertive role. Policy elites in Beijing have produced a number of articulations to deal with this issue, from Zheng Bijian's concept of 'Peaceful Rise' (*heping jueqi*),[17] to the blunter statements of China simply 'rising' that have figured since then.

This takes place against an awareness that while the US is possibly 'declining', it isn't likely to relinquish its top spot any time soon. The US's clear naval superiority has been mentioned already. But it is the reach of the US across the world that is perhaps the most startling. This is, as historian Bruce Cumings has written, 'an American realm with no name, a territorial presence with little if any standing in the literature of international affairs'. The US, he says, 'runs a territorial empire . . . of somewhere between 737 and 860 overseas military installations operating in 153 countries, which most Americans know little if anything about.'[18] The Chinese may well have increased their military expenditure by double-digit figures for most of the last twenty years, but in 2010, the US budgeted US$760 billion for its military spending – almost ten times that of China, and more than its closest 15 competitors put together. Crudely put, without sinking unsustainable amounts into its military over the next decade, it is hard to see how China will be able to compete with the US.

For this reason, the desire of some within the PRC to be more assertive has to be held in check by two big restraints, which are not going to disappear. The first is the real economic interdependence between the two countries. China will continue to grow and develop its internal market, but the US will remain hugely important to it, if for no other reason than because it owes so much US debt. The second is the strategic dominance that the US has in most of the region, and throughout the rest of the world. According to Beijing-based academic Wang Hui, 'Is America an empire or a nation-state? Does America have boundaries or not? It certainly has boundaries, since one has to go through customs when one arrives, yet its frontiers may also be in Turkey, Iraq, Afghanistan, and all along China's periphery. It has frontiers everywhere.'[19] How can China start to move against such a ubiquitous force in order to create its own space?

One idea that Chinese policymakers have worked with is to pick key strategic areas where at least there is competitive advantage with the US. 'Informationalisation' has been one priority, looking to becoming globally advanced for instance in cyber conflict. It is true that China has put plenty of resources into this area, recruiting many of its talented computer programmers, software designers and mathematicians. China has had success in compromising or infiltrating a number of civilian and military networks globally, even managing attacks on the British, US and German government systems.[20] Google's withdrawal from China (at least from providing censored results via *www.google.com.cn*) in early 2010 was partially connected to a number of penetrating and aggressive attacks mounted against Google and other companies in late 2009.[21] US Secretary of State Hillary Clinton responded a few days later by saying that 'Countries or individuals that engage in cyber attacks should face consequences and international condemnation . . . In an interconnected world, an attack on one nation's networks can be an attack on all.'[22] The Internet and cyber conflict has already become a large arena, where state-supported moves are viewed as a means of pursuing national objectives. This conflict is only likely to get more important and powerful as the years go on, and may well cause countries, in particular the US and China, to agree limitations on what they can do as these tensions start to work against each other's interests.

The world beyond the US

For many years the PRC has talked about multi-polarity, setting itself against, in particular, 'US hegemony.' It has, since 2009, resisted talk of there being a G20. It likes working in multilateral settings, and dislikes being in an isolated position. 'The Chinese leadership generally seeks to maintain a stable international environment in order to defuse instabilities, especially around its periphery, so Beijing can focus on critical economic, political and social challenges at home.'[23] In order to achieve this it has proactively taken part in multilateral diplomacy, and participated in 24 of the 61 UN peacekeeping missions between 1989 and 2006.[24] There is therefore no longer any strong resistance to China having influence and seeking to exercise that influence beyond its borders. In January 2010, following on from the deployment of two ships off the coast of Somalia to work against piracy, it agreed to join an international naval force combating piracy. But China's relationships and activities remain self-interested. It resists talk of a 'G2' because it does not feel ready, nor does it want the responsibility, of being a regional or global policeman like the US. Premier Wen Jiabao said to President Obama when he met him in Beijing in November 2009, 'China is still a developing country with a huge population and has a long way to go before it becomes modernised. We must always keep sober-minded over it.'[25]

In the last thirty years, China has built links with countries throughout the world. In 1967, it had only one diplomat still serving, in Egypt. Its international representation had been decimated by the Cultural Revolution being waged in Beijing. By 2010, it had one of the widest, best-respected diplomatic services in the world, and was able to preserve good relations with 50 of the 54 countries in Africa, all the countries in the Middle East, Latin America, and Europe. The drivers behind this were partly through the PRC's own economic and resource needs (for which see below), but also because of its desire to have a balanced international system, where no single power is overwhelmingly dominant. However, such talk in the years up to 2020 will come under much greater pressure, if only because China will find itself increasingly pushed into a counterbalancing role with the United States. Possible partners in this multipolar world are unlikely to be able to come close to the diplomatic weight of either the US or the PRC, no matter how much they, and China, might want this.

- The European Union (EU) is sometimes talked of as the most likely partner in a global triangular system. Economically it is larger than either the PRC or the US, accounting for 36 per cent of global GDP. It is China's largest trading partner. With the implementation of the Lisbon Treaty in 2009, the EU should have a more unified diplomatic service, and a stronger and more consistent voice. Its uneven relationship with the PRC over the last decade has been well documented elsewhere.[26] Were the EU to manage this better in the coming years, it could have much stronger leverage on the back of its huge trade interests in China, and might be a counterbalance to the US. But from its past behaviour, this is unlikely. It would need to resolve its approach to China, creating a unified understanding amongst the 27 member states of, for instance, policy about Tibet, attitudes to the maintenance of the arms embargo, and movement away from being a purely economic-centred relationship. To resolve this, the EU would need to answer some of its questions about itself to itself. There is no indication at the moment that the political will exists to do this within the EU. The key area of strong mutual interest is in climate change, and exchange of technologies to deal with this. This is likely to hugely intensify by 2020.

- Russia's relations with China remain complex, and scarred by the last century of history between the two. Commentator Bobo Lo has said that Russia and China are joined together in an 'axis of convenience'. There has, he writes, been a deep-seated mutual ambivalence between the two, with Russia regarding the PRC as a threat, getting much more out of the relationship than Moscow, and the Chinese becoming increasingly dismissive in recent years of the economic performance of their vast neighbour since it gave up on Communism: 'They [the PRC] value [Russia] as a supplier of advanced weaponry to the People's Liberation Army (PLA), as an important source of crude oil, and as a useful ally in balancing American power in Central Asia.'[27] Tentative Chinese investments in the energy sector in Russia since 2005 have shown how critical this aspect is, at least to the PRC. Even despite improved economic performance for the USSR under Putin and then Medvedev, however, it is unlikely that Russia will be able to keep up with the pace the PRC has set. Nor is any alliance which would be a threat to the US or the west likely either. Sino-Russian relations will be dominated by pragmatism, and mutual suspicion.
- India is a different challenge. Bill Emmott could state in 2008 that 'Chinese policy towards India has been successful in the past fifteen years in a way that is consistent with its broader foreign policy: China has ensured that relations are warm enough to facilitate trade, and that tensions are by and large kept under control.'[28] In 2009, however, tensions between the two countries escalated. Hosting of the Dalai Lama and a large contingent of exiled Tibetans is a constant source of irritation. The unresolved border disputes look no closer to being sorted out now than they did thirty years ago. Competition between the two powers has spread into fights for overseas markets, and increasing frustration in India at the ability of Chinese entrepreneurs to gain a competitive edge. There is a surprising lack of knowledge about India in China. This relationship, of all those on China's borders, offers the most potential scope for unpleasant surprises. That they are both nuclear powers, and that they also jealously guard their relationships with the US, is also worrying.

- Japan is also a source of contention. Historic issues have become, in fact, worse if not better in the last decade. There is no sign that they are going to go away any time soon.[29] Japan has been a huge partner in the economic development of China since the 1980s, and the largest provider of aid. But political relations between the two are frequently affected by the strong nationalist sentiment in the PRC, something that the government often colludes with, allowing demonstrations in 2005 when Japan attempted to join the Permanent Security Council of the UN. China's replacing Japan as the world's second largest economy in 2010 is a moment of huge symbolic significance. The likelihood of increasing tensions between the two countries as they readjust to a world in which Japan is no longer number two is high.
- Massive increases in aid and investment in Africa have given China immense new influence there. This will be a key area that will need to be worked out over the coming decade. China has become one of the largest investors in the continent, standing in 2009 just behind the US and France. Oil and resources are central to much of its interests in Africa: 'Getting hold of raw materials is integral to [the strategy for increased economic growth]; Africa, with its natural resources, thus fits squarely into Chinese policy both foreign and domestic. Indeed, it would be difficult to overstate the importance of Africa to China's own development.'[30] China has had something of a baptism of fire as it has increased its investments and interests in the continent in the last decade, coming in for heavy criticism for its relations with Sudan, Zimbabwe and other countries with poor governance and human rights issues. But China's interests in Africa can only intensify and increase by 2020. The question, which will be addressed more fully later, is to what extent this will bring China into conflict with other countries with interests in the region, and how it will choose to frame its new diplomatic prominence in an area where there will be increasing expectations of its role.
- China also has key interests in the Middle East and Latin America, largely centred on its resource needs. It will attempt to balance these against political pressures, for instance, for it to take a stand over Iran and its nuclear proliferation programme. The PRC's ability to remain neutral and either abstain on issues, or use its veto against action, will become increasingly difficult.

There are other groupings within which China has increasing leverage. The G77 developing countries continue to look towards it for leadership. They were to be disappointed at what they saw as the PRC's self-interested behaviour in resisting clear carbon emission targets in a final accord at the end of the Copenhagen Climate Change Summit in December 2009. Perhaps this is a sign of how China is now becoming more isolated, and less easy to fit into the existing developing country rubric. The PRC also works with the ASEAN countries. It will demand, and probably get, an increased role in international organisations like the International Monetary Fund and the World Bank.

For this rapidly evolving and increasing international diplomatic role, China will need to answer some of the questions about itself that were posed above. What does it stand for, as a country, beyond raw economic growth? Does it believe in a development model which it has used, which is transferable to other countries, through which it could exercise increasing influence? Can it really resist traditional realpolitik 'great power' behaviour, on the back of at least a significant military presence regionally, or will it become a new kind of power? These are questions that the second part of this chapter will now seek to provide some initial speculative answers to.

The two big problems: Taiwan and North Korea

There are two issues which are directly linked to China's interests, which will impact on its international role in the coming decade. The first is the unresolved issue of the status of Taiwan. The second is North Korea. The first is marginally more predictable in its likely outcomes than the second. But both are potentially highly destructive if they are mishandled. And in the coming decade, both will offer an increasingly urgent need for some kind of sustainable resolution.

Taiwan: consensus versus resolution

Taiwan's status has been the subject of consensus between the main players since the 1970s. When the United Nations seat passed to the PRC in 1971, paving the way for President Nixon's visit to China, it was agreed that Taiwan would continue to enjoy a security blanket from, primarily, the US. This was enshrined in the Taiwan Relations Act from 1979, which commits the US executive to consult with Congress over any issues relating to Taiwan's protection. This was passed in the same year that the US conferred full diplomatic relations on the PRC. Since the Shanghai Communiqué issued in 1972 as a result of Nixon's visit, the key understanding between the PRC, the US and other international partners is the One China Policy, where recognition is granted only to one China, without specifying whether that be the PRC or the Republic of China or Taiwan. This ambiguity has offered enough flexibility for the PRC to withhold from all-out aggression, Taiwan to develop largely independently, and the international community to maintain a distance from the dispute between the two, while ensuring that there is still a commitment to intervene should things get out of hand.

Taiwan's democratisation in the late 1990s changed the whole dynamics of the issue. While the Nationalist leadership in Taiwan continued their stance from the Civil War and before of threatening, one day, to reconquer the Mainland, and the Mainland responded in kind, a whole new dimension was introduced with the holding of the first fully free, multi-party elections in Taiwan in 1996, and then the coming to power of the Democratic People's Party (DPP) under Chen Shuibian in 2000 and 2004. The change in Taiwan's political system became, for many in Taiwan, and to commentators and policymakers in the Mainland, a sure sign that this was one step further along the road to complete independence. The initial Mainland response was bellicose and aggressive, holding military manoeuvres in the South China Sea in 1996 that were sufficiently worrying for the US to despatch two aircraft carriers there. The Mainland has now learned to deal with its new democratic neighbour with a little more sophistication, and with the re-election of the Nationalists under Ma Ying Jeou in 2008 they seemingly have a more biddable leadership to talk to in Taipei. That has still not prevented them from amassing over a thousand missiles along the Fujianese coast directly opposite Taiwan. They have also stifled Taiwan's attempts to have any proper international space, with their sole concession being to allow Taiwan observer status in 2009 in the World Health Organisation.

Both sides have set out a number of proposals for how to handle their relationship. On the part of the PRC there have been two major policy statements about the approach to resolving cross-strait issues. One was made by former President of the PRC, Jiang Zemin, in January 1995. This has been called the 'Eight-Point Proposal'. These points include adhering to the principle that one China is the basis and prerequisite for peaceful reunification and that China's sovereignty and territorial integrity must never be allowed to suffer division (this could be called the ultimate red line). Other principles referred to by Jiang were:

- allowing for the development of non-governmental economic and cultural ties between Taiwan and other countries;
- holding negotiations with the Taiwan authorities on the peaceful reunification of the motherland;
- aiming to achieve the peaceful reunification of China since Chinese should not fight Chinese, but being willing to use force to resolve the issue if necessary against the foreign forces who intervene;
- developing economic exchange and cooperation between the two sides separated by the Taiwan Strait;
- promoting cultural ties.

That the PRC has not renounced force in the issue of Taiwan remains a major symbolic block to pursuing deeper proposals for political dialogue. The vision of policymakers around paramount leader Deng Xiaoping in the 1980s was that of the 'one country, two systems' model. This was subsequently used to resolve the issue of Hong Kong's status after reversion to PRC sovereignty in 1997 from the British. However, once Taiwan had become a fully functioning democracy by 1996, this model became much harder to envisage ever working. Current President Hu Jintao has also made a six-point 'Proposition on Taiwan', supplementing the issues put forward by Jiang Zemin over a decade earlier. These included: (1) reaching a common understanding on the principle of one China; (2) ending hostility and reaching peaceful agreements under the one China principle; (3) starting discussions between the two sides about political relations as a preliminary to reunification; (4) stepping up contacts on military issues 'at an appropriate time'; (5) developing transport and communication links across the Strait; (6) promoting cultural exchanges.

For the Taiwanese side, with the return to power of the KMT party in the presidential elections in March 2008, new President Ma Ying Jeou was seen as pursuing a more conciliatory path with Beijing, and Hu's points have, at least in terms of creating transport and communication links between the two sides, been partially implemented. Ma's own position on the status of cross-strait relations was contained most recently in his National Day Address in October 2009. There he states that the objectives of policy towards the PRC were:

- acceptance of the 1992 Consensus (by which both sides accepted the 'One China' principle);
- support for links through visits to Taiwan by mainland tourists, direct air, sea, and postal links, food safety inspections, and cross-strait legal assistance;

- an attempt to extend these into the economic realm with a free trade agreement;
- defence of Taiwanese national sovereignty and interests, in particular protections of its democratic system;
- development of friendly relations between Taiwan and mainland China and the promotion of 'flexible diplomacy';
- a national defence strategy of 'effective deterrence and resolute defence' developing a professional military base to protect the security of Taiwan.[31]

The status quo suits both sides well at the moment. For the PRC, beyond the hawkish elements on the military, who were effectively pulled in in 1996, there is a strong awareness that any military activity would be immensely damaging. It would also be counter-productive in potentially destroying the very economic prosperity of Taiwan which would be one of the great attractions of reclaiming sovereignty over the island. For Taiwan, despite large arms supply deals in 2010 with the US, there is increasing awareness of their own military vulnerability before the PLA, which has increased its military capacity hugely in the last two decades. The great stumbling block of sovereignty for both sides remains. Taiwan enjoys de facto independence, but is not allowed the freedom to express this. It is impossible seeing a democracy being attacked by a non-democracy and the US and others just standing by. So the only option is that both sides continue talking and that there is enough space and flexibility for them to continue as they are.

The problem in the coming decade will be the increasing sense in Taiwan of being a separate nation. The only way in which any kind of unification, however loose, would be realistically possible in the future would be if there was a fundamental change of the political system in the PRC. Were Beijing to have a more democratic system, then this would give any talks between it and Taipei a completely new context. But the likelihood of that happening in the next decade is low. Outright conflict between both sides is also very unlikely, though it should never be entirely dismissed. Ma Ying Jeou's current administration has been far more conciliatory towards the Mainland, and talked of a common market, signing a highly significant Economic Cooperation Framework Agreement in June 2010. But the real benefits of this have yet to filter through to the Taiwanese economy, and on the whole, public opinion remains very sceptical about what, if anything, these links with the PRC will do. Elections are due in 2012, and it is possible the DPP might regain power. In that case, some of the fractiousness that dominated relations across the

Strait in the 2000s might return. There would also be a hard rethink in Beijing about how, and whether in the end it is possible, to gain the hearts and minds of a population in a democracy that show all the capriciousness and unpredictability of electorates elsewhere.

In fact, what is most likely by 2020 is that, as with other areas, China continues to use its economic leverage to buy influence, calm nerves, and build trust, making the foundations of a longer-term sustainable political settlement in the future. Already Chinese investment is starting to appear in Taiwan. Lenovo and others are involved in projects there. Taiwan was one of the big investors in the Mainland in the 1990s onwards. Now this tide might be reversed. And while there is a high awareness of the political price tag that some of this investment might have, and campaigns by lawmakers and others to ensure that there are restrictions in place to offset any insidious influence, in the end it will be a crucial issue of how far populations in Taiwan see their own economic fortunes being tied to those of the Mainland, and what leverage that might give Beijing in pushing more aggressively for some outcome that suits them. Unification is not remotely likely, but deeper links leading to some kind of federal system might well one day be possible. For cross-strait relations by 2020, therefore, it will be a tale of two cities – Beijing and Taipei – and of two key areas – politics and economics.

North Korea

The only link between Taiwan and North Korea's problems with the PRC is that they are results of the Cold War that still continue into the twenty-first century. In 2010, after a brief economic recovery, the DPRK seems to be sliding back into the parlous state of ten years before. It is tragically returning to the poverty and starvation of the 1990s, when perhaps as many as two million died of malnutrition and famine-related diseases. The key leader, Kim Jong Il, has reportedly suffered both a heart attack and a stroke – another of either might kill him suddenly. His third son, still only in his twenties, was promoted to the rank of four-star general, and also elevated into a position in the Korean Workers Party at the Congress held in October 2010, indicating the first real steps in a succession plan. But as one China analyst in Shanghai in 2009 said, his sons will not be able to exercise power the same way he does. Something has to change. And the likelihood of this happening in the next decade is high.

For China, North Korea presents endless frustration and problems. Its implosion would present a costly clean-up exercise, and involve huge amounts of funds. The expectation that the PRC would be involved in this would be high. Unification with South Korea, unless some formula for a neutral Korea was devised, would mean seeing a possible US presence come right up to China's borders. That, too, would be very unwelcome. North Korea could continue as it is, impoverished and isolated – and, without its huge military and nuclear weapons, that might be acceptable. But it has shown repeatedly, especially since the collapse of the Agreed Framework with the USA in 2003, that it is able and willing to engage in provocative acts which have included launching missiles over Japan, testing nuclear weapons, and sinking a South Korean naval vessel. Its relations with the PRC are complex, and often far more fractious than the warm rhetoric of senior leaders going backwards and forwards would have people believe. And China, for all its historical ties with the DPRK, has limited leverage there – as was illustrated by the DPRK nuclear test of 2006, carried out in the face of Chinese public urgings to the contrary. China can bring the DPRK economy almost to a standstill by halting oil supplies across the common border – but that risks precipitating collapse. It can talk, engage, wheedle and cajole, but that seems to have a limited effect. But it does not have many levers in between these two.

Without something dramatic, either in terms of wholesale economic reform from within (which might lead to political reform soon afterwards, and for which there seems to be little appetite in Pyongyang) or intervention from outside (and the historic precedents for this in Korea have not been good), it is hard to see a palatable, manageable outcome to the DPRK problem by 2020. The intrinsic instability of the situation there means that implosion is highly possible, even though the regime has shown itself brutally effective in surviving so far. For North Korea, it is not a question of whether it survives in its current form, but for how long. Succession worries have made it clear that even Kim Jong Il has an awareness of his own mortality. Whatever system will exist once he dies will need to appease the various military and party constituents, of which there is a vague awareness outside the DPRK but about which very little is known. Two things are pretty certain. The DPRK expectations of Chinese aid and economic assistance in the coming decade will grow stronger, just as demands on China's aid budget to lubricate its burgeoning relationships with Africa and Latin America are likely to grow. Very ironically, and in a different way, the PRC will be using the same economic powers it now has with Pyongyang as it will need to do with Taipei. Secondly, North Korea remains by far the most potentially destabilising issue on China's borders. For that reason, although its influence and power over the DPRK are more limited than is sometimes thought, there will be strong hopes that China will be central to discussions and actions relating to the DPRK, and that it will need to become increasingly proactive in dealing with this issue.

China as an international player by 2020

By 2020, the PRC's economic needs will remain its most important objective. These are linked intimately to the ability of the CCP to remain in power. But economic power will bring with it responsibilities and expectations. The question remains how far China is prepared, in its internal governance, for the decade ahead. The two examples of Taiwan and the DPRK given above are only the most direct, and central, to the PRC's interests, and the ones where the pressure on it to be proactive and clarify a position will be the greatest. There will be negative and positive aspects of this process as the decade moves on.

China's economic needs highlight two key areas – resources and overseas investment, where it can find new forms of influence, but also put itself in the way of new conflicts. The tension between its needs, and those of others, will be greatest. And there is a clear link between the two. Much of Chinese overseas investment so far has been in the area of mining and energy resources.

Resources

China's hunger for energy has been well documented.[32] Between 2000 and 2006, its energy demand grew by 76 per cent.[33] According to one report, 'While China is endowed with the world's fifth largest oil reserves, domestic production is set to decline. Beijing will have to rely increasingly on international sources for its oil.'[34] One of the key reasons behind this is not just industrial usage, but 'the unbridled rise in personal car ownership'. Two-thirds of China's imported oil comes in 2010 from the Middle East, from regions of great instability. But it is a highly inefficient user of energy, 'requiring almost five times more energy to create one unit of economic growth compared to the United States and up to twelve times more than Japan.'[35] One of the greatest problems in the coming decade is China's predicted continuing reliance on coal.[36] This will be one of the key drivers of China's environmental impact, a geopolitical issue in its own right. China has been working hard on improving its energy efficiency, one of the key priorities in the White Paper on Energy issued in 2007.[37] But without a significant technology breakthrough, it is hard to see how it would be possible to deliver such enormous efficiencies. It has also diversified its energy sources. But the fundamental reliance on fossil fuels will remain. In that case, the need to locate more of China's energy resources abroad, for all the talk of energy security and satisfying its key energy needs domestically, is strongly probable. While China will almost certainly be a key player in devising new energy technologies in the coming decade, and also look to invest in its own resources, its need for imported energy will, at best, level out. It is far likelier to increase dramatically. That brings with it sharper tensions with other competitors. The US and the EU are also big importers of energy. Already, they are competing for supply with Russia, the Middle East, and in Africa. Should there be a lack of a specific energy source, then the potential political fallout from this could be significant. It is not impossible, albeit unlikely in the time frame at which we are looking, to see this leading to out-and-out conflict.

Chinese overseas investment

Finding resources, from oil, to coal, to mineral and metals, has been a significant cause of China's outward investment since the 1980s.[38] The figures for Chinese overseas direct investment (ODI) have shot up in the last decade.[39] As of 2009, it stood as the world's sixth largest outward investor. Part of this was through its sovereign wealth funds, in particular the China Investment Corporation. Part of it was through its State Administration for Foreign Exchanges (SAFE). And part of it was through a host of state and non-state, central and provincial direct investments. These have started to appear in Europe, Africa, and Latin America, with one of the highest profile being the Geely acquisition of the Volvo brand in 2010. Chinese ODI has raised issues about its political nature (as with the attempt to acquire US energy company Unocal in 2005), its lack of governance (Chinese energy investment in Sudan), and its potential problems (environmental, lack of transparency, etc.). But with US$2.5 trillion of foreign reserves, as of March 2010, China's deployment of overseas capital is not likely to go away. And there are many areas where it has been viewed as welcome, and positive. Chinese ODI, in fact, will be one of the most tangible interfaces between the PRC and the outside world in the coming decade. We are likely to see the era of 'Made in China' being replaced by the era of 'Owned by China'. And while much of this investment will be in the resources and mining sectors, it is already diversifying. The political impact of this rapid increase of a new source of ODI will almost inevitably be significant.

International China in the coming decade – the two paths

China's rising prominence in the coming decades is almost inevitable. Beyond being felled by a massive pandemic, which causes huge social turbulence that sweeps the current CCP regime away and replaces it with a new, unstable and potentially disunified entity, or an international security or economic catastrophe which negatively impinges on the PRC, as things currently stand China's influence globally is only set to rise.

There are two potential responses to this by policymakers. One is to practise a form of containment, led by suspicion of China's long-term motives, its own internal stability, and its intentions towards the world. Containment, it is claimed, was the default specifically for US policy towards China from 1949 to at least 1972. Since then, it has been engagement. Could China's influence cause enough of a backlash in the US to mean that attempts were made to thwart its global intentions? Certainly, in the bad periods of US–China relations, such strategies start to look nastily possible. In late 2009 and early 2010, a series of issues, from arms sales to Taiwan, to President Obama meeting with the Dalai Lama, to Google lifting censorship on its main Chinese language website, crowned by the lack of agreement at the global climate change summit in Copenhagen in late 2009, all showed just how plentiful the areas for disagreement between the two were. Relations only began to thaw in April 2010.

There is increasing awareness in the US that China is now in a position to significantly impact on its interests. Talk of trade protectionism, and resentment over the economic imbalances, is starting to have real political impact. These will need to be dealt with in the next few years. China is likely to move, finally, towards full convertibility of its currency. There is need for a further round of global trade talks to address the inefficiencies of the world trade system. China is likely soon to have a more representative position on the International Monetary Fund and the World Bank. If, however, it exercises its new powers in ways which are too self-interested, then there will be a backlash, particularly in the US, but perhaps also in the EU and other countries that currently have large deficits. China's military expenditure will be watched closely. Its attitude to conflicts in other countries will be studied. Hardliners in the US may feel that China's increased prominence is a problem that needs to be dealt with. Their main levers for this will be trade. They will assert increasing restrictions over the sharing of technology with China. They will seek to build alliances that impede China's international space. They will seek areas of conflict, in order to place China under pressure.

The second alternative is to view China's new powers as positive, and something that brings benefit to the world. China's involvement in global issues in this scenario is embraced and encouraged. It is given greater representation in international bodies, and major technology cooperations are supported. Trade deficits are seen in the wider context of the benefits of having access to China's domestic markets, and to its pool of labour. It is given a leading role on resolving the issue of the DPRK, and is allowed to have increasing space in the Asian region, with improving military contact with the US and other leading powers.

While the first of these is too pessimistic, the second is too optimistic. In the coming decade, what is far likelier is something in between – a sort of 'third way' towards China. In that, while there will be substantial areas of common concern and cooperation, the fundamental fact that China maintains a political system markedly different from any major power in the West (and arguably from anyone else, for that matter), where one party maintains a monopoly on power, means that the possibility for misunderstanding and conflict in specific areas remains high. There need to be robust processes and mechanisms in place to deal with the high likelihood of these spats. As China becomes stronger, then it will also become more assertive, and the conflict within itself between those who want it to be more assertive with the world, and those who want it to be more compliant, will grow. On the way to 2020, the final possible rupture with needing to 'keep close to the US' will come nearer. But it will never finally happen because, in the next decade at least, the US will maintain its overwhelming military superiority.

More likely is a series of attritional battles over, for instance, resources, the Internet and trade, where China and the rest of the world will battle for influence, but in a way which does not get out of hand and lead to real conflict.

There are three key areas where China and the rest of the world need to agree what to do. Each has urgency, and failure to agree for both sides will pose significant challenges:

- *The environment.* Copenhagen 2009 was a taste of things to come. China's unwillingness to sign up to specific targets betrayed two things – the fears of the central government that they might commit to measures that impeded their ability to deliver the economic growth on which so much of their legitimacy is now based, and the strong feeling that the main responsibility for this issue lies with developed countries. These two issues need to be dealt with quickly, if the scientists are right and the world is facing imminent impact (meaning within the next decade) from the results of global climate change and greenhouse gas emissions. China's environmental problems have been dealt with in detail elsewhere. But their international consequences are considerable. This problem, therefore, while it begins within the borders of China, doesn't stop there. In the coming decade, China needs to work out a framework with the world where it can deal with the two issues that arose at Copenhagen – apportioning of responsibility for dealing with the problem, and handling the impact of whatever agreement is reached on China's own growth. Perhaps part of this will be a far deeper transfer of technology from developed countries to China than has been considered before. The only way this might be achievable politically is when something irrefutable happens which is as a result of climate change and strengthens the resolve and public opinion in the West that the costs of doing nothing are too high. If climate change is happening, and will have the environmental impact believed, then we are also looking at a future where there will need to be more equitable sharing of resources than in the past, and where Western consumer patterns will need to be adapted radically, unless some radical new technology is devised to prevent this. All of these will involve major political concord in the coming years. Copenhagen was only the beginning. (Jonathan Watts' contribution to this volume studies this in more detail.)

- *Energy.* This has been discussed above. Again, China's interests and their impact are indisputable. In the next decade, two issues will need to be addressed: how to balance the competing demands for security of supply by different countries on different supply sources, and also how to avoid conflict over failures in supply, if and when they happen. This might mean a carving up of the world into zones of influence, where China becomes the prime destination for investment in one area, and Europe and the US for another. Areas like the Middle East, however, with their rich reserves, continue to be hugely contentious, with supply going to anyone. It is likely that strengthening political ties in the coming decade will dictate that more energy goes more easily to China. Russia will play an increasing role in this. But how the West responds is important.

- *The global economy.* This is discussed in Peter Wood's chapter. But the need for an equitable, just global economic balance can't be underestimated. As China grows closer to being the world's largest economy, its non-convertible currency will be increasingly anomalous. It will want a great say in the global economic system. This is already partially being addressed. But a world in which China's banks and financial entities will be some of the most powerful in the world is growing closer.

A Beijing model

Will China's economic influence mean that it acts as a model for other countries, and starts to form a bloc of its own – developing countries, inspired by its performance, set against the developed world and westernisation? China talks of multi-polarity, and at least in its rhetoric seems to have set its face against such an outcome. But others have been keen to talk of a 'Beijing consensus' ranged against the Washington consensus.[40] 'China is marking a path for other nations around the world who are trying to figure out not simply how to develop their countries, but also how to fit into the international order in a way that allows them to be truly independent, to protect their way of life and political choices in a world with a single massively powerful centre of gravity,' Joshua Cooper Ramo argued.[41] The Beijing consensus is based on three postulates in his argument – rapid innovation, what Ramo calls 'chaos management', and self-determination.[42] For Martin Jacques, claims are even grander. On a whole range of fronts, from Beijing being a global capital to the Chinese economy presiding over something like a new commonwealth, the PRC will 'act as an alternative model to the West, embodying a very different kind of political tradition – a post-colonial, developing country, a Communist regime, a highly sophisticated statecraft, and an authoritarian Confucian rather than democratic polity'.[43] Jacques concludes his book with the statement, 'The arrival of China as a major power marks the end of Western universalism. Western norms, values and institutions will increasingly find themselves competing with those of China.'[44]

Getting clarity on what specifically a Chinese-led modernity might be like, however, has proved more difficult. There has been plenty of talk along the same lines as Ramo's about China offering a new model of how to do things. But as Zheng Yongnian, Chen Gang and Lye Liang Fook have noted, when talking about the huge display of military hardware on the anniversary of the PRC's sixtieth birthday in power in 2009, 'The display of military might is a clear indication that Beijing still looks at the world from the real politic perspective.'[45] It is hard to discern any grand claims to some new model on the part of the current elite leaders of the PRC, nor, for that matter, their chief ideologues. And with their highly self-interested behaviour at the Copenhagen Summit alienating members of the G77 group of developing countries, which China is ostensibly meant to lead, it is hard to even see them wanting to try to export a Chinese model for doing things – that was tried during the Maoist period, and led to the grotesque tragedy of Cambodia and the Maoist insurgency that continues to this day in Nepal. These are hardly things the current PRC is proud of.

The key factor: what happens within

Indeed, from whatever angle one looks at China's likely future international trajectory, it ends up almost invariably relating intimately to what happens within China. Political problems might provoke the government to push a more nationalist line, with knock-on effects on its relations with Japan and the US. Competing factions within the CCP elite might use foreign relations to stake out territory on which to attack each other. There might be a battle to prove who is working more in the national interest. Some might even try to address, finally, the sense of historic grievance from the 'century of humiliation' with a tougher, even more self-interested stand than prevails at the moment.

China's development of its own form of governance will be important, not only within the country, but beyond its borders. A reforming China, with some kind of democracy, would have a huge impact on issues like Taiwan, for instance. It would also allow more flexibility in dealing with related security issues, allowing even more cooperation and involvement than occurs at present, and alleviating some of the residual suspicion. China's internal governance will, of course, affect its stability, and its ability to create consensus across its complex population and the groups within it that have to be placated and appeased. An unstable China, where these issues are not properly addressed, or addressed too late, will be a major problem, for the world's economy, for addressing the economic and environmental issues of the coming decade, and for dealing with regional security issues. An unstable China and an unstable North Korea equates to an almost perfect storm. It is therefore, ironically, in the US and West's interests to have the current status quo, where China is stable, strong, and able to fulfil its role in the global order. Containment would be a self-defeating strategy.

China's international relations have been dominated since 1949 by the need to assert self-determination and self-reliance. As Wang Hui says, 'Absent this condition of self-reliance and it would be very difficult to picture how China's path to reform and opening up would have looked.'[46] Paradoxically, now the forces of globalisation are starting to subvert this. Perhaps a new vocabulary is needed for China to maintain its focus on autonomy, which addresses the historic grievances mentioned above, but allows it to move with greater confidence into the international arena. International relations theorist Richard Ned Lebow mentions three motivators for state actors historically – fear, interest and honour. The final one of these, honour, might have the most traction when looking at how China is likely to behave in the coming decade: 'When actors seek self-esteem through honour, standing or autonomy, they are often willing to risk, even sacrifice themselves or their political units in pursuit of these goals.'[47] Perhaps we are better looking at China as a country that has placed honour at the top of its priorities, and in any situation, even where it might be destructive to its interests, acts in order to preserve that honour. The clearer understanding, therefore, that policymakers have of the absolute non-negotiables of Chinese international engagement now, the less likelihood there is of misunderstanding, and the conflict that might arise from that.

As things stand, accommodation is going to be increasingly demanded. China is already encroaching on core interests of developed powers, through its economic behaviour, through its increased military capacity, through its actions in cyberspace, and through its proactive campaigns of soft power promotion. With interests so closely entwined, the fallout from any conflict would be hard to contain. In addition, China has bought most of the West's development agenda. This is the key complaint behind much of the anger in *China is Not Happy*. It would be an act of particular historic hubris to resent China's success when it is using the very things that, on the whole, the West was urging on it several decades ago.

Policymakers need, therefore, to be clear about where interests are common, where they are divergent, and where the territory is to be contentious. Cyber conflict is a good current example. It is likely that information will continue to be important to the economy and security in the coming decade. It is also likely that there will be increasing cases of aggressive, state-supported activity in cyberspace, compromising secure and public systems, and attempting not only to break and incapacitate those systems, but also to use them as a means of covertly getting information. At a certain stage, however, a wholly unregulated free-for-all in the international, largely boundary-free world of the Internet is going to impede individuals, companies, institutions and countries. As that becomes clearer, some ground rules, spoken or unspoken, for the operations of the World Wide Web are likely to become important. By 2020, we may we see a UN-supported convention on the legitimate and illegitimate uses of the Internet, just as we see international law grappling with just and unjust uses of conflict and violence between states.

Definition of areas of mutual self-interest is important. China's involvement in the global legal, economic and financial system now offers unique leverage. There are no more battles to be fought there. A new Cold War is almost unthinkable. Instead, there will be a series of attritional, low-level conflicts, in areas like trade, information flows and culture, where China will have to contend with attacks on a number of fronts. Without constantly excusing China, policymakers will also have to factor in a great deal of knowledge of the processes of how decision-making happens in the PRC. They will need to be as knowledgeable as they can about the background, systems of patronage, and structures of power within China, and see how these impact on decision-making. A knowledge-based framing of policy will be important.

Beyond this, policymakers will need to balance working to support stable change and a move to a more sustainable form of governance in the PRC, with understanding of the country's intrinsic vulnerabilities and potential sources of instability. There will need to be greater encouragement of PRC leaders explaining the position of their country to the world, and taking a higher-profile role. China has to get used now to being in a highly prominent, visible position. It can no longer speak like it is a small, developing country, when it carries US$2.5 trillion of foreign reserves. It must be encouraged to speak more clearly about its intentions, and to take a role, and explain that role, in issues that relate to it (and these now stretch from Asia to Latin America and Europe). Like the US, it is likely to become an object of attack by, for instance, international Islamic extremist terrorists because of its actions in Xinjiang. It is likely to become the constant target for requests for aid from African, Asian and other countries. Its assets abroad might become a target for disgruntled groups, either linked to those wanting political reform in China (unlikely) or those seeking to support the self-determination of border areas. It will increasingly be expected to participate, and fund, multilateral international peacekeeping activities, and be willing to involve itself in UN sanctions against proliferators or other international problem countries. The era of keeping a low profile is over. There is now need for a post-Dengist settlement, of building up its capacity and being high-profile.

China faces enormous challenges in the coming decade. It cannot face these alone. Nor can the world outside of China deal with key issues without China being involved. In the coming decade, there is the opportunity to frame a new international settlement, which replaces that put in place at the end of the Second World War. This is not going to be comfortable for those who see China as an intrinsic threat. Nor is it going to be easy to deal with some of the heavy-handed rhetoric of nationalism that is likely to emanate from China, and the response it may well get. But a pragmatic approach, based on mutual respect and understanding, is possible. After all, the CCP-led PRC is very rational in its prioritising of economic growth above all other things. It now needs to be encouraged, and given the space, to start taking a role in other issues. And while a world dominated by China and the Beijing model is not likely, one where the West and China needlessly clash and try to refight yesterday's wars should also be off the cards.

Notes

1. I am grateful for comments on earlier drafts of this chapter from Dr Rex Li, John Moores University, Liverpool.
2. This history is dealt with in Margaret Macmillan, *Seize the Hour: When Nixon Met Mao*, Harper Collins, London, 2006, with the transcripts of the discussions between the main parties which have been released in William Burr (ed), *The Kissinger Transcripts*, I B Tauris, New York, 2000.
3. Robert S. Ross, *Chinese Security Policy: Structure, Power and Politics*, Routledge, London, 2009, p. 71.
4. See M. Taylor Fravel, *Strong Borders, Secure Nation*, Princeton University Press, Princeton and Oxford, 2008, p. 1. 'In its territorial disputes, however, China has been less prone to violence and more cooperative than a singular view of an expansionist state suggests.'
5. See Gary Li's chapter in this volume for more on China's current, and projected, military capacity.
6. Ian Bremmer, 'China Knows the Time for Lying Low has Ended,' *Financial Times*, 29 March 2010, p. 11.
7. See Rex Li, *A Rising China and Security in East Asia: Identity Construction and Security Discourse*, Routledge, London, 2009, pp. 33–8.
8. William A Callahan, *China: The Pessoptimist Nation*, Oxford University Press, Oxford, 2010, p. 8.
9. Callahan, p. 9.

10. Wang Xiaodong, Song Shaojun, Huang Jilao, Song Qiang and Liu Yi (eds), *Zhongguo Bu Gaoxing*, Phoenix Publishing and Jiangsu People's Press, Jiangsu, 2009, p. 29. My translation.
11. Wang Xiaodong et al., p. 40.
12. Wang Xiaodong et al., p. 81.
13. Wang Xiaodong, et al., pp. 96–7.
14. Wang Xiaodong et al., p. 113.
15. Wang Xiaodong, et al., p. 87.
16. Ross, p 233
17. See Zheng Bijian, 'China's Peaceful Rise to Great Power Status', *Foreign Affairs*, September/October 2005.
18. Bruce Cumings, *Dominion from Sea to Sea: Pacific Ascendancy and American Power*, Yale University Press, New Haven, CT, 2009, p. 393.
19. Wang Hui, *The End of the Revolution: China and the Limits of Modernity*, Verso, London and New York, 2009, p. 132.
20. Stefan Halper, *The Beijing Consensus*, Basic Books, London, 2010, p. 13.
21. 'Google may pull out of China after Gmail cyber attack,' BBC News, 13 January 2010, at *http://news.bbc.co.uk/1/hi/business/8455712.stm*, accessed 29 March 2010.
22. 'Hillary Clinton calls on China to probe Google attack,' BBC News, 21 January 2010, at *http://news.bbc.co.uk/1/hi/world/americas/8472683.stm*, accessed 5 October 2010.
23. Bates Gill, *Rising Star: China's New Security Diplomacy*, Brookings Institution Press, Washington, DC, 2007, p. 10.
24. Gill, p. 118.
25. 'Wen: China disagrees to so-called G2', *China Daily*, 18 November 2009, at *http://www.chinadaily.com.cn/china/2009–11/18/content_8998039.htm*, accessed 5 October 2010.
26. Kerry Brown, 'China–EU marriage on the rocks but salvageable', *The Diplomat*, 12 January 2010, at *http://the-diplomat.com/2010/01/12/china-eu-marriage-on-the-rocks-but-salvageabl/*, accessed 5 October 2010.
27. Bobo Lo, *Axis of Convenience: Moscow, Beijing and the New Geopolitics*, Brookings Institute, Washington, DC, 2008, p. 3.
28. Bill Emmott, *Rivals: How the Power Struggle Between China, India and Japan will Shape Our Next Decade*, Allen Lane, London, 2008, p. 51.
29. For the history of this, see Susan Shirk, *China: Fragile Superpower*, Oxford University Press, Oxford, 2007, Chapter Five, pp. 140–81.
30. Ian Taylor, *China's New Role in Africa*, Lynne Rienner, Boulder, CO and London, 2009, p. 15.
31. President Ma Ying Jeou's National Day Address, 10 October 2009, at *http://www.mac.gov.tw/ct.asp?xItem=66641&ctNode=5909&mp=3*, accessed 5 October 2010.
32. See, for instance, James Kynge, *China Shakes the World: The Rise of the Hungry Nation*, updated edition, Phoenix, 2009.
33. Michal Meidan (ed.), *Shaping China's Energy Security: The Inside Perspective*, Asia Centre, Paris, 2007, p. 18.
34. Meidan, p. 18.
35. Meidan, p. 21.

36. Meidan, p. 101.
37. Full details at *http://www.china.org.cn/english/environment/236955.htm*, section three, accessed 6 April 2010.
38. Xiaohua Yang and Clyde Soltenberg, 'Institutional Considerations, New Pathways' in Ilan Alan and John McIntyre (eds), *Globalization of Chinese Enterprises*, Palgrave Macmillan, Basingstoke, 2008, pp. 63–4.
39. See Kerry Brown, 'No reverse gear,' pp. 8 to 12, for statistics up to 2008, at *http://www.kerry-brown.co.uk/files/clsa_paper_final.pdf*, accessed 7 April 2010.
40. The most famous example of this was Joshua Cooper Ramo in *The Beijing Consensus*, Foreign Policy Centre, London 2004, available at *http://fpc.org.uk/fsblob/244.pdf*, accessed 5 October 2010.
41. Ramo, p. 3.
42. Ramo, pp. 11–12.
43. Martin Jacques, *When China Rules the Waves: The Rise of the Middle Kingdom and the End of the Western World*, Allen Lane, London, 2009, p. 398.
44. Jacques, p. 434.
45. Zheng Yongnian, Chen Gang and Lye Liang Fook, 'China's politics in 2009: an increasingly confident leadership', in *East Asian Policy*, January–March 2010, p. 8.
46. Wang Hui, *The End of the Revolution: China and the Limits of Modernity*, Verso Books, London, pp. xix–xx.
47. Richard Ned Lebow, *A Cultural Theory of International Relations*, Cambridge University Press, Cambridge, 2008, p. 19.

3

The Chinese economy in the next decade

Peter Wood

The best way to predict the future is to invent it.

(Alan Kay)

Opening the US–China Strategic Economic Dialogue in June 2009, the head of the Chinese delegation, Dai Bingguo, set out the Chinese leadership's key priorities: 'China's core interests are first the maintenance of the basic system and national security, second national sovereignty and territorial integrity, and third the continued stable development of economy and society.'

Starting from this clear statement of China's current strategic priorities, in this chapter I will explore what it means to talk about China's future and what core elements we need to keep at the forefront of our minds as we do so. In sum this involves first considering why so much effort is put into looking into China's crystal ball and what impact that has on the real world. Second, it means reminding ourselves that any 'underlying' trends such as demography or urbanisation are not natural artefacts but rather deeply political issues. The economy, therefore, is always political economy. I will explore this by looking at some themes which will dominate China's growth over the next ten years: population structure and geographic dispersal; urbanisation plans; the role of the state; financial sector reform. Third, I will suggest that Dai Bingguo's statement as it plays out in policy tells us that the government aims to insulate China as much as possible from external turbulence while at the same time extracting benefit from growing, but still partial, integration into the global economy. Growing but partial integration creates delicate and often unstable balances across a range of policy sectors, pushing and pulling the government in a variety of different ways.[1]

An essay on the prospects for the Chinese economy might reasonably begin by setting out the global macroeconomic context. Such a discussion would be a book all of its own. Nevertheless, I do argue in conclusion that those who wish to think about China's future need also to think about the global context in which that future unfolds, including, of course, their own futures. We all need to become more reflexive rather than assuming that the future is ours alone to invent.

Forecasting China

All those forecasts about China emanating from banks, investment institutions and multilateral organisations have real effects in the real world. Their impact on policymaking, inside and outside China, is more interesting than the forecasts themselves.

Forecasts have four elements: they try to shape the future that is being forecast; they build a consensus behind that forecast that can be monetised; they problematise areas and issues which the forecaster believes need to be corrected to achieve his or her desired outcome; and they act as a political justification for policies in other places that see themselves as already in competition with China or, depending on the forecast, that expect to be engaged in such competition in the near future. Forecasts tell us as much, if not more, about the forecaster than about China.

It has become an accepted commonplace that something has changed in the past decade or less, a change that the financial crisis served to accelerate but not to initiate. Niall Ferguson describes this as 'the end of 500 years of western ascendancy'.[2] There is something apocalyptic about this that ought to give us pause for thought, not because shifts of power do not happen but because it is not entirely clear what might be meant by economic power in the twenty-first century. Parsing the anxiety brings out concerns that China – whatever we might mean by that word – might use the size of its market and/or foreign exchange reserves to effect unilateral changes in the global economic system.[3] It is this that prompts much peering into the economic tea leaves to see whether China does indeed offer, consciously or unconsciously, an alternative model of political and economic development that can rival the dominant western neoliberal model, forgetting that that dominant western model is itself of recent origin.

Simplifying matters, it is states and their citizens that feel this anxiety. Institutions of private capital see only the possibility of profit. Predictions about the Chinese economy range from doom, most recently put forward by STRATFOR,[4] to world supremacy, with one commentator forecasting that by 2040 China's per capita income would reach US$85,000, double the forecast for the European Union.[5] It is a measure of the inflation built into the forecasting process that the prediction made by Goldman Sachs that the size of China's economy would exceed that of the US in 2040, a date subsequently brought forward to 2027,[6] now looks moderate and mainstream.

Mixed in with this is optimism or fear, depending on where we are in the cycle between the twin poles of sinomania and sinophobia,[7] representing a more complex set of constructions and responses that are mediated into the language of economists. The dialectic of yellow peril and the hard-working Asian turns on economic efficiency or, as Arif Dirlik, paraphrasing Colleen Lye, has put it, 'over the century and a half of relations between the United States and China, it has been an American dream to convert China to capitalism, which turns into a nightmare the moment the conversion begins to show signs of success'.[8]

The irony is that, seen from within China, the view looks different. Chinese policymakers are grappling with a complex set of issues without historical parallel. No doubt when the moment arrives that the Chinese economy is bigger than the US economy there will be much angst in the international media but for the Chinese government the key indicator will remain per capita GDP and income figures. Even on the most optimistic forecasts these will remain low for some time, an average that in itself will mask wide differences between richer eastern China, where per capita GDP in Jiangsu, Zhejiang, Fujian, Shandong, Guangdong and Shanghai could reach US levels in the mid 2020s,[9] and the poorer west. Within China, debate at present is dominated by anxieties about social stability and other immediate problems.[10] It often seems, when putting side by side the way Chinese write about their own country and the way others write about it, that there are two very different Chinas.

Nevertheless, much of what happens in the real world of politics is driven by perceptions based on forecasts. The Chinese government responds to other governments and corporations responding to forecasts that are themselves responses to something that one or other of the players in this merry-go-round might have said. Suddenly South Africa announces that it has approached China to be included in the BRICs, giving us the spectacle of the five biggest developing economies shaping themselves according to Goldman Sachs. Anthony Bolton of Fidelity decides to move to Hong Kong on the grounds that China is too good an opportunity to miss, not just to get ahead of the pack but more to lead the pack in the same direction, not so much following the money as hoping to attract more of it. The aggregate consensus becomes an important variable in any discussion of the future direction of China's GDP, the structure of China's economy, and China's economic policy.

We have to begin, therefore, by recognising that forecasts are important not because they might – or more likely might not – be right but because nevertheless they act as templates for the making of decisions now. China's economy in 2020 is already in the price. As Alan Kay said, albeit in a different context, the best way to predict the future is to invent it.

The Chinese state

Politics matters because where China will be in 2020 depends on where we think China is now. To call the current structure of power in China 'state capitalism' does not take us very far. France and China may both pursue policies that favour industrial champions, and both may reject some aspects of Anglo-Saxon capitalism, but they are, of course, very different. One way to look at this is to contrast the development of capitalism in the West and in East Asia. In the former, capitalists dominated the state, while in the latter market exchange was promoted by the state but large-scale capital was held in check. Japan created a mixed system by grafting elements of the western capitalist model onto its own economy. Arguments about whether the Chinese political system will become more 'western', therefore, are as much about whether the Chinese economy will become not so much more capitalist but whether control of its commanding heights will be handed over to globalised capital.[11] Phrased in this way, the answer to the question is of course a clear negative. It is not on the agenda of the Chinese Communist Party (CCP) to hand power over to another institution in China, let alone foreign capital. The first step, therefore, is to remember that the Chinese leadership is focused on Chinese interests, as defined domestically, including in this the maintenance of control over the key levers of power.

This is not the place to undertake a full-scale discussion of prospects for China's political system but again this matters in economic terms because these debates in turn influence decision making. Scenarios tend to offer three possible outcomes: the emergence of a democratic China; prolonged chaos; or a resilient, authoritarian China.[12] The impact of the middle scenario on the rest of the world, economically and politically, would be enormous. Every other forecast about the nature of the global economy in 2020 would have to be thrown out of the window. On the less apocalyptic forecasts the nature of economic growth would be different during what has been dubbed a democratic transition from that under the so-called resilient and authoritarian leadership.

In the democratic transition argument it is the weight of a growing Chinese middle class, finding its voice and defending its economic and property interests, which pushes the leadership to change. In the resilient authoritarian scenario it is the leadership, and the CCP, which defends its own economic interests and maintains its position, if not necessarily its legitimacy, as the sole institution capable of defending China's national sovereignty overseas and maintaining stability at home.

These scenarios assume that it is only China that will, or has to, change, while western states will remain as they are, but there is no reason to treat China as the sole independent variable. Inequality has increased and middle-class living standards have stagnated in the US for more than twenty years. In listing what the new Chinese middle class can apparently look forward to – 'The middle class usually enjoy stable housing, healthcare and educational opportunities (including college) for their children, reasonable retirement and job security, and discretionary income that can be spent on vacation and leisure pursuits'[13] – Homi Kharas has merely set out the very items increasingly problematic in western societies. This, of course, is without discussing issues of chronic poverty. The irony is, therefore, that the very class expected to generate demands for shifts to an ill-defined liberal political system in China is itself beleaguered in the west.

Politics, policy and the state

Within this overall framework of political structures and the interests they may represent, the issue for foreign analysts of the Chinese economy is simple: does China develop institutions familiar to a western capitalist economy and thereby become more intelligible or does it continue to achieve high levels of growth with its own set of institutions? Analysis of the early stages of China's reform suggested that it was possible to achieve similar ends through radically different institutional means.[14] China had managed to achieve high levels of growth, at least in the short term, without many of the institutions deemed necessary for development by western scholars. Will this remain the case? Indeed, how far was the specific growth model pursued by China itself a function of its set of specific political institutions, and will, therefore, a shift in that growth model, as called for by many in Washington, be impossible without fundamental changes in those political institutions?

This takes us to the question of different economic interests. In *The Pitfalls of Modernisation*, He Qinglian argued that divorcing analysis of China's economy from China's politics led to distorted and misleading conclusions.[15] Her solution was to draw on the public policy school of research and look at the motivators driving Chinese officials and senior political figures. He's call for a political economy of China remains as necessary as ever. Issues are never purely economic, nor are they ever purely political.[16]

The Chinese leadership is now taken up with preparations for the transfer of power to a new generation in 2012 according to mechanisms that are well established and that will take China through to 2022 (a process dealt with in detail by Kate Westgarth elsewhere in this book). Conventional wisdom divides the political elite into a faction which espouses welfare policies to support the poor and one which advocates continuing a more thoroughly Dengist line of letting some grow even richer in the interests of overall economic development, the two factions coexisting and cooperating. The two positions would, of course, generate alternative policies on taxation, investment, and the role of the state in the economy. Even as there is a handover in the leadership, changes in China's economy and society are creating new interest groups and lobbies, inside and outside the system.

The question then is how state, Party and economy will shape each other in the coming decade. None are variables independent of the other. The state and the Party possesses mechanisms to influence and direct enterprise behaviour, either through the State-owned Assets Supervision and Administration Commission (SASAC) and the Organisation Department of the CCP which controls senior appointments in the case of state-owned enterprises or through Party committees in the case of private enterprises. State and Party interests operate not just at the level of central government but also at lower levels, influencing, directing and shaping all forms of business behaviour.

The state directs the operations of enterprises both as regulator and in many cases as owner. Huang Yasheng's recent work,[17] focusing on changes in the share of investment in the economy, suggests that state intervention in the economy has if anything increased in recent years and that since the early 1990s the share of investment by private business has fallen sharply, a phenomenon that he goes on to re-cast as a shift in the balance between entrepreneurial, market-driven rural China in the 1980s and state-led urban China in the 1990s. This is the phenomenon much discussed in the Chinese press of '*guo jin min tui*' or 'State advances private withdraws'.

The state advances in a wide variety of ways. The state is a source of investment funds, either through budgetary allocations or through the banks that, for all their listing on various stock exchanges, remain state controlled. As a consequence, private firms face considerable difficulty in accessing bank credit.[18] The state is also owner of enterprises at every level of government. As policymaker the state sets to direct not just macroeconomic performance but industrial growth, latterly through long-term 'Plans for Adjustment and Rejuvenation' of ten sectors (steel, auto, shipbuilding, machinery, IT, light industry, textiles, petrochemicals, logistics and metallurgy). Finally, the state and the Party act as regulator in a variety of ways, from the more transparent and technocratic end of the financial regulators to the opaque operations of Party committees. Here there is anecdotal evidence that the financial crisis allowed even officials in regions where private enterprise had flourished to interfere in the operations of non-state enterprises.[19]

The complex of interacting interests operating today suggests that whatever the direction of evolution of the Chinese economy it is certainly not in the direction of something that would look familiar to proponents of markets in the West. Governments at local level have strong-armed private enterprises into agreeing to takeovers by poorly performing SOE counterparts.[20] Efforts by SASAC to direct central SOEs to focus on their core areas of business can be read as evidence either of the state taking a firm line or of the state failing to impose its will. Industrial SOEs have shown an eagerness to join the rush to get into whatever sector appears to be booming, including real estate[21] but also, and of much greater concern, finance, with Sinopec acquiring a bank in Xinjiang and State Grid expanding its own investments in China's banking sector.[22] The consequence of this is the creation of a tangle of cross-cutting SOE investments and government-influenced market interests that only clear policy objectives and determined political intervention would be able to unravel, even if such unravelling was considered desirable.

I began by suggesting that the future shape of the economy depends on how we characterise the Chinese state. This is precisely the point of what Dani Rodrik has termed the policy trilemma: one can have any two of national sovereignty, democracy and globalisation, but not all three.[23] Forecasts of the trajectory of either the political system or the economy cannot ignore the question of the relationship between the state and capital. But even if the scenarios of political change pointing to increasing moderate and stable political openness played out as predicted, it is by no means clear that this would automatically involve untangling the existing web of cross-cutting business and political interests. Privatisation, advocated as the standard route for extricating government from business, has had mixed results in other transition economies and might well result merely in the widening of inequality in an already unequal society.

China and the global economy

We can look at the relationship between state and economy in China in another way by thinking about China's interactions with the global economy. The picture that emerges here is that of a guarded embrace of globalisation. It is unlikely that this embrace will turn into full-scale union but the status quo is dynamic rather than static. What will emerge is likely to be a hybrid, the product of policies responding to conflicting domestic and international pressures.

China's interactions with the global economy over the past 30 years have been marked by a number of shifts, the result of domestic policy changes – opening up in 1978, Deng's Southern Tour in 1992, resumption of sovereignty over Hong Kong, accession to the WTO – and exogenous events – the Asian Financial Crisis and the globalisation of industrial supply chains. The specifics of China's development should not distract us from a broader trend, the growth of developing economies in general, leading to the latest OECD forecast that by 2030 these will account for almost 60 per cent of world GDP. To a degree that is perhaps unprecedented, China's economic future will be a function of global macroeconomic developments. But this is not a shift between the West and China. It is a shift between developed and developing and between economies within the developing category, hence the fluidity of movement from G3 to G7 to G20 to G77.

This is why comparisons with the past, and in particular the most commonly made comparison between China now and Japan thirty years ago, are of limited value. Japan, so the argument runs, built an economy based on exports, recycling the consequent foreign exchange surpluses into US dollars, a model which caught Deng Xiaoping's attention during his 1978 visit to Japan and which China has successfully emulated. But the present is not exactly like the past. Japan was a client state of the US. And if the Chinese state is profoundly different from the Japanese state the degree of financialisation of the global economy in 2010 is markedly greater than in 1980. This is also why comparisons with

China in the past are also of limited use. China now is far more integrated with the global economy than it was at the height of the Qing Dynasty. This is entirely new territory, both for the rest of the world and for the people of China.

If China is in uncharted waters, so too is the global economy. The consensus at present is that the focus of global asset growth has shifted, or is shifting, from developed to developing markets. A recent McKinsey report[24] suggested that the exceptional expansion in financial assets – a quadrupling – between 1980 and 2007 and the associated increase in global capital flows had come to an end. Mature financial markets are likely to see slower growth than in the past, reverting to a rate in line with GDP growth, while growth in developing markets will continue and continue to accelerate. The growth in capital flows will therefore not just slow but also change in form and direction. Western governments will have to repair fiscal imbalances. Western consumers will rein in their spending habits. Western financial institutions must look for profit either to regulatory arbitrage in their home markets or to growth in developing markets. Capital will flow to developing countries and in particular to China.

The weakness in this argument is that it assumes that the structure of the global economy will be able to continue unchanged, with merely a reshuffling of some of the cards in the pack. This is mistaken on two levels. The first, of course, is that business as usual is the least likely outcome of recent, or even not so recent, events. A range of views, from Brenner's account of the falling rate of return on capital as a long-term secular trend creating successive systemic crises,[25] to Simon Johnson's description of a 'doomsday cycle',[26] show that if one thing is certain it is that business is going to be unusual. The whole point of pushing the Chinese to consume more is precisely an attempt to make the future indistinguishable from the past. But that past was built on disguising stagnating incomes through higher levels of leverage, a process that has run its course.

Beyond this, however, reshuffling the cards in itself changes the pack. As described by Arrighi, the financialisation of recent years represented 'the autumn of a particular material expansion, centring on a particular state'.[27] It is not necessary to subscribe to the idea that China is about to become some sort of global hegemon to understand that China's growing power and influence changes the way markets work, from China's role as a setter of rules to the re-engineering of capitalism that the mere fact of China's significance will bring about. In part this stems from efforts by the Chinese leadership precisely to manage the process of financialisation within China. Those efforts, born out of the focus on social and economic stability, dictate on the one hand that financialisation to some degree is to be allowed because it raises living standards in general and generates capital for powerful sections of Chinese society, but on the other that it is to be controlled and channelled both because it is necessary to maintain Chinese elite control over the circulation of capital and because not to do so is precisely to create the conditions for the shocks to stability that must be avoided.

That there is going to be another crisis following on from that of 2008–9 ought to be obvious, even if the form it will take is not. Dai Bingguo's statement of China's national interests tells us both how the Chinese government might seek to avoid becoming embroiled in the next crisis and reminds us that integration comes in many different guises and will have its limits. As with every other area of Chinese policy the strategy of the Chinese leadership is to encourage interaction without relinquishing the state and Party control considered essential to maintaining social stability and national sovereignty.[28] The maintenance of social stability requires insulation from external shocks as much as possible. This in turn requires continued control by the Party of key economic interests. This will not change without a seismic shift in Chinese political institutions. Conversely, the maintenance of political legitimacy requires continued economic growth. These two requirements dictate the current semi-integration of China into the world economic and financial systems. How this develops will determine the range of possible different economic trajectories.

One facet of integration or semi-integration relates to trade, the decoupling debate analysed by Jonathan Anderson at UBS.[29] China's integration into global supply chains has, of course, proceeded at a rapid pace since WTO accession. Foreign trade now constitutes some 38 per cent of GDP, by any standards a high degree of openness.[30]

This trade and industrial integration might be expected to deepen and change over the next decade. It will change because it is government policy to encourage Chinese enterprises to move up the value chain, a process that will also be driven by increases in wages and the so-called demographic tipping point, forecast for 2015. The government also wishes to see the creation of Chinese industrial enterprises with a global reach of their own to match that of the western and Japanese multinationals that currently dominate the landscape. Chinese enterprises themselves prefer to create a solid domestic platform first by eliminating domestic competition before moving overseas. Competition within China is going to remain fierce, putting downward pressure on profitability.

The threat to the continuation of this trade globalisation comes from the prospect of protectionism. The terms under which business is done have changed. On the one hand the Chinese leadership is well aware that for many multinationals profitability hinges on the China market, a reliance that the prospect of slow growth in the next decade only deepens. Uniquely, however, China is not dependent on foreign capital and therefore is in a position to pick and choose while dangling the carrot of access to an enormous potential market. If foreign multinationals need China, western governments need jobs, investment and growth. For them the shift of economic power creates only difficulties that ultimately set them at odds with corporate interests. Growth in China does not help the US unless it translates into growth there too.

The difficulty for foreign corporations seeking to invest in China or do business there is that uniquely this is a market that does not need to bend over backwards to make itself a favoured destination and it is most unlikely that the multilateral instruments that have prised open markets elsewhere, particularly the IMF, will be called in to resolve macroeconomic difficulties. Foreign corporations, therefore, cannot rely on their own governments or international institutions to come to their aid. The solution put forward by some, particularly banks, to become in some way part Chinese by listing on the Shanghai stock exchange is purely cosmetic. Corporations therefore face a situation in which they are genuinely on their own for the first time in decades.

The result of all this is likely to be a shift in the constellation of forces over the next decade as western governments seek to ensure that mobile multinationals are both encouraged, by measures that protect domestic markets, and compelled, by tax and other legislation, to continue to contribute to social stability in western societies. Corporations will have to find their own ways to survive in an environment in which they enjoy less political protection than in the past. The Chinese government will remain willing to negotiate as it sees its interests threatened or furthered.

China is of course integrated into the global economy not just as an exporter and supply chain hub but also as an importer of raw materials on a massive scale. Driven so far by a model of development based on the development of heavy industry but in the future increasingly by the demands of urbanisation, Chinese commodity imports are forecast to grow at an exponential rate. The long-term impact of this on commodity prices is far from clear. Chinese demand has been of great benefit for commodity producers. Chinese global resource procurement serves to expand and diversify supplies of natural resources and to make the market more efficient.[31] This need for resources will shape China's foreign

Table 3.1 China's import dependence for major minerals[32]

Product	Import Dependence (%)		
	2000	2010	2020
Oil	31	41	58
Iron	33	34	52
Manganese	16	31	38
Copper	48	72	82
Lead	0	45	52
Zinc	0	53	69

policy, both at the level of the government and at the level of the activities of large state-owned enterprises. In the absence of currency reform it is also already shaping some exchange rates, as we have seen with the Australian Dollar.

The financial sector

While the integration into global trade has proceeded apace, integration of the financial sector has been much slower, a process designed to insulate China from external financial shocks and retain Party control of key financial levers while at the same time allowing the government to take some steps to increase domestic liquidity. Capital account liberalisation has moved slowly. This is the narrower version of Rodrik's trilemma: how to pursue an independent domestic monetary policy and limit exchange rate flexibility, while at the same time controlling international capital flows.[33] Policy on the exchange rate continues to see a key role for government control. For all the stakes in Chinese banks taken by foreign financial institutions the banking sector has remained largely protected. The experience of 2009 has shown that in the last resort China's banks remain instruments of central government policy and credit allocation, albeit with the new twist that this time round they will seek to replenish their depleted coffers with funds raised from investors, both Chinese and foreign. But if the banks escaped the effects of subprime in the US, China's stock markets did react to events in US financial markets.[34]

Setting aside what western analysts see as the causes of the crisis, the Chinese leadership formulates policy on the basis of lessons learnt from the

Asian Financial Crisis of 1997, lessons reinforced by recent experience. Zhou Xiaochuan attributes Asian trade and savings imbalances to a response to that crisis which he has described as an 'attack of speculative capital'. Substantial foreign exchange reserves are merely 'defensive reactions against predatory speculation', speculation which the international community subsequently failed to take steps to curb. A key element, therefore, in Zhou's list of steps needing to be taken is increased regulation of cross-border speculative capital flows.[35] The message is clear: liberalisation inside China should be matched by tighter regulation outside China.

For all the technical reforms such as a gold futures market and a NASDAQ equivalent in Shenzhen, the core of the Chinese financial system remains state dominated. State control here means policy settings, regulation, ownership, as in the banks, and/or management veto. Key areas of policy control remain interest rates, which have yet to be liberalised, and full RMB convertibility, which remains a distant prospect. One source of pressure on this will come from a wealthier and older population. Households will need stable long-term savings options and pensions, a shift from the current position in which it is the state that saves. Misallocation of resources is endemic, as we have seen with the surge in government-inspired corporate lending in 2009. With real deposit rates at or close to zero this in turn depresses consumption by limiting returns to households on savings, supports an inefficient banking sector, and by effectively removing interest rates as a tool to control the economy forces the government to resort to administrative measures and leads to inefficient investment.[36] The IMF solution to this stresses the importance of financial intermediation to the performance of modern market economies and the limits of traditional banking systems and calls for the liberalisation of interest rates and the development of capital markets.[37]

Managing this shift would be a considerable regulatory challenge alone but this pales into insignificance when we consider the political consequences, as interest groups see established positions threatened and the Chinese leadership seeks to maintain core state and Party control.[38] The banks remain dominated by state and Party interests, despite IPOs and the selling of stakes to strategic investors. SOEs are both major beneficiaries of the current arrangement and also investors in financial institutions. Reform is also not likely to appeal to sections of the central government that were relieved to be able to use the banking system as a lever to deliver stimulus to the economy in a manner far beyond anything western governments could manage. Such reform would also require granting independence to the People's Bank of China and allowing it to make decisions about rates without seeking the approval of the State Council.

In addition to the policy settings, state control over the financial sector through ownership and management veto will also remain a cornerstone of policy. The aim is both to facilitate the raising of funds and to maintain direct control. Foreign private equity firms have signed agreements with local governments to establish RMB denominated funds.[39] There is debate within China about setting up an equivalent of SASAC for Chinese financial institutions that hitherto have managed without supervision by any body that might claim to represent the interests of the state as the majority shareholder.[40] The reasons for this should be obvious by now. Liberalisation will have to fit into Dai Bingguo's statement of China's national priorities.

This is not to say that reform of interest rates will not take place over the coming decade, but it is highly unlikely to be anything other than extremely gradual. Experience in other areas of the economy is a helpful guide in this respect. The exchange rate is the most sensitive area of state control of prices at present but continued controls over factory prices should also remind us that abandoning controls over prices deemed fundamental to economic growth or to social stability is difficult at the best of times.

There is, however, another aspect to all this that will drive Chinese policy in new, and unexpected, directions: the acquisition of foreign assets. China's foreign assets position swung from a position of net debtor of around 9 per cent of GDP in 1999 to that of net creditor of more than 30 per cent of GDP at the end of 2007. In absolute terms China's net foreign assets at the end of 2007 ranked second only to Japan. Some estimate that China's gross foreign assets and liabilities could triple by 2020.[41] By any standards this is a remarkable position for China to be in. This is an issue that will shape Chinese integration into the global economy over the next few decades. Dai Bingguo's formulation should lead us to expect that the commanding heights will remain under Chinese political control in order to maintain stability, while the growth in the accumulation of foreign assets will also continue, as the BIS paper predicts.

Multilateral policymaking is also going to change under the impact of China's shifting semi-integration. The engagement of the Chinese government and of Chinese institutions in the changes to the global financial architecture will become increasingly obvious. Even as the IMF makes a push to raise its profile and change its image in Asia it argues that international monetary policy must seek to dissuade countries from accumulating substantial reserves as insurance against shocks. Clearly Chinese agreement to this will be essential but it is hard to see that agreement being forthcoming. At another level future changes to the Basel accords will need to take into account concerns among Chinese banks about the scope of international banking regulation. Jiang Jianping of ICBC has already made negative comments on the exclusion of land use rights from the capital account.[42] Just as there are many inside China who talk about there being a need to set a China price, so the government and the banks will aim to ensure that global rules are tailored to meet Chinese concerns.

We can sum up by saying that the one constant over the next decade and more will be that the Party, acting in defence of China's interests as it sees them, will act both to maintain its own leading role and subordinate foreign economic interests to the maintenance of that role, even as it also pursues on behalf of its population the growth that has become the basis for its legitimacy. In the West the idea that economic efficiency trumps all else has achieved the status of hallowed orthodoxy, at least in theory if not in practice. It is by no means a given that China will follow suit.

Inequality and consumption

Analysis of trends in China's economy has focused almost exclusively on consumption. Partly this is because increasing domestic consumption is seen by many as the principal, if not sole, means of redressing global imbalances; partly it is because foreign corporations see China's consumer goods market as having the biggest growth potential.[43] But the number of Louis Vuitton bags sold in China is a trivial index of any country's economic development. Consumption is but a part of bigger questions about the future of the Chinese development model, poverty and inequality.

China's progress in lifting people out of absolute poverty has been impressive. Measured against the revised international poverty standard of $1.25 per person per day, poverty has declined from 85 per cent in 1981 to 27 per cent in 2004.[44] This decline has continued since then. In addition to absolute poverty, however, there is vulnerability to poverty as a result of income shocks. Seventy per cent of income poverty and 40 per cent of consumption poverty in rural areas is attributable to risk,[45] leading to high levels of rural saving. If transient poverty is one new aspect of the problem, the geographical dispersal of the poor is another, rendering area-based programmes less effective. Furthermore, poverty in China is much less responsive to GDP growth than in the past.

While poverty has declined, inequality has increased, in part because access to a much wider range of services than hitherto depends on income, in part because urban labour force participation rates have declined, between 1999 and 2003 by 10 per cent, both factors in turn increasing vulnerability to transient poverty. Transient poverty is, of course, a particular issue for rural migrant workers, of whom at the last official count there were 157 million.[46] One important aspect of the solution to the problem involves increasing the returns to labour. What poor households 'lack are adequate returns to their main asset, which is their labour, and what they need is greater and more rewarding employment'.[47] Migration of labour to urban areas has been an important part of that solution but it has in turn created a number of problems that threaten to entrench poverty among those left behind.

Do poverty and inequality matter? Even if the capacity of GDP growth to reduce poverty is reduced, surely the glittering future anticipated for the Chinese economy will ensure that the problem will vanish of its own accord in due course. This has been the Deng philosophy, one shared with mainstream western economics for the past thirty years. But for China and the current leadership they do matter in two ways. First, eradication of poverty is central to the Party's legitimacy. Second, He Qinglian argued in *Pitfalls of Modernisation* that inequality arose not from the distribution of national income but from the intervention of holders of power in the allocation of national resources. Inequality is both an issue of social justice and an index of the misallocation of resources.

Rather than ask, therefore, as many do, how big the Chinese consumer market is going to be in ten years' time we should be asking what will be the level of poverty and inequality. By so doing we will also be asking how, if at all, China's growth model might change.

Inequality today takes many forms. One is the gap between wages in state-owned enterprises and private enterprises.[48] The China Justice Survey of 2004 showed mean per capita incomes for urban workers of 10,558 RMB, migrant workers of 4,889 RMB and rural workers of 4,033 RMB.[49] This speaks to the gap in access to funding for investment between state-owned enterprises and private enterprises. It also speaks to the lighter regulation that smaller private enterprises can sometimes enjoy from their local governments in contrast to central state-owned enterprises that are more likely to observe centrally instituted standards. Another is rapidly growing inequality in the distribution of wealth. Savings deposits in the names of Chinese millionaires constituted 40 per cent of total savings deposits in 2009.[50] In 2007 household saving among the top two income deciles accounted for 48 per cent of total household saving, compared with 3 per cent among the lowest two deciles.[51] This inequality in income and savings is reflected in activity in the real estate sector, one of the few investment options open to those with savings. Real estate has become a key means for those who already have savings to increase their wealth.

This is the context for discussion of the reasons for China's high savings rate and low consumption rates and widespread enthusiasm among foreign observers in particular for the prospect of China developing into a major consumer society. The debate about the causes of China's high savings rate has yet to reach a conclusion, with government, state-owned enterprises and households variously blamed.[52] There is, however, widespread agreement that the solution involves a range of policies to improve social security, pension provision, public health care and public education. A separate category of required reforms, as we have seen, involves the financial sector, liberalisation of interest rates and the facilitation of new forms of saving that will allow households to earn a better rate of return on their investments. A final category focuses on the governance of SOEs which pay minimal dividends and enjoy easy access to low-cost financing. The result is high levels of investment, not always in profitable ventures, as the volume of SOE funds in real estate have shown.[53]

This list of reform measures alone ought to indicate the complexity of the issue. They do not all point in the same direction. Those who call for policies to increase retail consumption, for example, also warn against increasing taxes on the better off to pay for increased provision of public services on the grounds that this would stifle such consumption. The provision of a range of improved public services raises the question of accountability at all levels of government.[54]

Tackling these problems over the next decade and more, therefore, will involve reshaping not just the country's economic growth paradigm but also the relationship between government and governed. Such changes will be shaped by perceptions of national interest and the interests of interest groups both within the Party and in industry and will in turn determine trends in inequality. The Party has justifiably cited as a core achievement the lifting of huge numbers of people out of poverty. To this unfinished task is now to be added the facilitation of a full-blown consumer society. Combining policies for poverty alleviation and to increase consumption has proved challenging for other governments. This is not to say that it cannot be done but we certainly cannot predict what any outcome might look like in 2020.

Demography

One factor highlighted by commentators as a significant influence on future economic growth is China's demographic structure, itself a policy artefact because of the 'one child' policy under Deng.[55] The geographical distribution of that population is in turn the result of policy decisions: the shift in the Cultural Revolution of urban populations into the countryside, not all of whom succeeded in returning to the cities in the late 1970s; and the *hukou* system which inhibits free movement of labour. Demographic structure, the distribution of the population and migration all therefore create a policy nexus. Unravelling this will require difficult policy decisions.

Discussion of China's demographic structure has come to be dominated by the idea that the Chinese will grow old before they grow rich: that China's population will age while still at low levels of per capita income. According to United Nations projections[56] the percentage of the population under the age of 15 will have fallen from 22.1 per cent in 1985 to 12.6 per cent in 2020, a trend that will then stabilise before falling again to 10.4 per cent in 2050. The percentage aged over 60 will have risen from 8.0 per cent in 1985 to 16.7 per cent in 2020, projected to reach 31 per cent in 2050. Xinhua cited estimates suggesting that the number of people over 60 in 2020 would reach 248 million.[57] The sharpest rise occurs in the over 80 age bracket, rising from 0.6 per cent in 1985 to 2.0 per cent in 2020 and 7.2 per cent in 2050. Projections for changes in the demographic structure of the United States suggest that by comparison China will be worse off.

These numbers indicate a change in the dependency ratio. Under the impact of the one-child dependency and other factors relating to fertility China's overall dependency ratio fell from 55 per cent in 1985 to 38 per cent in 2007 as the number of young people relative to the working age population declined. This falling dependency rate lifted the savings rate of households for the simple reason that more members of the household were working, even though the growth in household incomes was slower than the growth in GDP. The higher labour supply also boosted corporate profits by putting downward pressure on wages. Nevertheless, the effects of dependency are asymmetric, depending on whether it is youth (under 15) or old-age dependency that is increasing.[58]

Declining youth dependence boosts saving and investment but the consequences of rising old-age dependency are less clear. The decline in the dependency ratio between 1985 and 2007 reflects a decline in youth dependency as more people entered the work force. This has been identified as a major determinant of the increase in China's foreign assets. The effects of an increased old-age dependency ratio are less clear, although Barry Eichengreen was unambiguous in asserting that a higher old-age dependency ratio has a larger negative impact on savings than investment and therefore a positive impact on the current account.[59]

What will this do for labour costs? There has been much debate about whether China has reached a Lewis Turning Point or when it will do so.[60] This understates the role of government policy in creating the supply of surplus rural labour. It has been government policies that caused a widening gap in rural–urban incomes, with the inevitable consequence that labour migrated from the former to the latter. Those policies in turn reflect an overwhelming bias within the leadership in favour of urban industrial growth. Nevertheless, it also appears that insofar as the most mobile segment of the rural population – that segment aged under 40 – has now joined this migrant labour force the main gains have been achieved. As a result the Chinese population can be divided into urban, rural and rural-migrant, each with different economic, social and political characteristics.[61]

Bullish forecasts for the Chinese economy make two assumptions about China's demographic future: that the 'one child' policy will be abolished; and that the *hukou* system will be reformed or abolished. Rather than treat these two policy moves as inevitable, however, we should regard them as variables. It is true that coastal areas are reported to have begun to experience shortages of labour. It is also true that labour costs are rising, presumably a reflection of a reduced supply of labour.[62] Some cities have taken steps to reduce barriers for migrants to access services.[63] It is also true for every example of piecemeal and ad hoc measures to change both the 'one child' policy and the *hukou* system there are other examples to the contrary. The pressures against change, deriving partly from a belief that such change would have massive unpredictable consequences, partly from a belief that some would take it as a sign that one or both policies had been mistaken, are powerful. For every local government that wants to facilitate at least a modest increase in the labour supply there are others concerned about the impact on local budgets of an increase in the number of people with a claim on local services.[64]

How much growth potential is left in the economy on the basis of cheap labour? Comparing China's growth trajectory with Japan, Korea and Taiwan, Carsten Holz concludes that there is potential for a further thirty years' low-cost labour-fuelled growth.[65] Cai Fang concludes that

China has already reached the Lewis Turning Point.[66] Hung Ho-Fung[67] makes the sensible point that none of this is about the number of physical bodies but rather it concerns policy decisions relating to freedom of movement and a policy establishment dominated by interests favouring exporters. He Jianwu, Li Shantong and Sandra Polaski calculate, however, that the contribution from the growth of the labour supply will decline to close to zero in 2020, while the contribution from capital accumulation, although also declining, will still be between 68 and 75 per cent in 2020.[68] But with the price of labour remaining the last bastion of corporate arbitrage between markets, the threat to China will come from the tens of millions of other young, well-trained, low-paid workers coming onto the labour market in Indonesia, India, Mexico and elsewhere. Perhaps at this point the unified control of the Party becomes part of China's comparative advantage.

Urbanisation

The fate of the *hukou* plays straight into a second domestic determinant of growth over the coming decade, urbanisation. At the 17th Party Congress in 2007, Hu Jintao announced that China's GDP would quadruple by 2020. To achieve that China has to urbanise. Since 1949 the rural sector in China has served as a source of surplus for urban and industrial development, first in providing low-cost food, later in providing cheap labour. The political underpinning for this transfer has been a concentration of power in the major urban centres, in contrast to the experience elsewhere in East Asia where ruling elites were forced to reach accommodations with farmers. The economic underpinning for this has been the fact that all land remains the property of the state. Critically relevant to China's future political trajectory, this also means that the division between 'princelings' and 'populists' that has now become standard in discussion of Chinese politics indicates only a distinction between different groups within that urban elite. The rural population has never had representatives at the top level of political decision-making and is most unlikely to get them now.

Even as the population age structure changes, where that population is concentrated will also change. In 1978 the urban population made up 17.9 per cent of the total population. By 2007 this percentage had increased to 44.9 per cent. Urban population growth of 422 million in this period outstripped total population growth of 358 million. The number of cities in the same period increased from 193 to 655. China now has twenty cities with a population in excess of five million.

It is government policy that this trend will now accelerate. The motive behind the policy is explicitly to expand domestic demand and therefore grow the economy, as Li Keqiang explained in a recent speech.[69] He went on to set the policy in the Dengist context of China's continuing drive to modernise. The forecast is that between now and 2025, 350 million rural residents will move into cities, either existing cities or newly constructed cities. The urban population will increase from just over 600 million to one billion. In 1978 more than 80 per cent of Chinese still lived in the countryside. By 2002 this percentage had fallen to 60 per cent. It took only six years for it to fall to below 50 per cent. By 2025 China will have at least 221 cities with a population over one million. Six new megacities with populations in excess of ten million will have emerged.[70]

Although these are called cities, the word urbanisation points us towards what is both old and new in all this. As Wang Kai and Chen Ming point out, the shape of China's urbanisation is determined by China's economic growth model.[71] They might have added that it also reflects the political structure. Urbanisation has tended to proceed through the extension of jurisdictional boundaries, a process driven by urban elites and developers rather than economic processes. Larger cities campaign for autonomous status, with the twin aims of detaching themselves from provincial authorities and reducing obligations to transfer resources to surrounding poor areas. Once autonomous status is achieved the newly independent city can then seek to expand its boundaries. The result is massive consumption of raw materials. The economic benefits for the mass of the population, however, have been less obvious. As Huang Yasheng has pointed out, the rapid increase in the pace of urbanisation in China since the early 1990s coincided precisely with a sharp decline in household consumption as a ratio to GDP.[72]

The enthusiasm within the bureaucracy for urbanisation also points us to another feature, the changing political role of cities.[73] Cities are transmission belts for globalising capitalism. For millennia they coexisted with the surrounding countryside in a relationship that was exploitative but also symbiotic. Cities today, and in particular megacities, are more isolated from that surrounding hinterland, the functions of which as supplier of food and cheap labour are now performed by a range of global entities. The corollary of this is that the relationship of megacities in particular with national political elites is radically changed.

Urbanisation, then, brings with it the potential to reshape political structures. Conversely it is by no means inevitable that urbanisation in

China will bring with it the transformative economic growth benefits looked for by some. There is of course a massive shift of population from the rural areas but, as we have seen, this population does not acquire full urban citizenship rights. Indeed, if Shanghai is a model the prospects for the private economy are poor. Indigenous private sector businesses in Shanghai are among the smallest in the country and self-employment business income per capita is about the same as in Yunnan.[74]

Redistribution of population on a massive scale, reshaping of political relationships between urban elites and national and international political and business elites, and the reconfiguration of urban economic processes; to all this must be added urban governance itself. It is forecast that giving rural migrants access to the level of resources currently enjoyed by urban *hukou* holders will require an additional 2.5 per cent of urban GDP by 2025. This will increase fiscal pressure on city authorities. Indeed, it is one factor behind resistance to abolition of the *hukou* in some quarters. Urbanisation to date has been overwhelmingly funded by sales of land taken from peasants and bank loans, the latter a particular feature of the recent stimulus package. McKinsey highlight the importance of fiscal transfers for many cities today. Going forward the creation of a stable basis for local government funding is a priority if urbanisation is to succeed.[75] A stable funding basis in turn implies tax reform and governance reforms.[76]

The McKinsey study outlined four alternative urbanisation scenarios, each associated with different economic growth outcomes:

- the development of a small number of megacities with populations in excess of 20 million;
- a hub and spoke development, with clusters of small and medium-sized cities around larger cities;
- distributed growth with large numbers of cities with populations between 1.5 million and 5 million;
- a pattern of a very large number of towns with populations between 500,000 and 1.5 million.

So far the trend in practice has been towards a more distributed growth pattern. This was also the thrust of Li Keqiang's recent speech that included a particular focus on the need to grow county-level towns. An outcome that is not optimal in terms of the McKinsey economic analysis should not surprise us. A high degree of local autonomy in areas of decision making related to the economy is likely to produce precisely this result. This in turn generates a patchwork of differing urban development plans and outcomes.

It is also creating new networks of interest groups, most particularly in the links between local officials and developers, with the latter assuming a dominant role in the urbanisation process.[77] Such a process led by private developers is only going to deliver what Zhu Xiaoyang has called, in the context of the growth of Kunming, 'the transformation of cities into dinosaurs',[78] the proliferation of socially divided, and socially divisive, gated developments designed to keep out non-residents and entirely dependent on the private automobile for transport.

All these urbanisation plans will run into one major barrier, in north China at least: water. Northern China already ranks as a water-scarce region. Some 380 million people have access to some 7 per cent of China's surface water. Northern rivers are also subject to serious levels of pollution and sedimentation. China as a whole will soon join the group of water-stressed countries. Already, 400 of China's existing 660 cities are short of water, including Beijing, Shanghai and Tianjin. Water shortage in Beijing has now reached a critical state.[79] Available water per capita in the city has fallen from 1,000 cubic metres in 1949 to 230 cubic metres in 2007. Uncontrolled development causing pollution of the groundwater, undercharging for water use, and competing jurisdictions are manifestations of political difficulties arising from competing interest groups and government objectives. Finding a solution is by no means easy but waiting until the landscape of north China is dotted with parched new cities is not an option.

That urban development will make a major contribution to China's economic growth over the next decade and more in terms of increasing consumption of raw materials and developing infrastructure is indisputable. What contribution to economic growth the urban centres thus created might then make is, however, less clear. The mix of motives, many of them non-economic, means that it is likely to be some time before we are in a position to judge. In the meantime China's new urban landscape will reshape not only China's economy but also its environment and its politics.

Conclusion

One odd strand in western twentieth-century thinking about China was a focus on 'why not' questions: why did China not develop capitalism; why did China not develop western science? China was seen as lacking, measured against the achievements of the west. The 'why not' questions may not be asked as often as they used to be but the underlying teleology is still there: China will develop into something like the West.

Of course this is not the case, not least because the future of western economies is far from clear. Even if it were clear, the specific historical circumstances of China would ensure that the country develops into something different. Recognising that difference is the first essential step.

Once the difference is recognised, however, we need to move on to understand that all the parties in a globalised economy are shaping each other in very specific ways. Shifts of economic power to Asia, the hollowing out of the western middle class with all sorts of currently unimaginable consequences for western political systems, all this changes China even as China changes the world. This is not merely a matter of recognising that the global macroeconomic and geo-strategic environment in which the Chinese leadership operates is itself changing rapidly. It is not even merely a matter of recognising that the interaction between China and the rest of the world is multi-dimensional. Instead we should be taking a relational view rather than one that starts from the premise of economies founded on nation-states. China's future is not a moving target plotted against a static West. Equally, the West's future is not a moving target plotted against a static China.

There is yet a third layer in this, starting with a recognition that the current conjuncture makes predictions about the future shape of western economies problematic. That current conjuncture is not simply the recent economic crisis. Taking such a short view ignores the fact that crises have been endemic rather than contingent. An economic structure that both globalises and is subject to regular bouts of collapse must itself be factored into the equation before we can make confident predictions about the future direction of any one element in the global macroeconomy.

It should also be clear that China's future involves an enormous number of interconnected policy variables. Confident predictions of the shape of the Chinese middle class or urbanisation skate over that complexity. It is time to abandon the search for a single linear future, represented by one large number or another, and instead think in terms of interlocking futures, none of which are inevitable, many of which are not even probable, but all of which are possible.

Returning to Dai Bingguo's statement one conclusion is clear: the Chinese leadership will do everything they can to preserve the leading role of the Party in order to protect China's national interests. China's national interests include not exposing the country to the risk of any infringement of national sovereignty. Economic issues are always also political issues.

Notes

1. I am grateful to Arif Dirlik and a peer reviewer for their comments on a draft of this essay.
2. Niall Ferguson, 'The decade the world tilted east', *Financial Times*, 27 December 2009.
3. See John Whalley, *Shifting Economic Power*, OECD Perspective on Global Development Background Paper, June 2010.
4. STRATFOR Top Predictions for the Next Decade at *http://www.businessinsider.com/stratfor-predictions-for-the-next-decade-2010-1#china-doomed-1*, accessed 28 January 2010; more sober thoughts about China's future are included in the National Intelligence Centre report, *Global Trends 2025: A Transformed World*, November 2008.
5. Robert Fogel, $123 000 000 000 000, *Foreign Policy*, January–February 2010.
6. Goldman Sachs Global Economics Paper 99, 2003.
7. Perry Anderson, 'Two Revolutions', *New Left Review* 61, January–February 2010.
8. Arif Dirlik, *Global Modernity*, Paradigm Publishers, 2007, p. 145, based on Colleen Lye, *America's Asia: Racial Form and American Literature, 1893–1945*, Princeton University Press, 2005.
9. Carsten Holz, 'What we know today about China's economic growth tomorrow', December 2006, available at *http://papers.ssrn.com/sol3/papers.cfm?abstract_id=756044*, accessed 5 October 2010.
10. See for example, Sun Liping, 'The biggest threat to China is not social turmoil but social decay', *http://chinadigitaltimes.net/2009/03/sun-liping-%E5%AD%99%E7%AB%8B%E5%B9%B3-the-biggest-threat-to-china-is-not-social-turmoil-but-social-decay/*; Yu Jianrong, Shouzhu shehui wending de di xian (in Chinese), at *http://www.chinaelections.org/printnews.asp?newsid=169507*, both accessed 5 October 2010.
11. Giovanni Arrighi, *Adam Smith in Beijing*, Verso, 2007. See also Joel Andreas, 'Changing colours in China', *New Left Review,* 54, November–December 2008. See also Simon Johnson's various critiques of the capture of the American political system by Wall Street.
12. Cheng Li, 'China in the year 2020: three political scenarios', *Asia Policy,* 4 (July 2007), 17–29; similar trios of possibilities were discussed at the Centre for Global Affairs, CGA Scenarios 3, Winter 2009; Wang Zhengxu prefers a formulation of 'semi-democracy' by 2020. See Zhengxu Wang, *Nation Building, State Building, and the Road to Democracy: Political Development in 60 Years of the People's Republic*, China Policy Institute Briefing Series Issue 54, September 2009; an offering of four alternatives can be found at 'China in the year 2020', *Asia Policy,* 4, July 2007.
13. Homi Kharas, *The Emerging Middle Class in Developing Countries*, OECD Development Centre, Working Paper No. 285.
14. Yingyi Qian, 'The institutional foundations of China's market transition', 1999, available at *http://siteresources.worldbank.org/INTABCDEWASHINGTON1999/Resources/qian.pdf*, accessed 5 October 2010.
15. He Qinglian, *Xiandaihua de Xianjing*, Jinri Zhongguo Chubanshe, 1996.

16. I recognise that is a superficial sense of the term political economy, far from the subtle discussion in, for example, Foucault's *The Birth of Biopolitics*.
17. Yasheng Huang, *Capitalism with Chinese Characteristics*, 2008.
18. OECD, Economic Surveys: China, 2005.
19. See the case of the Rizhao Steel Mill, discussed by Zhou Biao, Guodu ganyu min qi bu ke qu (in Chinese), at *http://www.21cbh.com/HTML/2009-7-25/HTML_U1XGVI474QRG.html*, accessed 26 July 2009.
20. Barry Naughton, 'Loans, firms, and steel: is the state advancing at the expense of the private sector?', *China Leadership Monitor*, 30 (Fall 2009).
21. For an example of the difficulties this caused government ministries see the comments of a vice minister in the Ministry of Housing and Urban Construction (in Chinese), at *http://www.21cbh.com/HTML/2009-9-29/148546.html*, accessed 30 September 2009.
22. Zhong Shiyou Jinjun Yinhang Ye (in Chinese) at *http://money.163.com/09/0427/17/57U2UD9E00252KFB.html*, accessed 30 April 2009; Guojia Dianwang Jinrong Bantu Di Diao Kuozhang (in Chinese) at *http://www.21cbh.com/HTML/2009-8-21/HTML_NC12D7NYK3SA.html*, accessed 22 August 2009.
23. Dani Rodrik, *Feasible Globalisations*, NBER Working Paper 9129, at *http://www.nber.org/papers/w9129*, accessed 5 October 2010.
24. *Global Capital Markets: Entering a New Era*, McKinsey Global Institute, September 2009.
25. Robert Brenner, 'What is good for Goldman Sachs is good for America: the origins of the current crisis', April 2009, at *http://escholarship.org/uc/item/0sg0782h#page-1*, accessed 5 October 2010; also David Harvey, *The Limits to Capital*, Verso, 2006.
26. Peter Boone and Simon Johnson, 'The doomsday cycle', at *http://www.voxeu.org/index.php?q=node/4659*, accessed 23 February 2010.
27. Giovanni Arrighi, 'The winding paths of capital', *New Left Review* 56, March–April 2009, p. 90.
28. For a particularly trenchant statement of the threat to China's autonomy from what is described as western monopoly capitalism see Shu Zhan, Jingji Quanqiuhua yu Guojia Jingji de Zizhuquan, Qiushi (in Chinese), at *http://www.qstheory.cn/hqwg/2010/201011/201006/t20100611_32986.htm*, accessed 15 June 2010.
29. 'The recession and China', UBS Investment Research, 23 January 2008; 'Decoupling update', 15 January 2010; 'The real decoupling', 17 August 2009.
30. See Eswar Prasad (ed.), *China's Growth and Integration into the World Economy*, IMF Occasional Paper 232, 2004.
31. Theodore Moran, *China's Strategy to Secure Natural Resources: Risks, Dangers and Opportunities*, Peterson Institute, 2010, p. 2.
32. Denis Pamlin and Long Baijin, 'Re Think: China's outward investment flows', World Wide Fund for Nature, April 2007, p. 35.
33. Reuven Glick and Michael Hutchison, *Navigating the Trilemma: Capital Flows and Monetary Policy in China*, HKIMR Working Paper 25, December 2008.
34. Tao Sun and Xiaojing Zhang, *Spillovers of the US Subprime Financial Turmoil to Mainland China and Hong Kong SAR: Evidence from Stock Markets*, IMF Working Paper, WP/09/166.

35. Zhou Xiaochuan, 'Some observations and analyses on savings ratio', Speech at the High Level Conference, Kuala Lumpur, 10 February 2009, at *www.bis.org/review/r090318c.pdf*, accessed 30 March 2010.
36. See OECD Survey China, February 2010, pp. 47–99 for a summary of China's monetary policy framework and financial reforms.
37. See the speech by John Lipsky, 'Managing financial innovation in emerging markets', 12 February 2010, at *http://www.imf.org/external/np/speeches/2010/021210.htm*; Kai Guo and Papa N'Daye, *Determinants of China's Private Consumption: An International Perspective*, IMF Working Paper WP/10/93; 'Huobi zhengce gaige wu chiyi', Caixin Online (in Chinese), at *http://magazine.caing.com/2010-02-19/100117952.html*, both websites accessed 20 February 2010.
38. Interest rate reform, for example, will benefit small banks over large banks. See Tarhan Feyzioglu, Nathan Porter and Elod Takats, *Interest Rate Liberalisation in China*, IMF Working Paper, WP/09/171.
39. Blackstone's signing in August 2009 of an agreement with Shanghai Municipality was followed by Carlyle's with Beijing Municipality in January 2010.
40. 'Jinrong guozi guanli', 24 March, 2010, (in Chinese) at *http://www.21cbh.com/HTML/2010-3-25/170150_2.html*, accessed 25 March 2010.
41. Ma Guonan and Zhou Haiwen, *China's Evolving External Wealth and Rising Creditor Position*, BIS Working Paper 286, July 2009; The extreme view of this is put forward by John Ross in 'China – the world's financial superpower', at *http://www.china.org.cn/opinion/2009-11/10/content_18861607.htm*, accessed 5 October 2010.
42. See *http://english.caing.com/2010-07-12/100160135.html*, accessed 5 October 2010; see also initial attempts to create a competitor to western ratings agencies in the form of Dagong International. This is, of course, but part of a much broader trend that includes technology standards. See Scott Kennedy, Richard Suttmeier and Jun Su, *Standards, Stakeholders and Innovation*, NBR Special Report 15, September 2008.
43. For an amusing discussion of the impact of the Chinese market on one particular sector see Lawrence Allen, *Chocolate Fortunes: The Battle for the Hearts, Minds, and Wallets of China's Consumers*, Amacom Books, 2009.
44. World Bank, *From Poor Areas to Poor People*, March 2009, p. 15.
45. World Bank, *From Poor Areas,* p. v.
46. According to the Ministry of Human Resources, 26 July (in Chinese), at *http://www.ciudsrc.com/chengshihuaxinwen/xinwentoutiao/2010-07-26/6377.html*, accessed 5 October 2010.
47. World Bank, *From Poor Areas*, p. xv.
48. See *http://www.stats.gov.cn/tjfx/jdfx/t20100716_402657779.htm* and *http://www.stats.gov.cn/tjfx/jdfx/t20100716_402657787.htm* for the most recent Chinese government breakdown of wage data, both accessed 5 October 2010.
49. Quoted in Feng Wang, *Boundaries of Inequality*, Centre for the Study of Democracy, UC Irvine, p. 6, available at *http://escholarship.org/uc/item/1v62q8pw#page-1*, accessed 5 October 2010.

50. *'Zhongguo caifu kuaisu xiang shao shu ren jizhong'* Liaowang Magazine (in Chinese), at *http://news.qq.com/a/20100213/000010.htm*, accessed 15 February 2010.
51. Louis Kuijs, 'Policies drive Chinese saving', *China Economic Quarterly,* 13(4), December 2009, 32.
52. For a clear recent statement of differing positions see the various contributions to the Saving Debate in *China Economic Quarterly,* 13(4), December 2009. Also Calla Wiemer, 'Explaining China's high saving', available at *http://www.eai.nus.edu.sg/BB476.pdf*, accessed 19 October 2010; Louis Kuijs, *Investment and Saving in China*, World Bank, WPS3633; Jahangir Aziz and Li Cui, *Explaining China's Low Consumption*, IMF Working Paper, WP/07/181; Jonathan Anderson, 'The myth of Chinese savings', *Far Eastern Economic Review*, November 2009; Zhou Xiaochuan, Governor of the People's Bank of China, takes a contrary view, placing emphasis on cultural factors as determinants of China's savings rates.
53. One recent study found that SOEs' bids for residential real estate land exceeded those of rivals by an average 27 per cent. Jing Wu, Joseph Gyourko and Yongheng Deng, *Evaluating Conditions in Major Chinese Housing Markets*, NBER Working Paper 16189, July 2010.
54. A recent CASS study noted the pension fund was already running a deficit of 130 billion RMB. See *http://www.caijing.com.cn/2010-07-14/110478935.html* (in Chinese), accessed 15 July 2010.
55. For a fascinating analysis of the 'one child' policy see Susan Greenhalgh, *Just One Child: Science and Policy in Deng's China*, University of California Press, 2008.
56. United Nations World Population Prospects: The 2008 Revision.
57. *http://news.xinhuanet.com/english/2009-08/01/content_11808683.htm*, accessed 19 October 2010.
58. Ma and Zhou, *China's Evolving External Wealth.*
59. Barry Eichengreen, 'Global Imbalances: the blind men and the elephant', The Brookings Institution, *Issues in Economic Policy* 1, January 2006, available at *http://www.brookings.edu/papers/2006/01macroeconomics_eichengreen.aspx*, accessed 19 October 2010; Kai Guo and Papa N'Diaye ('Determinants of China's private consumption: an international perspective, IMF Working Paper, WP/10/93), however, point out that in China the elderly continue to save.
60. See Cai Fang, Du Yang and Wang Meiyan, *Migration and Labour Mobility in China*, UNDP Human Development Research Paper, 2009/09; Cai Fang, *Approaching a Triumphal Span*, UNU-WIDER Research Paper 2008/09.
61. Just how different can be seen in Yasheng Huang's initial study of rural migrants in Guangdong, *Urbanisation, Hukou System and Government Land Ownership*, OECD Background Paper for Global Development Outlook 2010. See also Feng Wang, *Boundaries of Inequality.*
62. See the increase in the minimum wage in Jiangsu, Chinese Province Raises Wages 13 per cent, *Financial Times*, 7 February 2010, at *http://www.ft.com/cms/s/fa86afe4-1418-11df-8847-00144feab49a*, accessed 5 October 2010.

63. See most recently moves in Chongqing to unify rural and urban development plans (in Chinese), at *http://news.xinhuanet.com/local/2010-07/06/c_12301224_3.htm*, accessed 5 October 2010.
64. Willy Lam, 'Powerful interests stifle reform at National People's Congress', *China Brief,* 10(6), Jamestown Foundation, 18 March 2010, accessed 5 October 2010.
65. Carsten Holz, What We Know Today About China's Economic Growth Tomorrow, at *http://129.3.20.41/eps/dev/papers/0512/0512002.pdf*, accessed 5 October 2010.
66. Cai Fang, Du Yang and Wang Meiyan, *Migration and Labour Mobility in China.*
67. Hung Ho-Fung, 'America's head servant', *New Left Review*, 60, November–December 2009.
68. He Jianwu, Li Shantong and Sandra Polaski, *China's Economic Prospects 2006–2020*, Carnegie Papers, Number 83, April 2007.
69. 'Zhongguo chengzhenhua chu yu kuaisu fazhan jieduan' (in Chinese), at *http://www.ciudsrc.com/chengshihuaxinwen/xinwentoutiao/2010-06-07/5506.html*, accessed 10 June 2010.
70. See McKinsey Global Institute, *Preparing for China's Urban Billion*, 2009; for a more anxious discussion of Chinese urbanisation plans and prospects see 'Zhongguo chengshi fazhan baogao', Chengshi Lan Pi Shu, CASS, 2010.
71. 'Zhongguo chengshi fazhan baogao', p. 65.
72. Yasheng Huang, *Urbanization, Hukou System and Government Land Ownership*, OECD Development Centre, June 2010.
73. I am grateful to Arif Dirlik for sharing with me a draft of a paper to be published by the Institute of Urban Studies in Seoul which has prompted much of this paragraph.
74. Yasheng Huang, *Capitalism with Chinese Characteristics*, Cambridge University Press, 2008.
75. For just one of the many challenges in this see Wei difang rongzi pingtai sheli 'fang huo quiang', *Caijing Wang*, 11 March 2010 (in Chinese), at *http://www.caijing.com.cn/2010-03-11/110394063.html*, accessed 12 March 2010.
76. Richard M. Bird, 'Getting it right: financing urban development in China', *Asia-Pacific Tax Bulletin*, March/April 2005; World Bank, China, *Urban Services and Governance*, WPS 5030, 2 September 2009.
77. The urbanisation process to date is also seen as being a significant contributor to widening inequality. See for example 'Zhongguo caifu kuaisu xiang shao shu ren jizhong, fangdichan cheng zhuyao caiyuan' (in Chinese), at *http://news.qq.com/a/20100213/000010.htm*, accessed 13 February 2010.
78. Zhu Xiaoyang, Jingti Chengshi Konglonghua (in Chinese), at *http://www.infzm.com/content/43327*, accessed 10 April 2010.
79. 'Beijing's water crisis', *Probe International*, June 2008.

4

China's military in 2020

Gary Li

Introduction: robust economy

The People's Republic of China has seen extraordinary development since Deng Xiaoping's 'Reform and Opening Up' policy of the 1980s. Double-digit growth and a massive foreign currency reserve since 2006, coupled with its unique version of the free-market model, has seen the country weather the 2009 global financial crisis much better than the rest of Asia. Alongside China's economic strength, its military power has also grown within the past three decades, but as the new century progresses China finds itself having to adjust in the face of new challenges and strategic dilemmas.

China continues to increase its defence spending, rising to $77.9 billion in 2010, an increase of some 7.5 per cent from 2009.[1] However, this increase did signal an end to a long run of double-digit growth such as the 14.9 per cent increase in 2009 from 2008.[2] In proportion to its GDP, China's spending is still low compared to that of the US and Russia, coming in at 1.4 per cent compared with 3.6 per cent in the US and 2.8 per cent in Russia.[3] This slowing down of defence spending shows that China is content on continuing its growth model adopted during the reform and opening-up period in which the economy is seen as a higher priority than the armed forces.

The global financial crisis, in combination with previous large budget increases, means that the Chinese Communist Party (CCP) leadership can slow down spending on the People's Liberation Army (PLA) for the time being. Furthermore, more money is now being spent on pay and living conditions rather than expensive R&D programmes, further reducing defence expenditure. Any changes in the future will therefore be related to China's economic development.

Arms embargoes

In terms of foreign technological assistance, China remains under two arms embargoes – by the European Union and the United States – following the 1989 Tiananmen protests. While the US arms embargo stems from geopolitical calculations, and it is unlikely that the US still considers Tiananmen or human rights as the major justification for the continued embargo, the fact is China is no longer a potential ally in a confrontation with the Soviet Union, but rather a potential adversary. Therefore Chinese access to US technology will continue to rely on the extensive and relatively effective cyber espionage networks it has in place.

The EU embargo is a much more archaic affair, with several countries arguing that it should be lifted in recent years. However, no consensus has been achieved even with the governments themselves, let alone unanimously in all 27 member states. The previous attempt at lifting the embargo buckled under US pressure in 2004, and it remains unlikely that any attempts will be successful by 2020.

Having said this, it is important to point out that the EU embargo is little more than a political gesture. The original 1989 declaration after the Tiananmen crackdown was not legally binding, and each EU member defines and implements the arms embargo differently. This has allowed China to acquire numerous dual-use technologies from Europe for military purposes. Companies su ch as Aérospatiale have provided China with production licences for helicopters, which have been converted from civilian to a variety of military attack configurations. Similarly, Eurocopter and Turbomeca (Safran Group) have all contributed to the Chinese military helicopter industry.

Combat experience

One of the largest challenges facing an assessment of the PLA's military capabilities is the lack of actual combat experience of the forces. The last great military confrontation between the PLA and another regular army was the Sino-Vietnam war in 1979, followed by a series of border clashes in the early 1980s. It has remained a peacetime army since then. In fact, none of the fruits of modernisation have been tested in a combat situation.

However, the PLA has gained valuable experience through dealing with what it calls 'Military Operations Other Than War' (MOOTW), commonly described as non-traditional security issues. The Sichuan earthquake in 2008, followed by another earthquake in Qinghai in 2010, as well as several other natural disasters in the past few years, stretched PLA capabilities to their limit. Furthermore, MOOTW also includes the People's Liberation Army Navy (PLAN) Gulf of Aden anti-piracy flotillas, operating on a six-months' rotation.

These operations provide the best insight into PLA operational capabilities and potential combat readiness. These however, are not always positive. The sluggish response to the earthquakes – the difficult terrain notwithstanding – showed that the PLA command and control capabilities still had a lot of room for improvement. The lack of hardware such as helicopters was also a major handicap. Similarly, the PLAN flotillas showed that Chinese forces still had a long way to go in terms of long-range deployments, with the crew suffering from a lack of fresh food and fatigue caused by long periods at sea. However, the situation is improving as more ports in the region are offering the PLAN berthing and resupplying rights.

Confidence and change

With the changing security environment and varying development priorities, China has had to change its armed forces in their composition, organisation, training and mission objectives. This chapter will examine the factors which precipitated these changes, what has already been achieved, and what will continue in the next decade. The following sections will place PLA modernisation within China's wider development and strategic context.

What is certain is that the world will find itself faced with a China growing in confidence and becoming ever more assertive. For the countries of East and South-east Asia, this will be particularly worrying as China has many unresolved border disputes with its neighbours. Another danger stems from Beijing's paranoia concerning encirclement, which could lead to heated diplomatic confrontations backed up by aggressive military sabre rattling. However, China has not yet displayed the signs of a revisionist power, and is restricted in action due to a multitude of interdependent factors such as economics – so crucial for its continued growth. Therefore the more assertive China of 2020 will not be a closed China, and many avenues for approaching this rising giant will remain.

PLA: the armed wing of the Party

The PLA is a unique force, different from the armed forces of most other nations. True to Mao Zedong's maxim, 'power grows out of the barrel of a gun', it is not a national defence force but rather comes under the direct control of the Chinese Communist Party (CCP), rather than the government. Therefore it swears allegiance not to the country but to the CCP. It is nominally under the control of the Ministry of National Defence, but in reality this is not so. Instead control comes from the Central Military Commission (CMC), which is currently chaired by President and Party General Secretary Hu Jintao.

The PLA is organised into four branches: the ground force, the air force, the navy and the second artillery corps. Service is through selective conscription where provincial governments are asked to fill a quota each year. However, in reality the number of places is limited due to the employment security offered by the armed forces. The army has always been a route to a job if a young person is unable to carry on to higher education. The army offers not only security and pay, but also a promise of a state-assigned job at the end of the service term of 24 months.

Since the founding of the PRC, the ground forces have always been the main branch of the PLA, but this has now changed. Beginning with Deng Xiaoping, the PLA has been drastically cut over the past three decades in an effort to streamline the force, which stood at a bloated 4.7 million personnel in the early 1980s. Around one million personnel were cut by 1987, with some of the demobilised troops going into the People's Armed Police (PAP). Deng stressed the need for quality over quantity, and the cuts continued into the 1990s when Deng's successor, Jiang Zemin, had reduced the numbers by another 500,000 by the end of the millennium.[4]

As the PLA entered the twenty-first century, the ground forces were at the forefront of the comprehensive reorganisation and modernisation programme. There were two reasons for this: firstly, it is much cheaper to modernise ground-based military equipment such as main battle tanks, armoured personnel carriers and small arms than it is to modernise the air and naval forces. This is mainly due to the costly research and development processes needed for the latter services.

Secondly, the US-led coalition victory in the first Gulf War of 1991 over the Iraqi army came as a rude awakening for many PLA officers and the Chinese leadership. China's decision-makers and the PLA rank and file watched in horror as a modern, Soviet-equipped army – with many items of equipment far superior to those of the PLA of the 1990s –

became mere cannon fodder for the modern western forces. PLA planners realised that a comprehensive modernisation programme was needed in order to build up a force with even the most basic of defence capabilities on a modern battlefield. The priorities were focused on improving the ground force's equipment, as well as improving its capability for fighting a war in a digital age. Jiang Zemin implemented a new doctrine calling for the PLA to be able to 'win localised wars under hi-tech conditions'[5].

However, the priorities for PLA modernisation have shifted over the past few years, and the emphasis is once again focused on the technology-heavy forces of the air force (PLAAF) and navy (PLAN). This is due to the need for China to be able to contest disputed regions such as the South China Sea, which in turn called for a building-up of power projection capabilities. This will allow the PLA to be able to be deployed not just within China but also in the peripheral regions. As Chinese overseas interests and its domestic economy continue to grow (see Peter Wood's chapter in this volume), it is becoming increasingly vital for the PLA to be able to defend the lifeblood of Chinese development – energy. To this end, possessing a force capable of defending vital sea lanes is becoming a core focus for the modernisation process.

With the shifting of priorities, and in China's changing economic and security environment, President Hu Jintao redefined the PLA's mission statement in December 2004.[6] The priorities were:

- consolidate the ruling status of the Communist Party;
- help ensure China's sovereignty, territorial integrity, and domestic security in order to continue national development;
- safeguard China's expanding national interests;
- help maintain world peace.

It is important to stress that these new guidelines do not contradict the one long-standing priority for the PLA, which is the possibility of an armed conflict with Taiwan in the event of secession. This comes under the point of sovereignty and territorial integrity, and, by relation, CCP legitimacy. This has a direct link to the drastic build-up of amphibious combat forces as well as various naval and air assets required for a rapid conflict with Taiwan.

Furthermore, although the first of these points calls on the PLA to safeguard the CCP's power, it has, however, become the ultimate taboo for the CCP to use the PLA in the event of political or social unrest. This is a result of the international and internal backlash caused by the Tiananmen crackdown of 1989, which has arguably tarnished the image of the PLA in the eyes of the Chinese people for good. This is demonstrated by the lack of PLA troops at either the Tibetan or the Xinjiang riots in 2008 and 2010 respectively.

As will be discussed later, the side-effect of possessing high-tech armed forces is the erosion of a blindingly loyal officer corps, as educational and technological abilities have replaced ideological purity as the most important asset for the PLA. In the event of another Tiananmen-like large-scale social disturbance, it would be highly unlikely for the PLA to be deployed in the same fashion as in 1989. In fact it would be questionable if the officers would even follow such orders even if they are given.[7]

According to China's official defence white paper in 2008, the next decade will see the PLA pursue 'the RMA[8] with Chinese characteristics', and to 'accomplish mechanisation and make major progress in "informatisation"[9] by 2020'.[10] China will also seek to better organise its defence industry, develop independent R&D capabilities, as well as cost-effective manufacturing of military equipment of better quality. This systemic shake-up will also include better integration of civilian infrastructures into military logistical planning, and more centralised and efficient defence mobilisation laws.[11]

The PLA ground forces

The ground forces makes up the bulk of the PLA. As of 2010, it has 800 000 serving personnel organised into 18 Group Armies (GA).[12] These are deployed in seven Military Regions (MR), which are further divided into 28 Military Districts (MD). The seven MRs consist of Shenyang (3 × GA), Beijing (3 × GA), Lanzhou (2 × GA), Nanjing (3 × GA), Jinan (3 × GA), Guangzhou (2 × GA) and Chengdu (2 × GA).[13]

Modernisation efforts

The modernisation of the ground forces included personnel cuts, but also focused on changes in doctrine, strategy and tactics. The previous 11 MRs were reduced to seven in 1987,[14] with combined-arms Group Armies replacing the obsolete Field Army formations. These new Group Armies focused on improving the mobility of formations by gradual mechanisation of infantry units. This was done by increasing the number of armoured personnel carriers, infantry fighting vehicles and self-propelled artillery support. Some formations also began to receive integrated army aviation assets in the 1990s in the form of helicopter regiments.

One of the most important aspects of the modernisation programme is the recruitment of a new, well-educated and highly skilled officer corps. The PLA has relinquished political reliability as the most important factor in officer candidates and is replacing it with technical competency, for it needs a new cadre of technical experts in order to utilise the upgraded hardware to its full potential. The active recruitment of university graduates and the subsequent torrents of political indoctrination is evidence of a continuing worry about this shift from political to technical ability and whether it will cause problems for the reliability of senior army leaders.[15] A similar process is taking place with the recruitment of non-commissioned officers (NCOs),[16] with the barely literate peasant soldiers of previous years replaced with high-school graduates. Better pay and other incentives have also been brought into place to entice NCOs to sign on for longer terms of service.[17]

Hardware

Over the first decade of the twenty-first century, the modernisation programme of the ground forces began to bear fruit. The various formations have retired large quantities of obsolete equipment, and are well on the way to meeting the goal of total mechanisation and partial informatisation by 2020. The 60th anniversary of the founding of the PRC in 2009 saw a massive parade which displayed a modernised ground force equipped with indigenously developed hardware.[18]

The PLA ground forces at the start of the reforms consisted largely of obsolete 1950s and 1960s vintage Soviet designs. The chief main battle tank (MBT) was the Norinco Type-59, a derivative of the Soviet T-55, a design dating back to the 1950s. Large quantities of the Type-59 and its upgraded successor, the Type-69, were exported to Iraq in the 1980s. The subsequent coalition victory in 1991 demonstrated the absolute vulnerability and obsolescence of these vehicles as thousands were knocked out by US tanks, aircraft and helicopter gunships.[19]

By 2010, the PLA ground forces had built up a substantial force of third-generation MBTs. Currently the most numerous is the Norinco Type-96 and its modified/upgraded version, the Type-96G. This vehicle is armed with a 125mm smooth bore main gun, and protected by advanced laminate armour as well as an outer layer of explosive reactive armour (ERA) plates.[20] The latter is designed in a modular fashion to ease field replacements.

The Type-96 entered service in 1997, and production continues to this day with approximately 1500 vehicles in service as of 2010.[21]

The most advanced Chinese MBT in service with the PLA today is the Norinco Type-99. It is considerably heavier than the Type-96, at around 54 to 58 tonnes versus the latter's 42-odd tonnes. It is also better armoured and possesses advanced electronic countermeasures such as the active laser suppression system on the turret. The 125mm main gun can fire both standard ammunition as well as laser-guided anti-tank missiles.[22] Despite its qualities, the Type-99 remains a costly item, and only around 250 to 300 are in service with PLA ground forces as of 2010.[23] However, an improved version, dubbed the Type-99A2, is thought to be nearing the completion of its field trials.

Perhaps the most vital part of PLA ground force modernisation has been in the area of armoured personnel carriers (APC) and infantry fighting vehicles (IFV). The former have consisted of poorly designed, thinly armoured Type-63 APCs for the past three decades, and the latter was more or less non-existent until a decade ago. While the majority of formations still retain the Type-63, large quantities of Type-04 and Type-05 IFVs had been built by 2010.[24] This new generation of vehicles possesses excellent cross-country performance and is totally amphibious, allowing a high degree of flexibility in future potential deployments.[25]

The artillery arm has also been modernised, though the ground force still relies on large quantities of towed guns. As of 2010, more than 1200 self-propelled artillery pieces are in the PLA inventory,[26] giving the ground force a level of mobile fire support that simply did not exist at the start of the reforms. A wide range of long-distance multiple rocket launchers (MLR) have also been developed, after the US system was seen as being so effective in 1991. Some of these vehicles, such as the Type-03/PHL-03 300mm MRL, have an astonishing range of some 200km,[27] allowing them to provide cross-regional indirect fire support, even having the ability to hit Taiwan when deployed along the Fujian coast.

The expanding arm of helicopter regiments is currently hampered by the lack of aircraft due to the under-developed domestic helicopter R&D infrastructure. Currently some 500 attack, transport and utility helicopters are spread in ten army aviation regiments attached to various armies.[28] The PLA's ultimate goal is to possess somewhere in the region of a thousand.[29] The lack of a dedicated attack helicopter – the Z-9 being a conversion of a French civilian model – will soon be remedied as the indigenous-designed Z-10 comes into service. However, the Z-9 and Russian Mi-17/171 helicopters are likely to remain the aerial mainstay of the future PLA ground formations.

Doctrine and training

The doctrinal framework for the hardware modernisation programme lies in the concept of 'cross-regional deployment', where regions denote MRs or provinces. This is reflected in the War Zone Campaign (WZC), which calls for a rapid, surgical and intense conflict with a clear political objective.[30] This calls for highly mobile and well-trained rapid reaction units (RRU), capable of being deployed over long distances and possessing integrated combined arms elements.

In order to achieve this, the PLA ground force has been experimenting with 'brigadisation' of its units. This involves downsizing the previously overstaffed divisions into combined arms brigades, similar to the US brigade combat team (BCT). However, the lack of initiative in the officer corps caused by decades of highly restrictive and hierarchical command structure meant that this process has been slowed down. Nevertheless, seven divisions have been designated as RRUs, not including the three RRU Airborne divisions of the 15th Airborne Army under the PLAAF and the two marine brigades of the PLAN.[31]

The ground force has been engaged in rigorous training according to several training directives that have been issued by the CMC in recent years. These are generally focused on integrated joint operations, and stress the importance of training with realistic scenarios. In terms of joint operations, the new training directives called for improvements in not just multi-unit, but multi-arm and multi-service joint training. The other main focus has been on the ability to conduct operations under 'complex electromagnetic conditions'. This highlights the importance the PLA places upon Electronic Warfare (EW) in future conflicts. All of these training concepts will remain the focus for the PLA ground forces for at least the next decade.[32]

In 2020

Over the next decade, the PLA ground force will continue with its mechanisation and 'informatisation'[33] programmes although not on as large a scale as the previous two decades. As funding is shifted towards the PLAN and PLAAF, the ground force will be focusing on building more rather than newer vehicles, with the focus on amphibious capabilities. The trend of training will continue to focus on combined arms and force projection for a Taiwan invasion scenario.[34] As China's own information infrastructure grows, such as optical fibres and satellite navigation systems, so will the ground force's C4ISR (Command, Control, Communications, Computers, Intelligence, Surveillance and Reconaissance) capabilities.[35] This will allow the 2020 force to be able to better respond to an ever-evolving security environment.

The new hardware and training of the ground formations will not only allow them to possess the capability of mounting an amphibious assault on Taiwan in the event of succession, but also highly mobile forces to be deployed to troublesome border regions such as Arunachal Pradesh on the Sino-Indian border. Aside from these, the ground force will make up the large majority of units sent on UN deployments, which will continue to provide the PLA with valuable overseas deployment experience.[36]

The force of 2020 will also possess much more competent and professional officer and NCO corps. These will be composed largely of university and high-school graduates, often with a technical expertise such as software engineering. However, the preference of technical ability over political reliability will continue to be a matter of concern for the CMC. The lack of any real combat experience since the 1980s will also make the actual combat capabilities of the 2020 PLA an unknown quantity.[37]

The People's Liberation Army Air Force (PLAAF)

As of 2010, the PLAAF has around 300 000 personnel, divided into aviation, air defence and airborne troop types. Over 1 600 combat-capable aircraft in 29 air divisions are stationed in the various MRs, and are divided into fighter, bomber and transport divisions.[38] The PLAAF operates numerous surface-to-air missile (SAM) and air defence (AD) divisions in the country, the majority being stationed around Beijing and the major cities along the cost. Three rapid-reaction airborne divisions are also under the jurisdiction of the PLAAF, and are organised under the 15th Airborne Army.

As with the navy, the PLAAF had a low priority at the start of the reforms in the 1980s. As discussed previously, this was due to the costly nature of aeronautical R&D and the lack of a sophisticated electronics industry which could support avionic development. This situation changed in the 1990s when the Jiang Zemin leadership purchased numerous Su-27 fighters from Russia. This was triggered by the 1996 Taiwan Strait Crisis, when the PLAAF found itself at a qualitative disadvantage.[39]

Modernisation of the PLAAF over the past decade has focused on two areas. Firstly, the PLAAF embarked on a large-scale demobilisation of obsolete aircraft, replacing them with both imported and domestically manufactured models.[40] Secondly, the PLAAF has re-orientated its doctrine from local air defence to an offensive defensive strategy.[41] This called for drastic improvements in PLAAF C4ISR capabilities as well as combined arms experience.

In order to achieve these aims, the PLAAF has been intensifying training programmes since 2000. These often take the form of long-range confrontation exercises, which include mid-air refuelling and other capabilities needed for future force projection or area denial strategies.[42] The use of flight simulators has also grown in popularity over the past decade, as it is believed that this can complement actual flying hours in a trainer aircraft as well as being economical.

However, the PLAAF has been faced with several development problems, which mostly stem from technological bottlenecks. One of these is the difficulties faced by the Chinese aeronautical industry in developing a successful domestically designed jet engine. This is due to a lack of a high-tech industrial base and expertise in the manufacture of high-tolerance materials needed for engines, which have proved highly problematic. The lack of a suitable large aircraft design has also hampered the PLAAF's attempts at transferring doctrinal changes into operational reality.

Currently the PLAAF still relies on imported jet engines for its new third-generation fighters, as well as attempting to import more Il-76 transport aircraft. While these issues remain, the PLAAF will not be able to achieve substantial force projection capabilities over the next decade, despite the progress made in other areas. It will, however, be able to conduct long-range fighter cover for any regional actions, often in coordination with the navy. It already has a substantial quantitative and qualitative advantage over the Taiwanese, and has also made significant contributions in asserting Chinese sovereignty in the South China Sea.

Hardware

Over the past decade the PLAAF has retired thousands of aged J-7 and J-6 fighters (Mig-21 *Fishbed* and Mig-19 *Farmer* derivatives). These obsolete models have been gradually replaced by newer, domestically manufactured models. The bulk of the PLAAF fighter force now composes of J-8, J-10 and J-11 fighters, while the aging Q-5 *Fantan* ground attack aircraft is being rapidly phased out and replaced by the JH-7/7A *Flying Leopard*, which also equips the naval air force (PLANAF).[43]

Despite the great leaps taken by the Chinese aviation industry over the past two decades, and producing excellent indigenous fighter designs such as the J-8 and J-10, the best PLAAF units are equipped with imported or upgraded Russian aircraft in the form of Su-27 and Su-30 *Flanker* units.[44] The former has been reverse engineered and manufactured under the new designation of J-11. As of 2010, there are six J-11/J-11B regiments serving in the PLAAF, with two more of Su-27s and one of Su-30s.[45] The production of J-11 and J-10 fighters will be the priority for the next decade.

The production of China's rapidly modernising and expanding fighter force has been severely restricted by the dependence on imported engines, such as the Russian AL-31FN for the J-10 and J-11 aircraft. The manufacture of aircraft bodies has occasionally outpaced the number of available engines in recent years.[46] The Chinese attempt at an indigenous replacement has proved problematic. The WS-10A turbofan engine has begun equipping J-10 units but has proved to be unreliable, causing two near crashes and one actual crash over the past two years. The JH-7A's WS-9 engines, which are reverse-engineered Rolls-Royce Spey engines, have also proved to be problematic, with several fatal crashes occurring in recent years.[47]

The biggest problem facing the future development of the PLAAF is the lack of a viable large aircraft airframe. This has hampered the development of bomber aircraft as well as new transport planes for the airborne forces. Incredibly, PLAAF bomber units are still equipped with derivatives of the Soviet 1950s vintage Tu-16 *Badger* bomber in the form of the H-6. This more than anything highlights the effects of a technological bottleneck. Although upgraded many times, the ageing airframe of the H-6 is proving to be of limited value in any future conflict as it does not stand a real chance of penetrating modern air defences.

The PLAAF is attempting to balance out this defect by arming newer models of the H-6 with long-range anti-shipping or cruise missiles. The H-6 also provides the airframe for a somewhat improvised tanker aircraft in the form of the H-6U. This aircraft provides the PLAAF and PLANAF forces with a modest mid-air refuelling capability. The lack of a suitable large aircraft airframe has also restricted the PLA's overall force projection capabilities dictated by China's new strategic doctrine. The limited number of Il-76 transports can only transport one out of the three airborne divisions at any one time. During the Tibetan riots in 2008, the government had to resort to chartering domestic civilian airliners in order to ferry troops to Lhasa.

Despite these technological limitations, the PLAAF has cause for optimism for the future. Already, in 2010, former Soviet states such as the Ukraine have proved to be keen on selling China the required technology, and various foreign firms have also pledged technical support for the Chinese domestic large aircraft programme. However, the biggest success story for the PLAAF has been the development of a comprehensive and formidable air defence network, which has moved rapidly from the gun-heavy force of the 1980s to one composed of advanced SAMs.

The importation of Russian equipment has been a great boost for the PLAAF.[48] Already a substantial amount of Russian S-300 *Grumble* SAMs are serving with the PLAAF, with licensed copies (HQ-9) also being manufactured. With a range of around 200km, the S-300s can engage not only aircraft, but also ballistic missiles in the terminal phase. The deployment of several S-300 batteries along the Fujian coast opposite Taiwan has proved to be controversial as the units' range easily encompasses Taiwanese air bases in the north of the island and thus gives PLA forces a distinct advantage.[49]

Another area where the PLAAF has made great inroads is the field of airborne surveillance and electronic warfare (EW). It was apparent to PLAAF chiefs that in order for the air divisions to conduct wide-ranging missions, a more robust and extensive C4ISR network was needed. This came in the form of a new generation of AWACS (Airborne Warning and Control System) aircraft such as the KJ-2000 and the KJ-200. Both are modified transport aircraft and offer the PLAAF considerable support in a whole variety of missions. Numerous exercises in recent years have also highlighted the prominence of AWACS and ELINT (Electronic Signals Intelligence) aircraft in PLAAF doctrine.[50]

The final aspect of the PLAAF is the airborne element in the form of the three parachute divisions – 43rd, 44th and 45th. These units have been gradually re-equipped with a new generation of light armoured vehicles such as the ZBD-03 infantry fighting vehicle and other specialised equipment. These greatly enhance the combat capabilities of the airborne forces, and allow them to conduct a much wider range of missions. However, the lack of transport aircraft makes it difficult to train paratroopers and conduct airborne operations.

The next decade will see the PLAAF continue its rapid modernisation process. It is now no longer a localised defence force but a highly capable army that can conduct aerial support for the PLA's other branches, as well as preventing aerial penetration by hostile forces through its elaborate

SAM network. The rumoured progress and insider claims of a fourth-generation stealth fighter programme also sheds light on a potential war-winning weapons platform entering the scene by the next decade.[51]

In 2020

By 2020, the PLAAF should have more or less completed the phasing out of its previous generation of fighter aircraft. The force will be largely divided into the heavy fighters, equipped with the J-11, and the light fighters in the form of the J-10. However, it is difficult to see a new large aircraft replacing the existing bombers and transports in the space of a decade. Therefore the PLAAF will continue to employ H-6 variants in the long-range bomber role, or replace it altogether with much more capable dedicated ground attack aircraft like the JH-7/7A, carrying an ever-expanding array of long-range missiles. The reliability of Chinese engines will also improve over the next decade, and they could be equipping the majority of Chinese aircraft by 2020.

C4ISR and inter-service cooperation will also have greatly increased by the end of the next decade, as more AWACS aircraft are built and integrated into the PLAAF operational network. The changing character of PLA doctrine and the development of dedicated forward air observers embedded with ground units will see the PLAAF enter into a much more symbiotic relationship with the other services. The PLAAF will also be a common sight in the South China Sea as it continues its coordination with the PLAN as seen in recent years. Fighters from the PLAAF will provide long-range air cover for Chinese fleets, as well as conducting patrols over the disputed islands.

Chinese air defences will also continue to grow and consolidate. By 2020 the majority of Chinese cities and other economic centres will be well protected by advanced SAM systems, including the Russian S-400, which is thought to possess anti-stealth technologies.[52] These advances will have the dual advantage of both protecting the Chinese mainland and being an effective part of the PLA's area denial strategy regarding Taiwan.

The People's Liberation Army Navy (PLAN)

The PLAN in 2010 has around 255 000 personnel and is divided into three regional fleets.[53] These are the North, East and South China Sea

Fleets. The first is based in Qingdao in the Shandong peninsular, the second in Shanghai, and the last is primarily based in Hainan. The fleets also possess six naval aviation divisions as well as two marine brigades.

The PLAN was one of the branches of the PLA that took second place during the initial reforms of the 1980s. Primarily this was due to a lack of a sophisticated technological and industrial base. Naval research and development was also prohibitively expensive at a time when China was desperately trying to rebuild the economy after the turbulence of the Cultural Revolution.

The real turning point came under Jiang Zemin, when the 1996 Taiwan Strait crisis pushed naval development forwards as a major issue. Jiang realised that the humiliation suffered by the Chinese leadership during the crisis – during which the USS *Nimitz* carrier task group sailed through the Taiwan Strait – was unacceptable and potentially could threaten the legitimacy of the party. Therefore the late 1990s saw an influx of modern equipment and an increase of funding for the PLAN. The period of 'forbearance' was finally over. Since the 1990s, the East China Sea Fleet has received the most investment, due to its importance in resolving any future incidents over Taiwan.

However, this has changed during the Hu Jintao period. This was due to the much more stable relationship between the KMT government under Ma Ying-jeou since 2008 and the mainland. Hu was much more focused on energy security, which relies on the PLAN being able to keep open China's access to oil via the Sea Lines of Communication (SLOC) such as the Malacca Straits. To this end, the South China Sea Fleet has been greatly upgraded and was the best equipped of the three fleets by the start of the twenty-first century.

As the 60th anniversary of the establishment of the PLAN dawned in April 2009, Hu Jintao inspected a large naval review in Qingdao. The review demonstrated the fruits of reform as well as acting as a platform for Hu to announce a 'new historical starting point' for the PLAN as a part of the continuation of the 'new historical missions' Hu set out for the PLA in general, the most important element of which is the focus on maintaining Chinese territorial sovereignty and continued economic development. This is not a surprise as these two factors are the only remaining legitimising factors for the Communist government. To this end, PLAN development for the next decade is going to continue the current pattern of asserting Chinese sovereignty claims in the South China Sea, and ensuring the safety of SLOCs.

The main aim of continued modernisation will be to achieve capabilities in joint warfare in the littoral, conduct sea control operations in near peripheral waters and sea denial operations at extended ranges in regional seas, and deploy and sustain naval formations in support of non-combat or low-intensity operations in distant seas. This last capability can support mutually desirable stakeholder objectives, such as international law enforcement, peacekeeping and humanitarian relief operations.[54]

In March and April 2010, the world saw the first signs of a more assertive Chinese navy in a series of dramatic confrontations in the East and South China Seas. After weeks of tension between Chinese Fisheries vessels and Vietnamese 'fishing boats' in the disputed Spratly Islands, the PLAN dispatched first a flotilla of six ships from the North China Sea Fleet, quickly followed by another flotilla of ten ships from the East China Sea Fleet. Both sailed directly through the Miyako Straits – a mere 140km from Okinawa – and prompted the Japanese Ministry of Defence to issue a statement requesting an explanation for such 'unprecedented behaviour'.[55]

This series of exercises heralded a new era of Chinese naval development. The confidence displayed by the PLAN flotillas was only made possible after years of planning and modernisation. The deployment of a rotational anti-piracy taskforce to the Gulf of Aden in 2008 has provided the PLAN with much-needed long-range power projection experience. The establishment of an elaborate network of Chinese communication and maritime observation satellites has greatly improved the PLAN's C4ISR capabilities. Finally, many new vessels have entered service over the past decade, replacing many obsolete models and considerably increasing the PLAN's ability to take on diverse missions.

Hardware

The East China Sea Fleet was the main beneficiary of modern equipment under Jiang Zemin. As already discussed, it was deemed vital to station the most advanced weaponry with this fleet as a deterrent against Taiwan. The late 1990s saw three Russian-made *Sovremenny* class destroyers and the state-of-the-art *Kilo* class diesel attack submarine being placed with this fleet.[56]

However, as the PLAN's missions shifted towards possessing a power projection capability, priorities were placed upon building larger vessels. From 2003, the PLAN began to receive the newer, indigenously designed Type 054 and 054A frigates (*Jiangkai* I/II). These multi-role missile frigates now form the backbone of the three fleets, offering the PLAN a vessel that is suitable for long-range deployment. Alongside these, China has also developed a whole series of highly capable naval vessels such as the Type 051C (*Luzhou*) and Type 052B/C (*Luyang* I/II) destroyers. Surface combatants are further supplemented by the ever-growing submarine force of both nuclear and conventionally powered submarines such as the Type 094 *Jin* and the Type 039 *Song*.

The most substantial and significant development in the PLAN in recent years has been the aircraft carrier project. First officially announced in 2009, although having been in development since 2002, the first Chinese aircraft carrier will be based on the former Soviet ski-jump carrier *Varyag*, which is due to be launched around 2012 after its refit in Dalian.[57] This vessel will primarily be a training ship, in order to allow the PLAN to train up a cadre of experienced captains and carrier pilots, as well as helping the PLAN to accumulate experience in the complexities of carrier operations.

The issue of a suitable carrier aircraft has been a bottleneck for the project as Russian objections to Chinese reverse engineering of the Su-27 fighter (with the Chinese variant called the J-11) soured talks over the purchase of 30 or so Su-30 fighters.[58] It is highly unlikely that the *Varyag* will ever be part of a line taskforce as China is currently working on a more conventional catapult take-off carrier programme.

Aside from naval vessels, the PLAN has also been placing considerable investment and effort into the modernisation of its naval aviation arm, the PLANAF. Naval aviation has long been regarded as the poorer relation to the PLAAF, but over the past decade the two branches have developed specialised roles in any potential future conflict. While the PLAAF is rapidly replacing its ageing fleet of J-7 fighters with newer J-10 and J-11 aircraft, the PLANAF is upgrading with JH-7/7A ground attack aircraft. The former is taking on the role of air dominance, while the latter is focusing more on surface attack.

In 2020

The PLAN in 2020 will not be considerably different from the one in 2010. However, the doctrine and missions of this force will have drastically changed. While still remaining primarily a defensive navy, and still 30 years from the 2050 blue water navy target, the PLAN will be a much more confident and assertive force in the region. The Chinese leadership will be more willing to exert its influence and support its claims of sovereignty over the various disputed maritime regions through the PLAN.

The training carrier *Varyag* will have already provided the PLAN with several years of valuable operational experience, and a new indigenous carrier construction programme will be in full swing. Various support vessels capable of making up the other vital components of a carrier task group – frigates for anti-ship and destroyers for anti-air defences – will continue to be launched from China's busy shipyards. Submarines, too, will be quieter and better integrated with the surface fleet.

Most significantly, the PLAN will most likely have moved beyond the three-fleet method of operation – a legacy from the Soviets. It will be replaced by a centralised naval command, able to coordinate and command mixed task forces from any of the three forces according to mission requirements. Coupled with the completion of the *Beidou* satellite system, as well as the newer generation of over-the-horizon radars, the C4ISR capabilities of the 2020 PLAN should be formidable.[59]

The 2020 force will continue to participate in UN-sanctioned deployments. The benefits from such collaborative exercises are well known to the Chinese leadership. Unilateral and multilateral exercises with China's neighbouring countries will be common, as the PLAN leads the way in building up trust in the region. The nations of the first island chain should also be prepared to see many more PLAN exercises in the Western Pacific.

The Second Artillery Corps (SAC)

The Second Artillery Corps (SAC) is China's strategic missile force, and its main nuclear deterrence force. It currently has around 100 000 personnel organised into 27 launch brigades.[60] These are subordinated to six army-level missile 'bases'. It was originally set up in 1966 and has developed from a silo-based deterrence force to one that is becoming increasingly mobile. It controls all of the PLA's land-based strategic missile assets, both nuclear and conventional. The Corps comes under the direct supervision of the CMC, and its launch personnel are considered elite troops.

The transformation of the original SAC has been a core focus for the PLA's modernisation programme. The move away from static silo-based missiles to more mobile ICBMs, MRBMs and SRBMs have made it a more flexible and effective deterrence force.[61] The addition of conventional strike capabilities since the 1990s has also increased the operational capability of the SAC. These stemmed from the 1996 Taiwan Crisis when the PLA realised that it lacked an effective strike force against maritime incursions by other nations that is not nuclear. It also saw an opportunity to overcome its limited amphibious and aerial capabilities in the event of a conflict with Taiwan by developing a long-range strike force in the form of SRBMs.[62]

The growth and diversification of the SAC, therefore, is closely linked with the PLA's area denial strategy which it began to develop after 1996. The number of launcher brigades opposite Taiwan has been increasing steadily since the late 1990s, as the SAC continues to upgrade the SRBM and MRBM forces with more accurate satellite-guided models such as the DF-21C. These have been augmented by a new force of Land Attack Cruise Missiles (LACMs) in the mid 2000s in the form of the CJ-10.[63]

However, in terms of grand strategy the SAC's primary mission has remained the same. That is, to act as China's minimal, hi-tech deterrent force. In this it has moved away from previous forms of static defence to increased mobility and hence survivability. This will allow China to possess a much more effective second-strike capability, which lies at the heart of nuclear deterrence strategy. All of this has created many challenges for the SAC's command and control capabilities, which centred on the CMC being able to maintain a line of communication to its more mobile and widely dispersed ICBM units in the event of an attack. Therefore continued EW and C4ISR training will be vital for the future development of the SAC.

Aside from continued development in its offensive capabilities, China has also been making great strides in space defence. The PLA realised from very early on the importance of both possessing a domestic satellite communications and surveillance network (such as the *Beidou* system), and the ability of denying an enemy use of theirs. To this end, the SAC and Chinese space agencies have been developing effective anti-satellite (ASAT) weapons for the past decade. The first successful test took place in January 2007 when a KT-1 solid-fuelled space launch vehicle destroyed a retired meteorological satellite in polar orbit.[64]

The ASAT test was followed by yet another landmark in the form of a successful anti-ballistic missile (ABM) test in 2010, three years to the day after the ASAT test of 2007. This test, which saw a converted DF-31 ICBM successfully intercept and kill a DF-21 target missile over Gansu province, was highly significant in that it saw China joining a very exclusive club of nations who currently possess ballistic missile defence (BMD) infrastructures. The interception occurred above the atmosphere and did not create the mass of debris which accompanied the 2007 ASAT test. A press statement from Xinhua also demonstrated a better level of transparency than before.[65]

As with the mobile ICBM force, the main difficulties faced by the future of the Chinese BMD programme will be C4ISR. China currently lacks the extensive infrastructure needed for a fully-fledged BMD system. Its space surveillance and tracking capabilities will not be ready until the full *Beidou* network is in place. Furthermore, China lacks a phased array radar network, which is also essential for the same reasons.

Hardware

The core of China's deterrence force of ICBMs has previously been the liquid-fuelled, two-stage *DongFeng* 5 (DF-5) ICBM. First introduced in the 1980s, it has a range of around 13000km and is based in launch silos. Despite its long range, the liquid-fuelled system means that the missile requires one to two hours' preparation time before launching, hence compromising its second-strike capabilities. This is one of the reasons why the SAC has shifted towards building up an ICBM force which can be fired from launch vehicles anywhere inside China.

The *DongFeng* 31A (DF-31A) ICBM is a road-mobile, solid-fuelled, three-stage ICBM with a range of around 11000km. It is an upgraded version of the original DF-31 project and can strike at any location in the US. The first successful test took place in 2006 and it has begun to equip the operational launch brigades of the SAC. As of 2010, two DF-31A and one DF-31 brigades are thought to be operational, with the latter thought to be earmarked for upgrade to DF-31As.[66] The fielding of this growing force, along with China's new submarine-launched ballistic missiles (SLBM), has provided the Chinese leadership with greater strategic options.

The most significant developments in the SAC have been the various intermediate range ballistic missiles (IRBM) coming into service over the past decade, the most significant being the *DongFeng* 21 (DF-21) family of missiles. These are land-based, road-mobile, conventionally armed missiles designed to deliver firepower quickly over extended distances. Both the DF-21 and the DF-21C upgrade have ranges of around 1700km, and can easily cover the Taiwan theatre as well as the disputed island regions in the South China Sea. Currently there are thought to be five brigades of DF-21s and two brigades of DF-21Cs, with the latter now receiving priority in production.[67]

One new addition to the SAC's impressive arsenal in recent years is the Land Attack Cruise Missile (LACM) and Anti-Ship Ballistic Missile (ASBM) projects. The former has already produced results in the

ChangJiang 10 (CJ-10). After years of speculation, it was finally unveiled publicly during the 60th anniversary parade of the founding of the PRC in October 2009. This too was a product of the 'rude awakening' of 1991, when US Tomahawk cruise missiles managed to strike with impunity inside Iraq with stupendous accuracy. It is thought that the CJ-10 might have been developed with Russian and Ukrainian assistance.[68] The missile is likely to be equipped with an inertial navigation system (INS), GPS and terrain comparison (TERCOM). This also means that, like much of the rest of the PLA, it is heavily dependent on the future *Beidou* satellite navigation network. Currently two brigades of the CJ-10 have been identified.[69]

Much speculation has been made on the ASBM project. Supposedly a derivative of the DF-21 IRBM, it can strike a large surface vessel, like an aircraft carrier, with high levels of precision. The task of the missile would not be to sink the ship, but rather to disable or to cripple its onboard air assets. According to a 2010 hearing, the commander of US PACOM Admiral Robert Willard described the ASBM as being in the testing phase.[70] The main worry for the US is that the Chinese ASBM system would be the world's first ballistic missile system capable of targeting a moving carrier strike group from long range. It would also be highly difficult to intercept. If successful, the ASBM will be the ultimate area denial deterrent and a potential game changer in the Pacific.[71]

In 2020

The SAC will continue to play a crucial role in Chinese defensive doctrine over the next decade. China will not deviate from its current stance on no first use of nuclear weapons, and will continue to pursue a development policy of vertical proliferation and minimum deterrence. This makes the SAC vital in allowing China to divert most of its revenues into economic development.

In matters of nuclear non-proliferation, it is unlikely that China will break its commitment not to sell nuclear equipment and materials abroad. It is simply not in China's interest to have more nuclear-capable countries, as it itself views nuclear weapons as an expensive venture, requiring constant upgrading and maintenance. Its current stance on achieving global zero has been mostly positive, although it responds badly to calls for disarmament. However, this stems from a legitimate view that China's nuclear weapons stockpile of around 200 warheads is nothing when compared with the thousands possessed by the US and Russia. This tendency to not encourage nuclear proliferation is set to continue as China finds itself more and more a status quo power, possessing more international interests which require stability.

Its privileged position in the PLA allows it to receive a large percentage of funding and to pick the best personnel for its units. These factors will ease at least some of the problems facing the SAC at present, namely the high level of élan and competence needed by its officers and men due to the sheer gravity of the task entrusted to them. High levels of education are essential for a force which, by its nature of being a second-strike option, implies the units responding on their own initiatives and while most likely being isolated from central command.

The level of coordination needed not just for command and control, but also to counterattack as defined in the 2008 Chinese Defence White Paper – 'either independently or together with the nuclear forces of other services' – will require a high level of training and a reliable communications network. This will depend heavily on the rapidly growing *Beidou* satellite system, which is on course to meet its target of having five geostationary and 35 orbital satellites by 2020.[72]

The majority of the Chinese silo-based DF-5 missiles will have been replaced by the mobile DF-31A ICBM in a decade's time. Already the former is deemed unclassified enough to pose for PLA pictorial magazines and other propaganda material. Official news reports surrounding the DF-31A brigades, on the other hand, are still very sketchy and few. The speed of launch, the flexibility and the range of the DF-31A makes it an excellent deterrent and an economically sound option.

Aside from nuclear deterrence, the SAC is also a highly effective tool in China's continued development of an area denial capability in both its littoral waters and beyond. The quality of the missiles arrayed opposite Taiwan will increase, with older models being superseded by newer ones. In this strategy, the DF-21C, CJ-10 and the yet unnamed ASBM weapons platforms will play a very important part in denying access to China's surrounding waters.

The People's Armed Police (PAP)

The PAP is a paramilitary police force tasked with dealing with internal security and unrest. It was created in the early 1980s by merging various internal security and public security units. Currently it has around 660,000 personnel, divided into internal security forces (400,000) and border defence forces (260,000).[73] The former are organised into 14 mobile divisions and 22 mobile regiments. These are stationed throughout the country, with HQ units being based in regional capitals. While not strictly a part of the PLA, the PAP does have a vital role to play in China's continued military reforms.

The majority of its personnel are demobilised PLA troops, which swelled its ranks following the massive cutbacks of the 1980s. It continues to recruit those with military experience as its functions often mirror those of the PLA. The mobile divisions of the internal security forces, for example, are light motorised infantry divisions in all but name, and possess high levels of training. Since the 1990s, the PAP has been under the direct control of the CMC, and has taken on more and more missions related to domestic unrest or ethnic tensions such as the Lhasa riots of 2008 and the Urumqi riots of 2009.

The various detachments of the internal security troops are responsible for guarding important locations, such as government and consular buildings, as well as strategic targets such as bridges and tunnels. The mobile units are stationed in bases and are only deployed during large-scale emergencies. These units were formed from the 14 demobilised infantry divisions transferred from the PLA to the PAP in 1996. They maintain their old systems of organisation but do not possess their heavy assets such as artillery. The mobile divisions are also not as well equipped as regular PLA infantry units, but do possess specialist riot control kit such as tear gas grenades and shields.

The rising prominence of the PAP has much to do with the aftermath of 4 June 1989, when public perceptions of the PLA became hostile after the troops cleared Tiananmen Square. To avoid any repeat of this, the CMC has placed all large-scale public emergencies into the jurisdiction of the PAP. This has grown to include anti-terrorism and natural disasters.[74] The utilisation of PAP troops during the Lhasa riots in 2008, and not those of the PLA, was a significant departure for the government. Also the tightening of mobilisation laws, allowing the PAP to be used only under direct orders from the State Council and the CMC, has made it a much more efficient tool of party policy.[75]

The PAP has been one of the slower beneficiaries from Chinese military reforms, mainly due to the fact that it does not come under the PLA, and possesses its own system of recruitment, training and education. However, reforms have been occurring in the form of better organisation and equipment. Over the past decade, the PAP forces have received much-needed upgrades for their second-line equipment such as new armoured personnel carriers and communications equipment. These have provided the mobile formations and the border units with much-increased command and control flexibility and more rapid response times.

The trend has been to turn the PAP into a much more specialised force, which can deal with the rise of non-traditional security threats. The centralised mobilisation laws that were brought into place in 2009 have also made the PAP more answerable to central authority, and not used by provincial governments as de facto local militias. However, funding for the PAP continues to come from the State Council and local governments, and not the defence budget.

One final aspect of the PAP's changing role is the area of overseas deployment. Personnel from PAP Special Forces units assigned to protect Chinese diplomatic personnel in high-risk countries have been highly visible in recent years. Their presence reflects the first stages of Chinese power projection, and provides valuable experience for future PAP deployments. Officers who have served at Chinese embassies in Iraq and Afghanistan are usually assigned to senior training positions on their return home. PAP units have also been participating in ongoing UN deployments, such as the UN mission in Haiti, significant in that it is the first time Chinese troops have been deployed so close to the US.[76] Finally, 'retired' PAP personnel have also been working in Afghanistan training up the local police force. This demonstrates the increased level of responsibility entrusted to the PAP for not just domestic security, but also security in China's periphery.[77]

In 2020

The PAP will continue to be streamlined and upgraded for the foreseeable future. The priority on hi-tech equipment emphasises the importance placed on the PAP's mission of securing Chinese borders and maintaining state control. This is especially true when considering the changing security environment surrounding China. The post-9/11 world and the war in Afghanistan have made it a priority for the government in maintaining a stable environment in the largely Muslim western regions of China.

The main fear is that Islamic militants in neighbouring Afghanistan and other Central Asian states such as Kyrgyzstan will filter through the border and provide technical assistance as well as training to domestic Uighur separatist groups such as the East Turkistan Independence Movement in Xinjiang province.[78] To this end, PAP units will be much reinforced along China's western borders such as the Wakhan corridor.

Following this, Tibet remains a high priority for China's internal security forces. As these regions see continued economic growth and an influx of workers from the Chinese interior, ethnic tensions are inevitable. The 2008 Lhasa riots have demonstrated that the Tibetan issue is now much more than merely concerning the Dalai Lama, and that a rapidly deployable and professional internal security force is needed in order to quell unrest which is set to continue.

By 2020 the mobile divisions of the PAP will have been upgraded into fully fledged light infantry units, with better vehicles and supporting arms. Already a limited number of helicopters are serving with the PAP, and this is set to continue as the PAP slowly acquires its own aviation force which will greatly assist with its deployment and tactical flexibility. The general increase in the mobility of these formations makes the PAP an essential rapid reaction asset, and its deployment in the event of natural disasters will be seen as the norm rather than an exceptional measure taken by the government.[79]

Cyber warfare

Perhaps the least known of China's military capabilities is the PLA's cyber warfare assets. Officially, China considers cyber attacks and computer hacking a crime, and disavows any involvement in it. However, it is commonly known that China possesses one of the largest cyber warfare capabilities in the world. The number of cyber attacks originating from China has also increased dramatically over the past decade, the types varying from industrial espionage to denial of service.

It has proved difficult to make any concrete linkages between the rising level of Chinese cyber attacks and official PLA commands or institutions, but clues do exist with which a picture can be built up of the general process of recruitment of 'cyber warriors' and the direction of attacks.[80] These include PLA-sponsored hacking contests and official press releases, as well as material produced by western IT security experts through open source intelligence (OSINT).[81]

According to a Taiwanese report published in the *ROC Defence Journal*, the PLA established a 'National Information Leading Group' in 1998, followed by the 'PLA Network Technology Research Centre' in 1999. These two institutions are the germ of the PLA 'cyber army'. In 2003 the CMC established the 'Information Mobilization Office', which is responsible for the mobilisation of a 'cyber militia' in the event of conflict.[82]

Chinese cyber warfare capabilities can be divided into two main types: electronic warfare and network warfare. The former involves the more commonly recognised forms of cyber warfare that take place on a battlefield. These range from disrupting enemy communications to mounting attacks on the opposition's C4ISR assets. The latter is focused on the disruption of enemy network infrastructure, as well as shoring up China's own cyber defences.

The doctrine that guides both 'wings' of attack is known as 'Integrated Network Electronic Warfare', which guides PLA Computer Network Operations (CNO). This doctrine calls for the combination of network warfare and electronic warfare tools at the start of a conflict in order to paralyse the opponent's C4ISR capabilities.

China's cyber assets fall under the command of two main departments of the General Staff Department (GSD). Computer network attacks and EW come under the 4th Department (Electronic Countermeasures), and computer network defence and intelligence gathering come under the 3rd Department (Signals Intelligence). The 3rd Department is also supported by a variety of 'militia units' – civilian hackers and cyber warfare personnel.[83]

The Taiwanese report quantifies Chinese cyber units as follows:

1. *Electronics Warfare Units:* company-sized units, responsible for resisting enemy electronic jamming and deception as well as attacking the enemy's EW capabilities.
2. *Network Warfare Units:* company-sized units, responsible for designing firewalls, maintaining network security, and the creation of electronic 'blocking points'.
3. *Hacker Units:* platoon-sized units, responsible for infiltrating enemy networks in order to disseminate false intelligence and viruses, and inflict general damage to the enemy's network infrastructure.
4. *Information Response Units:* company-sized units, responsible for network software and hardware maintenance and the resumption of network services following enemy attacks.

Therefore it is possible to assume that type 1 and 4 units come under the command of the 4th Department while 2 and 3 come under the 3rd Department. Apart from the units mentioned above, the 3rd Department also maintains at least six technical reconnaissance bureaus in the Lanzhou, Jinan, Chengdu, Guangzhou and Beijing Military Regions that are responsible for signals intelligence (SIGINT) collection against tactical and strategic targets and might also have CNO duties.

In 2020

The PLA is currently faced with a conundrum. It can either retain the decentralised network of 'cyber militia', consisting of talented hackers and programmers often operating on the margins of legality, or recruit them outright into its cyber units, but thus proving to foreign cyber security experts that the PLA is indeed behind them and these attacks are officially sanctioned. The alternative development path is to recruit graduates directly from university and train them in cyber attacks. However, this is not the best way to generate the level of talent needed for an effective cyber war.

It is obvious that the PLA is currently juggling the pros and cons of both of these methods, but much of this should be cleared up by 2020. China is increasingly aware of the double-edged sword that is cyber warfare, and the implications for its own network security to have large numbers of hackers loose around the Chinese Internet. The general trend suggests that the PLA will eventually try to formalise the massive resources it has into more efficient and better-directed units. Indeed, it was announced in July 2010 that the PLA had established an 'Information Security Base' – the first of its kind.[84] This is the first information of Chinese setting up security organisations of this type in the military which are similar to those in the West. It is not impossible that a specialised cyber command will be set up in the near future, now that many other countries are doing so, such as the US Cyber Command.

Strategic implications

This chapter has laid out the current changes that are taking place within the PLA. It is clear that Chinese defence spending will continue to grow, though it is still a long away from US standards. The strategic trajectory currently followed by the leadership will also continue to develop as China becomes increasingly dependent on energy resources from abroad, which in turn fuels domestic development and thus reinforces regime legitimacy.

The PLA in 2020 will not appear to be significantly different from the one we see in 2010. However, many systemic changes will have taken place. These include organisational restructuring – with smaller, leaner formations becoming more and more important – and training, with emphasis placed on force projection capabilities. Interoperability between various arms will also be better implemented by 2020 as China's *Beidou* satellite network becomes fully operational along with many other C4ISR infrastructures.

Force projection

In terms of strategic implications, the PLA in 2020 will possess more force projection capabilities than currently. However, these will be heavily dependent on several technological bottlenecks such as transport aircraft. Internally, the PLA and the PAP will both benefit from a highly effective and well-constructed road and rail network. This will allow light troops such as PLA motorised infantry divisions or PAP mobile divisions to be able to conduct cross-regional operations, i.e. moving from one province to another rapidly or concentrating along a threatened border region.

At sea too the PLAN will be more active and confident in asserting Beijing's territorial claims in the South China Sea. Long-range military exercises by naval vessels and routine patrols by armed Chinese Fisheries ships will be the norm, potentially raising tensions with Vietnam and other claimant nations in the region. The Chinese strategy in the region relies on routine patrols in order to maintain de facto sovereignty in the South China Sea.[85] The PLAN's submarine fleet will also have grown significantly by 2020, with additional SSBNs conducting exercises alongside the surface fleet and other submarine hunter-killers.

The PLAAF and PLANAF arms will be able to provide extensive air cover for both the ground and naval forces in 2020. More than a decade of intensive training in long-range confrontation, mid-air refuelling and air-to-ground strikes will have created a modern and deadly force which can project Chinese military might way beyond the country's borders. However, these air assets will still be mostly based on land, as the *Varyag* will not be integrated into the PLAN as a ship of the line and will remain as a training vessel, while the domestic carrier will still be under construction.

Aside from traditional security objectives such as territorial integrity and sovereignty in the South China Sea, China has been focusing extensively on what the CMC describes as 'Military Operations Other Than War' (MOOTW).[86] The leadership increasingly sees non-traditional military missions such as humanitarian relief and peacekeeping as appropriate to China's greater power status and as a way to demonstrate its commitment to the international system.[87] These operations will continue to provide Chinese officers with operational experience while helping to alleviate a growing Chinese concern regarding the security of Chinese personnel and infrastructure abroad.[88]

Defence in depth

With all of these advances in the PLA, China in 2020 will have achieved most of its goals and acquired all of the technologies for its area denial strategy. It is doubtful whether the US would risk a carrier task force in the South China Sea in the event of conflict with China. Even in 2010, the thought of sailing a carrier through the Taiwan Strait is no longer a viable option. The PLA in 2020 will have built up a robust defence in depth, consisting of aircraft, submarines and, above all, ASBM missiles. These will allow China to offer layers of defence through various ranged weapons platforms. Even if the naval barrier is breached, the mainland will still be protected by a web of air defence networks, well trained in resisting enemy jamming and other forms of electronic warfare.

The main element of deterrence will remain as the PLA's nuclear arm. The SAC in 2020 will have acquired several more brigades of DF-31A mobile ICBM launchers as more and more silo-based missiles are retired. However, China's nuclear doctrine will not change from its second-strike strategy – there will be no long-range SSBN strategic patrols like the US and the USSR during the Cold War.[89] The main offensive arm of the SAC in 2020 will instead be its conventional missiles, such as the DF-21C. The completion of the area denial package would be the successful deployment of ASBM missiles along the Chinese coast.

Policy implications

The long list of PLA capability building and expansion does signify a more assertive China by 2020. This will be particularly felt in the field of foreign policy, especially over disputed territories such as the South China Sea islands which China sees as an internal issue. However, as mentioned at the start of the chapter, this does not mean that China is closed to reason, nor does it necessarily imply that China is a revisionist power. Policymakers in other countries such as Britain can still engage with China, but will need to bear certain points in mind when doing so.

Firstly, it is important to remember China's cultural memory of the 'one hundred years of humiliation', which is the period between the first

Opium War in 1839 and the founding of the People's Republic in 1949. During this period the weak Qing dynasty gave in to numerous treaties demanded by an aggressive, imperialistic West. These treaties – which are known as the 'unequal treaties' in China – were a catastrophic blow to the Chinese, who were used to a Sinocentric view of the international order. Much of current Communist dogma and legitimacy revolves around the party's ability to reverse this process. Therefore policymakers in the West should be wary of potentially 'lecturing' China.

Secondly, during the same 'one hundred years of humiliation', China saw much of her territory forcefully taken by foreign powers – Hong Kong, Macau and Shandong for example. This was another blow to Chinese prestige and national pride. Again, this forms a central pillar in CCP policy, and its mandate to rule stems from its ability to protect China's territorial integrity. The problem arises when such territories are disputed with other countries, such as in the case of the Senkaku Islands (Diaoyutai) in the East China Sea, and the Spratlys (Nansha) in the South China Sea. Of particular importance, of course, is the issue of Taiwan, which Beijing sees as undisputedly an internal Chinese issue. This is an important point to remember for foreign policymakers when engaging China, for it is a point on which the CCP will simply not back down.

Thirdly, as China increases its international standing and stature, it is also stepping into foreign diplomatic territory. The Chinese government is not as experienced in its international relations as some of the other more established powers, honed by centuries of realpolitik. Therefore China will be increasingly wary of any perceived 'plots' against its interests, the most likely form being strategic encirclement in the East Asia region. This causes Beijing to lash out at seemingly trivial security developments in the region such as the establishment of a US base in Tajikistan.

Finally, it must be remembered that China's military, although becoming stronger with each passing year, is still decades short of challenging the main military power in Asia – the US. If this trend is not to develop into an arms race, then China needs to be engaged in more bilateral military confidence-building measures. China has shown that it is particularly keen on this type of exchange, and has shown increased transparency in recent years in the form of dialogues, exchanges and white papers. In fact this process is now so well established that many consider the PLA as being a much more prominent face of Chinese foreign policy than the civilian diplomats of the Ministry of Foreign Affairs.

The danger of describing China as a revisionist power, and adopting policies of containment, is to turn this into a self-fulfilling prophecy.

Policymakers should therefore adopt a two-pronged approach to China: to engage the PLA in security dialogues and joint exercises while maintaining a close eye on its capability developments, all the time bearing in mind the unique cultural factors described above which play such an important part in China's self perception and its perception of the outside world.

Conclusion

In conclusion, the world must be ready to face a China with much strengthened armed forces in 2020. There will be two options available to established powers in the Asia-Pacific region, namely to continue a policy of containment through alliances and the first and second island chains, or to engage China in more multilateral cooperation such as peacekeeping and humanitarian deployments. The former can only increase Chinese paranoia regarding foreign powers' desire to crush China's 'peaceful rise, and potentially spark a dangerous arms race in the Asia-Pacific. However, the latter option can encourage China to become a more responsible power on the world stage.

China has already demonstrated since the 1980s that it is willing to participate in the international society, and has taken on UN missions with enthusiasm. However, it remains to be seen whether China will use its new military might to back up revisionist aims. Therefore it is vital that channels for dialogue are kept open between the main regional powers such as the US. Only through further confidence-building exercises and routine exchanges can China achieve its aims of a 'peaceful rise' in the Asia-Pacific and the world. One thing will be certain in 2020 – the days of military coercion against China will be well and truly over.

Notes

1. 'China slows rise in military spending', BBC News, March 2010.
2. 'China increases defense budget', *Defence News*, March 2009.
3. The Stockholm International Peace Research Institute gives a slightly higher figure of 1.8 per cent for China, while the US and Russia are listed as 4 per cent and 4.3 per cent respectively.
4. PRC Central Government, 'Zhonguo de junbei kongzhi yu caijun' (PRC Arms Control and Force Reduction), 1995.
5. C. Mulvenon and Richard H. Yang (eds), *The People's Liberation Army in the Information Age*, RAND, 1999, p. 127.

6. Wang Weihua, CCP News, 'Jianfu renmin jundui de guangrong shiming' (Shouldering the PLA's glorious missions), 2007.
7. Even in 1989 several senior generals were sacked due to their blank refusal to send troops to Beijing, with one general telling the then Premier Li Peng that the PLA would be 'cursed for generations' if they did so.
8. RMA stands for Revolution in Military Affairs, which can be generally defined as a US theory about the future of warfare, which is tied to modern information, communications, and space technology. Essentially RMA stands for the transformation of an armed force into something that can fight effectively in the information age.
9. The term 'informatisation' (*Xinxihua*), which is unique to official PLA vocabulary, denotes roughly the same as 'digitisation' in the West. The main concept is the ability for the PLA to conduct military operations in an information warfare environment. One of the main stresses in doctrine has been the need to ensure combat capabilities under 'complex electromagnetic environments', i.e. electronic warfare and network warfare (see section on cyber warfare).
10. Ministry of National Defense of the PRC, 'China's National Defense in 2008', 2008.
11. Ibid.
12. IISS, *The Military Balance 2010*, Routledge, London, 2010.
13. Ibid.
14. Xinhua Editorial, 'Zhongguo renmin jiefangjun jingli sanshinian libingmoma zhanli tisheng' (30 Years of PLA Reforms), 2008, (in Chinese) at *http://news.xinhuanet.com/mil/2008-10/13/content_10186136.htm*, accessed 6 October 2010.
15. Xinhua Editorial, 'Jiefangjun he wujin kaizhan peixun junren hexinjiazhiguan huodong' (PLA and PAP begin education in Core Values), 2009.
16. The previous Soviet system of recruiting NCOs from senior conscripts meant that the PLA suffered from a lack of long-standing expertise among the lower ranks. This is an identical problem to that suffered by the Soviet army.
17. PLA Daily, 'Shenhua shiguan zhidu gaige zhengce jiedu' (Deepening NCO reforms), 2009.
18. IISS, 'China's military might on display', *Strategic Comments*, 15(8), October 2009.
19. US Department of Defense, *Annual Report on the Military Power of the People's Republic of China*, 2002.
20. Christopher F. Foss (ed.), *Jane's Armour and Artillery 2010*, Jane's Information Group, 2010.
21. *Military Balance 2010*.
22. *Jane's Armour and Artillery 2010*.
23. *Military Balance 2010*.
24. Ibid.
25. 'China's military might on display'.
26. *Military Balance 2010*.
27. *Jane's Armour and Artillery 2010*.
28. China News Network, 'Zhongguo lujun hangkongbing muqian zhuangbei jin wubaijia gongji zhichengji' (PLA army aviation now has 500 machines),

2009, (in Chinese) at *http://news.cctv.com/military/20090525/102024.shtml*, accessed 6 October 2010.
29. Ibid.
30. Anthony H. Cordesman and Martin Kleiber, *Chinese Military Modernisation, Force Development and Strategic Capabilities*, CSIS, 2007.
31. *Military Balance 2010.*
32. Eric C. Anderson and Jeffrey G. Engstrom, 'Capabilities of the Chinese PLA to carry out military action in the event of a regional military conflict', Science Applications International Corporation, March 2009, at *http://www.uscc.gov/researchpapers/2009/SAIC – PLA Military Capabilities – Final Report 02June2009.pdf*, accessed 6 October 2010.
33. Roughly translated into 'digitised conditions'.
34. Dennis C. Blair, *Annual Threat Assessment of the US Intelligence Community*, February 2010, at *http://www.dni.gov/testimonies/20100202_testimony.pdf*, accessed 6 October 2010.
35. Carlo Kopp, 'Advances in PLA C4ISR capabilities', *Jamestown China Brief*, 10(4), 2010.
36. Andrew Higgins, 'China showcasing its softer side', *The Washington Post*, December 2009, at *http://www.washingtonpost.com/wp-dyn/content/article/2009/12/01/AR2009120104060.html*, accessed 6 October 2010.
37. Mark A. Ryan et al., *Chinese Warfighting, the PLA Experience Since 1949*, ME Sharpe Publishing, 2003.
38. *Military Balance 2010.*
39. Stephen J. Blank, *The Dynamics of Russian Weapons Sales to China*, US Army Strategic Studies Institute, 1997, at *http://www.strategicstudiesinstitute.army.mil/pdffiles/pub83.pdf*, accessed 6 October 2010.
40. Phillip C. Saunders and Erik R. Quam, 'China's air force modernization', *Joint Forces Quarterly* 47, 2007.
41. 'China's National Defense 2008'.
42. PLA Daily, 'Guangkong baiyujia junji ceng yuanhai xunlian' (Hundred plane long range maritime exercise), 2010 (in Chinese), at *http://mil.news.sina.com.cn/2010-03-12/0709586668.html*, accessed 6 October 2010.
43. *Military Balance 2010.*
44. Ibid.
45. Ibid.
46. *Hangkongbao* (Aviation News), January 2010.
47. *People's Daily*, 'Sino-Russian drill to begin despite crash', 2009, at *http://www.chinadaily.com.cn/china/2009-07/22/content_8456192.htm*, accessed 6 October 2010.
48. Carlo Kopp, 'Advances in PLA air defence capabilities challenge strategic balance in Asia', *Jamestown China Brief* 8(20), 2008, at *http://www.jamestown.org/programs/chinabrief/single/?tx_ttnews%5btt_news%5d=5232&tx_ttnews%5bbackPid%5d=168&no_cache=1*, accessed 6 October 2010.
49. *Taiwan News*, 'China air force covers North Taiwan with Russian-built missiles', March 2010.
50. *PLA Daily*, 'Wo kongjing-2000 yujingji yu duoxing zhanji biandui lian yuanhai zouzhan' (KJ-2000 conducts exercises over South China Sea), 2010,

(in Chinese) at *http://mil.news.sina.com.cn/2010-03-10/0733586398.html*, accessed 6 October 2010.

51. Russell Hsiao, 'China's fifth-generation fighters and the changing strategic balance', *Jamestown China Brief* 9(23) (note that western designations for fifth generation fighters are actually considered fourth gen by Chinese standards), at *http://www.jamestown.org/programs/chinabrief/single/?tx_ttnews%5btt_news%5d=35745&cHash=f88fba6a86*, accessed 6 October 2010.
52. Martin Andrew, 'China's conventional cruise and ballistic missile force modernization and deployment', *Jamestown China Brief* 10(1), 2010, at *http://www.jamestown.org/single/?no_cache=1&tx_ttnews%5btt_news%5d=35881&tx_ttnews%5bbackPid%5d=7&cHash=3fe474929a*, accessed 6 October 2010.
53. *Military Balance 2010*, p. 401.
54. Cortez A. Cooper, *The PLAN's New Historic Missions, Expanding Capabilities for a Re-emergent Maritime Power*, RAND, 2009.
55. Peter Brown, 'China's navy cruises into Pacific ascendancy', *Asia Times*, April 2010, at *http://www.atimes.com/atimes/China/LD22Ad01.html*, accessed 6 October 2010.
56. Gary Klintworth, 'Expanded horizons', *Taiwan Review*, 1998, at *http://taiwanreview.nat.gov.tw/fp.asp?xItem=438&CtNode=128*, accessed 6 October 2010.
57. Admiral Robert F. Willard, *Statement before the House Armed Services Committee*, March 2010, at *http://armedservices.house.gov/pdfs/FC032510/Willard_Testimony032510.pdf*, accessed 6 October 2010.
58. Gary Li, 'Towards a blue water future: *ToT*China's aircraft carrier programme', *RUSI Newsbrief*, July 2009, at *http://www.rusi.org/publications/newsbrief/ref:A4A57396C0F649/*, accessed 6 October 2010.
59. Kopp, PLA C4ISR.
60. *Military Balance 2010.*
61. Michael S. Chase, 'China's SAC: New Trends in Force Modernization, Doctrine and Training', *Jamestown China Brief*, 6(25), 2007, at *http://www.jamestown.org/single/?no_cache=1&tx_ttnews%5btt_news%5d=4012*, accessed 6 October 2010.
62. Andrew, 'China's conventional cruise and ballistic missile force'.
63. Ian Easton, *The Assassin Under the Radar: China's DH-10 Cruise Missile Program*, 2049 Institute, 2009, at *http://project2049.net/documents/assassin_under_radar_china_cruise_missile.pdf*, accessed 6 October 2010. Note: 'DH-10' was a Western designation before the official announcement of the SAC designation of 'CJ-10'.
64. Richard Fisher Jr, *IASC- China's Direct Ascent ASAT*, IASC, January 2007, at *http://www.strategycenter.net/research/pubID.142/pub_detail.asp*, accessed 6 October 2010.
65. IISS, 'China's Successful Anti-Missile Test', *Strategic Comments* 16(6), 2010, at *http://www.iiss.org/publications/strategic-comments/past-issues/volume-16-2010/february/chinas-successful-anti-missile-test/*, accessed 6 October 2010.
66. *Military Balance 2010.*
67. Ibid.

68. Easton, *The Assassin Under the Radar*.
69. *Military Balance 2010*.
70. Willard, *Statement*.
71. Mark Stokes, *China's Evolving Conventional Strategic Strike Capability*, Project 2049 Institute, September 2009, at *http://project2049.net/documents/chinese_anti_ship_ballistic_missile_asbm.pdf*, accessed 6 October 2010.
72. Andrew S. Erickson, 'Eyes in the Sky', *US Naval Institute Proceedings*, April 2010.
73. *Military Balance 2010*.
74. 'China's National Defense 2008'.
75. *Xinhua*, 'Renmin wujingfa caoan: diaodong shiyong wujing budui shixing anbao renwu xu yange shenpi' (Draft PAP law amendment: strict reassessment of the mobilisation of PAP forces), 2009 (in Chinese), at *http://news.xinhuanet.com/politics/2009-08/24/content_11936231.htm*, accessed 6 October 2010.
76. Drew Thompson, 'Beijing's participation in UN peacekeeping operations, *Jamestown China Brief*, 5(11), December 2009, at *http://www.jamestown.org/single/?no_cache=1&tx_ttnews%5btt_news%5d=3860*, accessed 6 October 2010.
77. Kevin Larkin, 'China risk: political and security risk in China: China in Afghanistan', *WorldAnalysis.net*, 2009, at *http://worldanalysis.net/modules/news/article.php?storyid=1164*, accessed 6 October 2010.
78. Gary Li, RUSI Commentary, 'A Sign of things to come: Ethnic tensions spark new challenges for Chinese government', *RUSI Commentary*, 2009, at *http://www.rusi.org/analysis/commentary/ref:C4A6D7CBD846CB/*, accessed 6 October 2010.
79. *China Daily*, 'Guojiaji zhuanye yingji jiouyuan budui chengli wuwangren yingji jouyuan chengxing' (National level professional emergency rescue force of 50,000 to be established), April 2010.
80. *The United States Cyber Challenge*, The White House, August 2009.
81. For an excellent account of the nature of Chinese hackers and the activities of the 'cyber militia', please refer to Scott J. Henderson's book *The Dark Visitor: Inside the World of Chinese Hackers*, which is available in pdf format online at *http://www.lulu.com/product/file-download/the-dark-visitor-%28ebook%29/2420426?productTrackingContext=search_results/search_shelf/center/4* (accessed 6 October 2010).
82. Xe Yuyi, 'Zhonggong "Taihuanzhan" siwei yu zhandoli fazhan yanduan', (PLA 'paralyse' tactic during combat operations), *ROC Defense Journal*, 2(24).
83. Bryan Krekel, *Capability of the People's Republic of China to Conduct Cyber Warfare and Computer Network Exploitation*, Northrop Grumman, 2009, at *http://www.uscc.gov/researchpapers/2009/NorthropGrumman_PRC_Cyber_Paper_FINAL_Approved%20Report_16Oct2009.pdf*, accessed 6 October 2010.
84. *PLA Daily*, 'Chen Binde awards unit colours to information security base', 20 July 2010.
85. Cooper, *The PLAN's New Historic Missions*.
86. 'China's National Defense 2008'.

87. Blair, *Annual Threat Assessment.*
88. Cooper, *The PLAN's New Historic Missions.*
89. Chris Buckley, 'China military paper spells out nuclear arms stance', Reuters, April 2010, at *http://www.reuters.com/article/idUSTRE63L0PR20100422*, accessed 6 October 2010.

China's environment in 2020

Jonathan Watts

By 2020, the strain on world resources is likely to loom large as the biggest issue facing global policymakers. National governments will struggle to balance two fundamental approaches to survival: international cooperation to conserve and nationalist competition to consume. In this international context, China and its environment will take centre stage with Beijing's approach raising both fear and optimism among the planet's population.

From 2010 to 2020, China will have staked a strong claim to be the world's greenest superpower thanks to a massive expansion of its renewable energy sector and other low-carbon technologies. But on current trajectories, it will also be a greyer, less biodiverse nation plagued by an increasingly hostile climate and frequent protests over shortages of water. Desertification, declining soil quality and rising oil prices generate sharp upward pressures on food costs and prompt mass migrations into cities, adding to social tensions.

Within China, as across the capitals of the world, the environment in 2020 is increasingly thought of as a security issue. Generals are no longer just worried about superpower nuclear confrontation and Islamic fundamentalist terrorists. They also increasingly talk about the threat posed to populations and economies by growing water shortages, rising populations and food security. Economists highlight the ecological walls constraining growth. Politicians who once took sides on the welfare–market divide will increasingly define their positions by whether they support eco-intervention (programs to restore degraded lands and polluted waters) or a laissez-faire approach of letting nature return areas to their wild state. Newspaper columnists talk of the need for longer-term budgets that factor in environmental costs and put environmental spending closer to military spending. For nationalists, the environment and 'ethnic survival' becomes a new rallying point, along with trade protectionism and territorial claims.

Today, it is no coincidence that the West is now more concerned with Beijing's environmental performance than its governance or human-rights record. Visiting foreign leaders still raise the maltreatment of dissidents, the restrictions on the Internet and suppression of religious groups, but these issues will slip down the agenda, further below climate change and talks on the new issue of the age – sustainable global consumption. China's environment is increasingly likely to prompt intense diplomatic activity, creating new business opportunities and sparking growing security concerns well beyond the country's borders.

Dust storms in Japan, deforestation in Russia and the increased extraction of oil from Canada's tar sands can all be traced back to China. With the population expected to peak at 1.46bn by 2034 (up from 1.26bn in 2005), resources will come under increasing demographic pressure. Water shortages and pollution are already causing unease in Russia, Kazakhstan and South-east Asia. Retired PLA generals are calling for rivers to be diverted away from India, which, if adopted (which is currently far from being the case), would raise a very real risk of a conflict. Unless China kicks its coal habit, scientists say greenhouse emissions will surge, global temperatures will rise and climate change will create millions more eco-migrants and food supply instability.

Predominantly urbanised and plagued by droughts, China by 2020 is increasingly reliant on grand water diversion schemes and imports of 'virtual water' from countries that produce the foodstuffs it can no longer grow for itself. Although China is likely to succeed in reaching the 40 to 45 per cent reduction in carbon intensity target (emissions relative to GDP) set in 2009, it remains by far the world's biggest emitter of greenhouse gases and overtakes every country in Europe even in per capita terms. Beijing is increasingly criticised overseas for not doing more to combat climate change, which is causing increasing havoc.

Pollution and dust from China will continue to be a problem for neighbouring countries. Amid criticism of its growing environmental footprint in Africa and South America (where it sources ever larger quantities of commodities, including timber and foodstuffs), the government is likely to engage more with non-government organisations (NGOs) and other stakeholders. The security of water supplies will be a higher priority than in the past for diplomats and generals, with major charm offensives aimed at persuading neighbouring nations that dams and diversion projects will not harm their interests. In science and technology, China seeks more collaboration with overseas partners and acquisitions of leading foreign companies in local-carbon fields, while fighting accusations of unfair trade and investment opportunities in the same areas. At climate talks, its involvement will continue to be determined by a mix of concern about the impact on its glaciers and farm fields, a strong sense of injustice about historical emissions, and suspicions that the carbon debate is another attempt to contain its growth. China increasingly hosts low-carbon conferences and workshops, engages in joint studies and tries to display leadership, particularly in the developing world – which it is looking less and less a part of.

But though the country is increasingly wealthy, it is also one of the worst affected by the increasingly degraded global environment. The government in Beijing is preoccupied with the domestic implications. By 2020, as commodity costs rise and waste becomes more expensive to deal with, the nation's leaders find it harder to maintain the 8 to 10 per cent economic growth rates that were once considered normal. Polluting, energy-intensive industries are 'insourced' to poor western provinces, which suffer a loss of resources, an increase in environmental health problems and an upsurge of social unrest. The state is also having to spend large sums on climate-related measures, including flood relief, drought alleviation and barriers to protect crops and businesses on the coast from rising water levels.

Science is the government's main hope for a solution. New model eco-cities in Tianjin, Beijing and Nanjing will, if constructed and operated as planned, nudge China closer to the government's goal of a circular, recycling economy. By 2020, much of the old Silk Road will have become a giant wind farm, the deserts of the west will be filled with solar panels, new techniques will have been developed and commercialised for burning coal more efficiently (an area where China is moving ahead more aggressively and effectively than the US) and ambitious large-scale experiments will be conducted in biotechnology, weather modification, algae breeding and cloud whitening that are likely to stir up hopes and fears across the world. But still China struggles to shake off an image as a global centre for energy-intensive, high-carbon, low-cost manufacturing.

By 2020, the populace will need to be convinced that they have reached the goal of a *xiaokang* (all-round, moderately well-off) society. Unless significant progress is made to reduce pollution as well as raise living standards, many are likely to yearn for lost ecological wealth and criticise those who have sold it off cheaply. The environment will become an increasingly divisive issue in domestic politics and economic policymaking.

Economy

Long-held economic expectations have undergone a traumatic change since the Great Crash of 2008. Globally, annual growth by 2020 could prove the exception rather than the norm, despite a decade of fiscal stimulus packages in all of the old major economies. China is likely to buck the trend by expanding, but more slowly than in the past and mainly by government spending on infrastructure rather than exports.

The world economic contraction is increasingly linked to environmental restraints. Commodity prices have surged, to the benefit of resource-supplying nations such as Brazil, Russia, Australia, Mongolia and parts of Africa. But shortages and price increases have dampened global growth and added to the volatility of international markets.

Treasury chiefs still talk of V and W and WW-shaped recoveries, but gloomy economists speak of a global version of Japan's 'lost decade' (which by 2020 could have stretched to its 30th year!). Politicians will only slowly and reluctantly face up to this possibility. Though it will be difficult to admit to electorates at first, a few brave leaders may start to tout themselves as experts in responsibly managing decline rather than recklessly promoting expansion. Even those politicians and media commentators who reject this perspective as overly pessimistic will be increasingly likely to blame the economic malaise on previous generations that over-spent the planet's eco-wealth.

Finding a new, sustainable growth path becomes an increasingly pressing task. As China's economy is among the first to hit a series of environmental walls, its efforts to build an alternative are studied with greater interest by foreign scholars and diplomats.

In the 2011–2015 five-year plan, the government is likely to introduce a carbon trading scheme. Work is also under way to place a hefty value on the country's forest ecosystems and to draft new regulations that would oblige rich urban coastal regions to pay compensation fees to unspoiled inland areas that provide carbon sequestration and other environmental services. These steps followed United Nation recommendations that environmental costs should be factored into the global economy. Even if adopted, these measures are unlikely to be perfectly implemented, but they will be scrutinised as a model that might be replicated on a global scale. Although factoring in environmental costs puts an extra burden on the traditional economy, it creates new opportunities for non-material growth and consumption in intellectual property and ecological wealth creation. Values may well move in this direction.

Among global policymakers, the debate about the pros and cons of consumption, particularly Chinese consumption, to the world economy is likely to grow more intense. China's consumers are currently seen as potential saviours of the global economy. International retailers spend a fortune encouraging them to spend more. But the energy use of the average person in Shanghai has already surpassed that of Tokyo, New York and London. The government aims to raise the lifestyles of the rest of the 1.4bn population to at least the same level as that of Shanghai, which means factories have to churn out an extra 159 million refrigerators, 213 million televisions, 233 million computers, 166 million microwave ovens, 260 million air conditioners and 187 million cars. This will add to the surge of commodity prices and carbon emissions – which have become the world's two great diplomatic challenges.

Resource constraints

Shortages of water, fossil fuels and other commodities will become more pronounced as the global population passes the 7 billion mark. There is likely to be increasing talk of tipping points. Global public opinion in this regard is influenced by China, which joined the ranks of rich nations living in excess of the planet's means sometime around 2008, according to the World Wide Fund for Nature.

As its own forests, fields and mines struggle to satisfy a growing appetite, China is depleting Siberia's Taiga, Mongolia's ore deposits, the Amazon's rainforest, South-east Asia's wildlife and Africa's mines.

Contaminated water from Jilin and Heilongjiang flows into Russia. Dams and diversion projects in Tibet and Yunnan affect hundreds of millions of people downstream in Thailand, Cambodia, Laos and Burma. Chinese cash and political support is accelerating the filthy extraction of oil from Canada's tar sands and propping up pariah governments in resource-rich nations like Sudan and Zimbabwe. On human rights and environmental grounds, this may be unpopular, but China – as a hungry latecomer to global resource extraction – can afford even fewer qualms than the West about where and how it does business.

The most strained resource is the most basic: water. River volumes and lake levels are affected by warming temperatures, changing weather patterns and over-exploitation of water resources for irrigation, factories and drinking supplies. While climate change has resulted in increased precipitation to some desert areas, elsewhere it has worsened already alarming levels of soil erosion and encroachment by sand dunes on farm fields and villages.

The two great aquifers in northern China have fallen to dangerous levels due to over-exploitation. Water conflicts could break out as more communities run so short they are unable to irrigate their fields. The South–North Water Diversion Scheme, which was supposed to solve this problem by bringing water from the Yangtze delta up to the arid plains north of the Yellow River, is plagued by delays, cost over-runs, social unease over relocation and engineering challenges. Of the three planned legs, the eastern and central ones ought to be completed by 2020. It is unclear if the benefits will be as great as expected because much of the water is polluted and costs a great deal to purify. Tianjin prefers to build desalination plants. Meanwhile the south has started to suffer increasingly from droughts. If this persists, politicians in Sichuan, Hunan and Hubei are likely to complain that their regions can no longer donate so much water to the north. The western leg – through Tibetan areas of Qinghai – remains on hold due to engineering difficulties and political sensitivities.

Transboundary water issues are also a growing source of tension with neighbouring states. The downstream Mekong River nations of Thailand, Laos and Cambodia suspect China is over-using water for rubber plantations and hydropower generation. Russia is concerned about the Amur River and surrounding wetlands which are drying up, partly as a result of water diverted for cold-resistant hybrid rice crops which are expanding in the Sanjiang region of northern Heilongjiang province. Kazakhstan will be furious if politicians in Xinjiang suggest diverting water for coal liquefaction (a plant is planned in the region and local officials have privately discussed using more of the rivers that currently flow to Kazakhstan). India and Bangladesh watch warily as China builds a cascade of dams on the Yarlung Tsangpo (Brahmaputra).

Nations as far away as Ethiopia and Brazil are also affected as the import of 'virtual water' becomes an increasingly sensitive issue across the globe. Unable to produce enough water-intensive crops for itself, China and many other dry nations such as Saudi Arabia have started to ship in more food from overseas. The result is that they are effectively outsourcing their water stress. This is particularly evident in the soya trade. At the start of the century, China was roughly self-sufficient in this staple, producing and consuming about 15 tonnes a year. By 2010, consumption had surged almost fourfold, far faster than output. This meant China had to turn to Brazil and Argentina, where forests and savannah are cleared for the cash crop used to feed cows, pigs and chickens.

The pressure to secure food and energy resources will intensify. Flashpoints include the South China Sea, where China, Japan, Vietnam and the Philippines vie for waters containing significant natural gas deposits.

International climate talks

The world will increasingly be focused on what might be called a 'Great Accommodation' – a term that describes the readjustment in lifestyles, international trade and wealth distribution that aims to achieve a sustainable balance between man and nature. In retrospect, the 2009 Copenhagen summit was one of the first efforts to move in this direction because it pulled together more of the world's leaders than ever before in a drive to allocate a global resource – carbon emission space. Though the climate summit was billed at the time as an effort to find a solution to global warming, future historians may well see it as the environmental equivalent of the Potsdam or Versailles Conferences. While those post-war gatherings of leaders aimed to carve up and share out geographic territory, Copenhagen tried to allocate development space in the traditional carbon economy.

It was a historic failure. Copenhagen marked a shift in power that matched the shift in carbon emissions, first from Europe in the nineteenth century, next to the United States in the twentieth century, and then to Asia in the twenty-first century. Among the 192 nations at the climate conference, the gap between Britain and China appeared the greatest. The UK, the first nation to carbonise its economy, arguably invested more political capital than any other country in pushing for strong, binding limits on emissions. But it was China – the most recent convert to capital-driven, carbon-fuelled growth – that played a more influential role in shaping proceedings from then on.

The acrimony and chaos of Copenhagen dissuaded Chinese leaders from returning directly to such a negotiation, though climate diplomats continue to meet and take small steps. It is hard to see much urgency being injected into the debate unless a major economy suffers an opinion-shifting climate-related catastrophe.

For the most part, however, the shift in climate patterns will be steady and pronounced rather than spectacular. Water is a major source of tension as changing rain patterns and rising temperatures disrupt supplies to population and industrial centres. This is likely to drive people across borders and raise transboundary disputes about the fair division of drinking water and hydropower resources. In this regard, the Mekong basin drought of 2010 may have been a taste of things to come as it raised questions in several countries about China's upstream use of water for rubber plantations and dams. Extreme weather events will become more frequent and intense. Glaciers will melt at an accelerated rate, initially creating a water surplus – and even floods – in downstream areas such as Urumqi. But the government is bracing for the droughts that will follow when the glaciers shrink by building underground water storage plants. This is part of a growing climate budget. An increasingly large share of the government funds will be devoted to disaster relief efforts, flood control, coastal barriers and resettlement of populations from the areas worst affected by floods and drought. Although Nicholas Stern and other economists point out that adapting to climate change is ultimately more expensive and riskier than mitigating the problem, the former is easier for governments to sell to their people and powerful interests in the construction and engineering sectors.

As the climate becomes more important – and a greater source of funds and prestige – different ministries vie with each other to lead policy. In China, the foreign ministry lost much of its responsibility – and transferred its top two climate negotiators – after being blamed for the poor endgame it played during Copenhagen. Since then the National Development and Reform Commission (NDRC) has reasserted its authority. The Environment Ministry continues to angle for a greater role, but remains on the fringes.

China has learned from the public relations disaster of the Copenhagen summit that it has to be more proactive in putting across its message. It will increasingly host international conferences on climate issues, invests heavily in related research institutes, injects billions of yuan into 'soft power' media organisations such as CCTV and Xinhua, learns to 'spin' global media organisations and builds stronger alliances with other nations at a similar stage of development. The BASIC group, initially comprising Brazil, South Africa, India and China, is likely to be expanded to include other nations. Among the candidates are Argentina, Indonesia, Pakistan and the leading representatives of the African Union and small island states.

It may also be forced to reshape its negotiating strategy. For most of the previous two decades, China argued that it should not have to accept constraints on emissions because its per capita greenhouse gas output was considerably lower than that in the United States or Europe. But thanks to the rapid growth in its coal-dependent economy, this is increasingly untrue. Certain cities – such as Shanghai and Tianjin – have already passed London, New York and Tokyo in per capita emissions terms. By 2020, the nation as a whole will probably do the same if current trends hold. Realising this has weakened their position, Chinese negotiators will stress other comparisons.

The two key measures of carbon responsibility are historic (accrued emissions over the past hundred or more years) and per capita (emission volumes divided by the size of the population). If China meets its carbon-intensity goals and its economy continues to grow by more than 8 per cent per year, it will overtake the UK in both per capita and historic emissions by 2020. But it will not be until 2030 that it overtakes the US in per capita emissions, and between 2030 and 2040 that it catches up with the US in terms of historic emissions. Put these two together and it probably will not be until after 2050 that China surpasses the US in historic, per capita emissions. But even this could be too optimistic. An earlier historic start date or the factoring in of emissions produced by exports could allow China to say it has not caught up with the 'carbon responsibility' of the West until much later.

A historical reckoning about emissions remains contentious. Most nations recognise that the greatest destruction from greenhouse gases has been wrought, mostly by the industrial powers of Europe, the United States and Japan, over the past 200 or so years. But China – the world's oldest civilisation – has been destroying forests and plundering natural resources unsustainably for millennia. This must have had an impact on the atmosphere. Worldwide, the loss of photosynthesising trees is estimated to contribute a fifth of the carbon imbalance.

Given these internal and external divisions, a comprehensive, legally binding global agreement could still be a distant prospect in 2020. But action is being taken by cities, businesses and in individual sectors. China boasts that it is leading the way in many areas, particularly adoption of renewable and low-carbon technologies. It may also claim that it has honoured its commitments (albeit those listed only as domestic targets) to reduce the carbon intensity of its economy by between 40 and 45 per cent between 2005 and 2020, and to increase the share of renewables in the nation's power supply mix to 15 per cent. The state's determination to achieve its goals was apparent in 2010, when several factories were forced to shut down periodically so the government could meet its energy intensity targets just before the end of the 2006–2010 five-year plan.

But the government remains reluctant to set a target for when its carbon emissions might peak. The science ministry – which will benefit from a shift to new technologies – is optimistic that this can be done between

2030 and 2035. The National Development and Reform Commission – which is more concerned with maintaining economic growth – gloomily predicts the date as 2050. But massive efforts are under way to reconfigure the country's energy mix, which have implications for the economy, trade, security and social stability across the planet.

Energy and renewable power

The development of a renewable energy industry is one of China's greatest modern achievements and a considerable source of both hard and soft power. Thanks to a massive expansion of nuclear, hydro, wind, solar, biomass and geothermal electricity generation, the government is likely to exceed its 2020 target to generate 15 per cent of the country's power from non-fossil fuel sources. To the shock of many in Europe, it may even have surpassed the 20 per cent goal achieved by the EU, which once thought of itself as a frontrunner in the green technology field.

As a result, China aims to become less dependent on its coal resources, which by 2015 are expected to account for 63 per cent of its power supply, down from 70 per cent in 2010. Its renewable industry is a source of international prestige, tens of billions of dollars in exports and enhanced energy security in an increasingly unstable world. Despite the initial high investment, the shift in this direction will look increasingly smart as global oil prices rise due to concerns about shortages, persistent conflict in the Middle East and shipping lines increasingly plagued by piracy.

China's turbine and photovoltaic panel manufacturers will, by 2020, be dominant global players, able to capitalise on cheap production costs and increasingly strong links with governments in developing nations in Africa, South America and South-east Asia. To boost domestic demand, the government in Beijing is likely to introduce a scheme of generous feed-in tariffs for solar power and solar thermal power generation. Along with the likely introduction of a carbon tax or carbon pricing system, this could mean the price of solar and wind power passes the point of 'grid parity' with coal-fired power well before 2020. The world's first solar billionaire, Shi Zhengrong, the founder and CEO of Suntech, boasts that his company is on course to be a true global energy giant on the scale of BP and Shell. Yinhe, a Hebei-based solar PV manufacturer, is now a World Cup sponsor (and could use this base to lobby for China to be awarded the tournament in the future).

Currently, though still notorious outside China for building a coal-fired power plant every week, China is also erecting a wind turbine every hour. In Gansu, Inner Mongolia and Xinjiang, the deserts of the Old Silk Road are now filled with massive wind and solar farms. Seven wind-based mega-complexes are under construction that will together provide 130 000 megawatts of electricity, equivalent to adding 260 coal-fired power plants of 500MW capacity. It is estimated that China still has enough harnessable wind capacity to expand harvestable onshore wind capacity sevenfold from 2005 levels.

There is also enormous potential offshore. Many coastal waters are already lined with turbines, though the government complains that German's Siemens company should share its salt-resistant alloy technology so this potential can be realised more economically.

If all goes to plan, then by 2020, in Nanjing, the world's biggest solar-powered community will have just celebrated its fifth anniversary. Sinohydro is ramping up hydroelectric development of Tibet's great rivers, the last in China to be dammed on a massive scale. Most controversial is the cascade of dams on the Yarlung Tsangpo – also known as the Brahmaputra – and continued efforts by industry lobbyists to build the world's biggest dam at the great U-bend of the river before it descends towards the flood plains of India and Bangladesh. With more and more power coming from remote deserts and mountains, the State Grid is in the process of an expensive expansion. The creation of a 'strong smart grid' is a pillar of central government policy for industry, the environment and climate diplomacy. It also becomes a new focus of the mainland's trade relations with Taiwan – the semiconductor capital of the world – which is a key supplier of smart grid components and energy-saving devices.

At a local level, geothermal and wind power is being tapped for the ten-year-old eco-city in the Tianjin Binhai area – one of a growing number of similar projects throughout the nation, though none are yet up and running. On an even bigger scale, biofuel projects, initially funded by the World Bank, are likely to be replicated and expanded in tens of thousands of villages. By 2020, farmers and nomads in remote locations will all be supplied with solar panels on their tents and homes. Thanks to this and excellent mobile phone network coverage, almost everyone in China will then have access to the Internet. Almost every city in China will have completed the switch of street lamps and lighting in public buildings from old-style incandescent to LEDs – many with motion sensors – which will trim their demand for electricity by more than half.

Several of the wealthier and more developed cities on the eastern seaboard are also pioneering ambitious and expensive programs in low-carbon public transport. High-speed rail is undergoing a massive expansion that has in the past two years pushed China's network above that of the rest of the world combined. Local transport is also being upgraded. By 2020, Dalian, Hangzhou, Tianjin, Shanghai, Nanjing and Beijing will have some of the most advanced and extensive subway systems in the world. Trams have also made a comeback, but perhaps the most pioneering development is the expansion of the fleet of electric vehicles and buses. Several companies have entered the field, but the leader is BYD (Build Your Dreams). The company's base city of Shenzhen has China's most advanced charging network for electric vehicles. Shanghai looks set to follow suit with a multibillion yuan program. By 2020, such vehicles can be mass produced at relatively low cost and with high specs, which will encourage a growing take-up among private citizens. But at this time it is possible that the government no longer encourages car ownership. It is recognised that even electric cars are a drain on diminishing resources and for the most part they end up being powered – via the grid – by coal.

This is not the only cloud over hopes for low-carbon economic growth. Private companies and local governments have been so quick to jump on to the renewable energy bandwagon that there are concerns that a bubble has formed. Oversupply of PV panels and wind turbines has depressed the price of these technologies within China, prompting domestic companies to look overseas for business. Worldwide, this has helped to accelerate the adoption of low-cost renewable energy technologies, but it has also led to trade tensions. US and European solar and wind companies complain that China is dumping subsidised products on the global market. Rivalries also hinder collaboration and technology sharing. Strategic affairs analysts increasingly make a connection between low-carbon technological prowess and national power. Companies and nations refuse to share patents with rivals, even though global adoption of those devices would be in the interests of humanity as a whole.

There is also a growing awareness of the environmental cost of 'clean technologies'. Journalists – by 2020 perhaps either working independently or for one of a handful of global Internet conglomerates in a massively consolidated industry – expose pollution associated with the manufacture of photovoltaic cells. Bird numbers are decimated by wind farms. The covering of deserts in solar panels threatens the habitats of rare arid-region species. Even a minor nuclear accident will raise public concerns of a major disaster and push up costs. Private companies are already reluctant to invest in nuclear reactors and even state utilities are hesitant to get involved because operating, insurance and clean-up costs are so high. Providing more energy also involves a social cost that will become more evident. Ethnic tensions in Tibet are heightened by the damming of rivers that locals consider sacred. The construction of supposedly clean dams is often followed by an influx of dirty, energy-intensive industries, which pollute pristine mountain areas and often require coal plants as a back-up for the dry season.

China is also still a very long way from kicking its coal habit. The fuel is being mined far more safely than in the past thanks to the closure of tens of thousands of small, private mines in Shanxi – which by 2020 will be almost empty of coal reserves – and the opening of huge automated pits in Inner Mongolia operated by Shenhua – the state-owned firm that is now the biggest coal mine company in the world. Even these will be surpassed by the mega-mines that are being eyed in Xinjiang, which is set to become the carbon capital of the world. This far western region, bordering central Asia, has long been the main provider of China's oil and gas. It also contains 40 per cent of the country's known coal reserves. For decades, extraction of this coal was uneconomical because road transport was too expensive. But advances in coal gasification and liquefaction mean that the fuel will one day be cheaply piped across the 3,000 kilometres from the western deserts to east-coast factories.

While this guarantees China's energy supplies for many decades, it worsens two long-standing environmental problems: greenhouse gas emissions and water shortages. Chinese officials want to reduce carbon dioxide output because their country is criticised for being the world's biggest emitter on a growing variety of counts and its people are increasingly affected by climate change. They have responded in a number of ways. Industrial planners have phased out most of the old, inefficient power stations and heavy industry. Among the new power stations are dozens of supercritical and ultra-supercritical thermal plants, which are among the cleanest and most efficient in the world. But they continue to belch out a growing volume of carbon dioxide.

Utilities such as Huaneng are developing a new generation of Integrated Gas Combined Cycle (IGCC) power plants that burn coal more efficiently and are equipped to capture the emissions. Their technology – developed in collaboration with US energy giant, Duke – is the best in the world. If current permit requests are approved by 2020, IGCC plants could be operating in Shandong, Shanghai and three other areas. It is expected that they will become the industry standard in China and across the world, creating a lucrative new export market.

Policymakers remain unsure, however, what to do with captured carbon. Sequestration pilot projects are being launched in Ordos, Inner Mongolia, with support from the US government. But dumping carbon is seen as an expensive waste. Diplomats argue that wealthy countries should pay for these projects until China's historical per capita emissions reach the level of the old industrial powers. In the meantime, a growing number of China's leading chemists and businessmen devote themselves to finding the Philosophers' Stone of the modern age: not turning base metals into gold, but turning CO_2 into a useable fuel. At the National New Energy Research Centre in Dalian, scientists focus on catalytic processes that use solar power to turn carbon into usable hydrogen fuel. In Ordos, the company ENN is building a massive experimental plant that feeds carbon dioxide to algae, which is then used for biodiesel and fertiliser. The hangar-sized facility full of huge pipes of bright green gunk resembles the set of a science-fiction film. None of these experiments is ready yet for commercialisation, but there is no limit on the willingness to try new ideas, including the splicing of algae cells with cancer genes to try to develop a super-fast-growing organism to consume CO_2.

Expect China to push further at the limits of science in the search for a solution to its environmental problems, either leading or collaborating in the development of technology for cloud whitening, ocean fertilising, salt-lake batteries and weather modification. One of the air force's chief responsibilities is to fly thousands of cloud-seeding missions every year to clear pollution for political events and to stimulate rainfall when clouds approach reservoirs. In the drought-hit north, rival communities race to shoot down clouds over their territory. To avert conflict, the National People's Congress may one day have to pass a law against cloud theft.

This is on the fringes of a now long-established tendency among Chinese officials to rely on science, technology and hardware to try to engineer a solution to the nation's environmental problems. This may change in 2012 when a politburo dominated by domestically trained engineers is replaced by a leadership with more social scientists. In academic institutions and local governments around the country, a new generation of decision makers and experts is cautious about replicating the mistakes of past mega projects. But there is still clearly also a strong willingness to experiment, despite frequent failures. China could soon be a leader in genetically modified crops. Approval for sales of GM rice is likely in the next few years.

Waste and pollution

By 2020, the government ought to have long since declared that China has passed the dirtiest phase of development. The clean-up of the worst-polluting industries should make good progress given the pattern of development seen in other countries at a similar stage. However, corruption and a lack of transparency and accountability may slow the process. On the east coast, air and water quality should become considerably better than they were during the dark days of the pre-Olympic era. Beijing's government will increasingly boast a larger number of 'blue sky days' for the year. Thanks to the relocation of the worst-polluting industries far outside the city boundaries, the levels of sulphur dioxide and nitrogen dioxide in the air have fallen significantly and smog is less of a problem. Rivers, such as the Huai and Songhua, which once ran black with factory discharges, have been restored to a level that allows their water to be used for irrigation and, if properly treated, is even fit for drinking along some stretches.

Industrial pollution has not gone away. It has been 'insourced' to poor western regions, such as Gansu, Ningxia and Inner Mongolia, which will probably witness a related uptick in respiratory diseases, cancer of the liver and social unrest related to chemical factories and incinerators.

Non-point pollution from agriculture remains serious. Continued overuse of fertiliser, pesticide and other chemicals results in the contamination of waterways with excess nitrates. The result is continued eutrophication of major lakes. The government may be able to partially alleviate the problem with a propaganda campaign aimed at educating farmers to use more organic techniques. Local authorities also use algae-eating carp to limit the spread of the green gunk that is a now familiar sight on the surface of Dianchi, Tai and other lakes.

More alarming still are the red and green algae tides in coastal waters, which are increasing in frequency and size. At first, they were only seen in the summer. But now, in the warmer south, the red tides appear all through the year.

In the worst areas, around the Yangtze and Pearl river estuaries, these harmful algae blooms create 'dead zones' where the water is so starved of oxygen it is unable to sustain other forms of life. Farms are the main source of this environmental stress. Fertiliser nitrates and phosphorus seep into streams and rivers, and eventually lakes and oceans. The primary benefactors are the organisms first in the food chain, such as algae and plankton. With the extra nutrition they grow quickly in the form of green slime on lakes or red tides in the sea, to their own benefit and their predators' detriment. Some algae have become toxic, but most kill by suffocation, choking off oxygen and sunlight.

Even with a future economic slowdown and deceleration of the migration to cities, urban centres will struggle to cope with transport-related pollution and the growing mountain of consumer rubbish.

Landfill sites are full. Incinerators are unpopular. A massive public recycling campaign would be enthusiastically adopted, but consumer lifestyles remain unsustainably wasteful and waste-producing. This is particularly the case with regard to the country's car culture.

Even though vehicle exhaust standards are the strictest in the world, tailpipe pollution is a problem because the number of cars on Beijing's streets passed the 4.5 million mark in 2010, up from 2 million at the start of the decade. It is the same story throughout the country. Having overtaken the United States to become the world's biggest car market in 2009, China will put increasing pressure on global fuel supplies. In the coming ten years, enthusiasm for cars will be tempered by the rise in oil prices, worsening traffic jams and increasing awareness of the problems of ozone and particulate matter. Electric bicycles, subway and high-speed rail are the main form of transport for commuters.

Efficient cities are increasingly seen as the answer to China's environmental problems. To alleviate the strain on the land and improve the efficiency of energy use, the government is building smart, tall eco-conglomerations, including one thick urban string that threads its way up the Yangtze from Shanghai to Chongqing by way of Nanjing, Hefei and Wuhan, and others joining Beijing and Tianjin, Shanghai and Suzhou, and Guangzhou and Shenzhen. Tying these conglomerations together is the world's most advanced network of high-speed railways, which are due to be completed in 2012.

During the first quarter of the century, half of all the world's new buildings are likely to be erected in China. Fifty thousand of them will be skyscrapers, equivalent to ten New Yorks. China boasts many of the world's most spectacular cityscapes. Beijing, Shanghai and Tianjin are dominated by 80- to 100-storey skyscrapers. Chongqing has erected a hundred supertowers. Guangzhou is home to what architects describe as the planet's most eco-friendly skyscraper, which is almost entirely energy self-sufficient thanks to the solar panels on its south face and two giant wind turbines in its belly. In Jiangsu, even the 'village' of Huaxi is building a mega-tower that is taller than the Empire State Building.

China also leads the way on the construction of eco-cities. The most advanced project is the Sino-Singapore Tianjin Eco-City, currently being built on a former dump site on the western shore of the Bohai Sea. The technocratic governments of China and Singapore are pooling expertise and finance to build this new, green urban community of 350,000 people, which they tout as the most environmentally friendly city in China and an example for developing nations across the planet. The eco-city plans to get 20 per cent of its power from renewable sources, mostly wind farms and a geothermal power plant. Domestic water use is kept below 120 litres per person per day, half supplied by rain capture and recycled grey water. For optimum energy efficiency, every building is insulated, double-glazed and made entirely of materials that reach the government's green standards. More than 60 per cent of all waste is recycled. To get car journeys down by 90 per cent, a light railway passes near to every home and communities are zoned to ensure everyone will be able to walk to shops, schools and clinics. It is ecologically richer than almost any other city in China, with protected areas for wild grasses, such as bulrush, hairy uraria and wild chrysanthemum, and wetland birds, including purple heron, flying snipes and black-winged stilts. Overall, there is an average of 12 square metres of parkland, grassland or wetland for each resident. Environmental health will be further enhanced by an on-site water treatment plant to ensure that all tap water is potable, by free sports facilities and by a commitment to keep particulate matter in the air below 100 parts per cubic metre for more than four out of every five days.

The government hopes to replicate this for the 400 new similar-sized communities being constructed nationwide. But in reality, most new real-estate projects abuse the 'eco- friendly' label to sell upmarket real estate. Many in the nation's environmental movement criticise mega-eco developments and 'green' skyscrapers for wasteful use of resources.

Food

Will leaders one day call a soil summit to address the degradation of arable land? This is a looming crisis. Ever more dependent on fossil fuels and chemical fertiliser, the declining fertility of the earth could put upward pressure on grain prices and once again raise the spectre of shortages in the worst-affected areas.

Desertification, heavy metal accumulation, urban sprawl and overuse of fertiliser and pesticides is blamed when food production fails to keep pace with the increase of the population. About a third of the organic carbon in the soil of northern China has been lost to drought and aeolian desertification. If the trend continues, the worst-affected areas, such as Gansu, could start to resemble sub-Saharan Africa and suffer a decline in harvests.

The government is struggling to defend the 120 million hectares of farmland that it set as a red line for food security. Urbanisation adds to the pressure on food security as farmers move off their fields and into cities, where the consumption of meat, grain and dairy products is higher. With the forecast expansion of the urban population from 430 million in 2001 to 850 million in 2015, the number of cities with over 100,000 people will increase from 630 to over 1,000. Although state planners are trying to offset the impact by promoting taller, more concentrated mega-metropolises, urban sprawl and road building have eaten into arable land. The growing transport infrastructure and car culture also adds to pressure on farm fields. According to the World Watch Institute, a hectare of land is covered in asphalt for every 15 cars added to the national fleet.

To offset this, officials have been forced to trim the 'grain for green' policy of rewarding farmers to allow marginal land to return to forest. China's greatest wetlands – at the Sanjiang (Three Rivers) area of Heilongjiang near the border with Russia – are increasingly turned into paddies thanks to new strains of cold-resistant hybrid rice. The state media boast that the Three Rivers area now provides enough food for three cities – Beijing, Shanghai and Tianjin – as well as the entire People's Liberation Army. But the loss of the wetlands has a devastating effect on wildlife and dramatically increases agricultural pollution in the north-east. Fertiliser run-offs create eutrophication problems in nearby lakes and coastal waterways that affect drinking supplies and fish stocks. But for the local population, the move to cultivate the former nature reserve unleashes an economic boom. The value of wetland rises more than thirtyfold once it is converted into farmland.

In addition to Heilongjiang, the agriculture ministry also aims to ramp up food production in Guangxi, Anhui and other eastern regions where it previously focused more on developing industry. Its biggest problem is soil quality. Although the land has sustained the world's biggest population for millennia, it was looking exhausted after a century of supercharged demographic growth and a 'green revolution' that often meant deep ploughing and reliance on chemical fertilisers. The soil is growing paler as it loses nutrients. Heilongjiang shows the most alarming deterioration. The province once boasted the most carbon-rich earth in China. The black soil was so valuable that it was protected. Under provincial regulations, townships were not supposed to build factories unless they first removed the loam and laid it down elsewhere. But this rule was usually ignored. The topsoil thinned and paled as a result of over-cultivation and excess use of fertiliser. In some areas in the south-west of the province, the land is suffering the same fate as much of Gansu, Ningxia and Inner Mongolia and turning into desert. Elsewhere, a mix of factory pollution and excess salt in the air (blown in from the beds of dried-up lakes) is creating giant white salt-alkaline patches on the earth. Once the soil has degraded to this extent, the only crop that can be grown is sunflowers.

A growing eco-lobby calls for a reduction of chemical inputs into the land. But the government is reluctant to leave land fallow or abandon fertilisers, which it says are essential for feeding a fifth of the world's population on only 7 per cent of the planet's arable land. An industrial lobby is pushing for even greater use of chemicals. It includes the huge power company CNOOC, which runs the country's largest nitrogen fertiliser factory in Hainan's Dongfang City.

Food production is likely to shift along with changes in the country's economic structure. As the inland west of China becomes an increasingly important source of energy and raw materials, the government may decide the water resources of Xinjiang, Gansu and Inner Mongolia should be used for industry rather than agriculture. This would mean phasing out the huge and wasteful irrigation schemes put in place to grow cotton and other crops in near-desert conditions. Instead, more and more water will be used to mine and process coal in these areas.

Grazing pastures have also declined. The grasslands that cover much of Inner Mongolia, Qinghai and Tibet are in a dire condition. The depletion of predator species – eagles, hawks, wolves and leopards – has left an imbalance in the food chain resulting in an annual plague of rats (including pika, gerbils and mice) that chew up the soil.

Nutritional intake from the ocean is increasing. China is now more than 50 per cent dependent on aquaculture for seafood, particularly carp and catfish. Wild fish are almost extinct in coastal waters. Chinese fleets travel further and further for catches, resulting in occasional conflicts with competing foreign fishermen. While toxic algae remains a problem, there may one day be an algae farming industry, which would be a new factor in discussion about territorial waters.

The strain on food supplies has international consequences. This was the case during the food crisis of 2008, when grain prices tripled and Vietnam and other countries restricted exports, causing panic and long food lines in net import nations such as the Philippines. Beijing is using its large foreign currency reserves to expand investments in African, Australian and South American land to try to secure ample supplies of arable land. This is a potential source of conflict in and with those nations during times of shortage. In Ethiopia there is particular resentment that China is using its land to produce palm oil for cars in Beijing and Shanghai, instead of crops that could feed local children. There could also be growing calls inside China for more land to be used for food production instead of growing crops for ethanol, but policymakers will be uneasy about a step that would increase fuel prices.

By 2020, to feed a population that will have swollen by 300 million – equivalent to the entire USA – since the start of the century, the government is likely to aggressively promote biotechnology. By 2015, half the country's agricultural produce will be genetically modified. After a long debate, GM rice is grown throughout the country, which has raised yields by about 20 per cent. The benefits may not be as great as expected because the GM crops require greater chemical inputs, which are becoming increasingly expensive due to rising oil prices. Even with conventional pesticides, the decimation of bee and other insect populations has knock-on effects. In parts of Sichuan, farmers have to hand-pollinate plants.

Biodiversity

In the future, conservation of biodiversity will no longer be perceived as a middle-class luxury aimed at saving cute mammals. Instead, it will be seen as an economic imperative to protect ecosystems and secure a sustainable source of resources and environmental services, such as carbon sequestration and water purification.

On the international stage, this leads to a similar set of conferences to those related to the climate. Eco-diplomacy involves inventory checking, rationing and compensation to protect what is left of the world's biodiversity. China is a key concern, both as a major market for illegally traded wildlife and as a home to many of the planet's most endangered species.

Its record is mixed. In Heilongjiang, the nation's greatest forests could start to recover thanks to a logging ban, an eco-compensation scheme (currently on the drawing board in the environment ministry), and massive imports of illegally felled timber from overseas. China plants more new forest than the rest of the world combined, but most of the trees are monocultures prone to disease and providing a poor habitat for wildlife. The same is true in the other major forest province, Yunnan, which is increasingly suffering from water shortages, partly because of its dependence on thirsty rubber plantations.

The Siberian tiger is on the brink of extinction, but it could be pulled back by coordinated action by the government, an infusion of cash from the World Bank and agreements with Russia to establish cross-border reserves. On the Tibetan plateau, chiru (Tibetan antelope) and argali (mountain sheep) have made something of a comeback. Exotic animal farms are used to keep other species alive if they are used in traditional medicine. But extinctions of other less well-known creatures accelerates in the wild. Overall, species are dying out at a faster rate than ever before because of the loss of their habitat to human development.

To address this problem, the government is likely to invest more in nature reserves and step up its efforts to move more people from the countryside into urban centres – a politically controversial course of action, particularly in Tibetan and other ethnic minority areas. Moves are also afoot to streamline responsibility for protecting wildlife. Instead of being fragmented and left mostly to the State Forestry Administration (SFA) – which is primarily interested in the economy rather than the ecology of nature reserves – jurisdiction could be given to the environment ministry. This has been mooted on several occasions, but resisted by the SFA, which remains a powerful force.

Politics

If concerns continue to grow about the climate and the loss of biodiversity, the environment will increasingly top the political agenda and it could become the main dividing line between 'left' interventionists and 'right' laissez-faire advocates of leaving the problem of ecological balance to the markets. On the global stage, China's environmental policy will be the subject of a fierce debate between nationalists, who argue the country needs to be more assertive in securing scarce supplies to maintain consumption levels, and internationalists, who favour closer cooperation with the United Nations and other bodies advocating a fairer, scaled-down redistribution of the planet's resources.

In domestic politics, the environment is a growing source of social tension. The pollution protests of the first decade of the century may have declined by 2020, but tensions will grow over water and food pressures. Demonstrations against relocations for dam projects may shift from Sichuan and Yunnan to Tibet.

Public attitudes will change. At the grassroots, it is not hard to imagine a new green socialist movement calling for a revolution in consumer values, greater national self-sufficiency and a return to the country's Daoist roots. Young nationalists want China to blaze a new low-carbon trail of sustainability and energy security – as long as it does not constrain the country's ability to develop, catch up with and overtake the West. Website news portals increasingly focus on green issues. They are encouraged by 'progressive forces' in the government, who realise the popularity of a 'clean up and redistribute' campaign. On the fringes, there may be moves to introduce a weekly 'day of rest' for the environment. Monasteries gain converts with 'recycle for society' campaigns modelled on similar programs by Tzu Chi in Taiwan.

The government prefers to rely on technology and science to boost supply. But with this becoming increasingly difficult, it may turn reluctantly towards demand-side reforms. One planned tool for adjusting competing claims for resources between provinces and cities is the 'ecological compensation scheme', which obliges rich, high-consuming areas to pay less-developed regions for environmental services, such as forests that produce oxygen and wetlands that filter pollution.

But continued environmental degradation will prompt calls for more radical action: the rationing of resources, an environmental court at the United Nations, carbon tariffs, car restrictions, an eco-currency, population controls and a mandatory day of consumer rest.

The government will resist such drastic measures. Officials will suggest that the stresses will ease once the population starts to fall in 2033 (for which it credits its family planning policy as a boon to the global environment). As in Europe, Japan, South Korea and Taiwan, they say a rise in incomes has already started to bring an improvement in the environment. Once China fully overcomes the dirty stage of its development, they argue it will be in a position to lead the world towards a new economic model.

Stretch the imagination a little further and, with the dollar declining, the euro wobbly and foreign exchange rates volatile, there may even be talk – perhaps originating in Beijing – of creating a new currency that better reflects environmental values, perhaps named the eco, or the carb. Would the British public be more willing to give up the pound for the eco than the euro?

Coping with the constraints imposed by resource shortages will be the overriding priority in China and on the international stage. No diplomatic challenge has ever been more difficult. It will proceed slowly, unhappily and with great suspicion. The world will be divided on familiar lines. On one side will be those who believe free markets are the solution because they will protect rare commodities by pricing them out of the reach of the consuming masses. On the other will be interventionists who want the United Nations to conduct a global eco-inventory and ration out the remaining resources. Most people are likely to find themselves seeking a combination of the two, but if this does not work extremists will thrive. The ultras of the laissez-faire camp will prepare for a war over resources that will cull the global population, survival-of-the-fittest style. Their counterparts on the left may argue that individuals should be allocated resources for two generations. If they agree not to have children, they will be allowed a double ration during their lives. Moderates will urge caution, but as the global population and individual consumption grows there will be a growing sense that time is running out for a solution.

Hopefully, however, by 2020 the search for a new global accommodation between man and nature will belatedly but finally be under way.

6

China's western regions 2020: their national and global implications

Tim Summers

This chapter examines the prospects for the western regions of the People's Republic of China (PRC). After reviewing developments over recent years, it argues that there are gradual structural shifts under way which increase the relative importance of these regions both to the PRC and to China's relations with the rest of the world, and that these are evidenced by recent changes in the geography of the PRC's economic development. These shifts flow firstly from evolution in the policy direction and practical reality of domestic development towards social and regional rebalancing, and secondly from the changing structure of China's global relationships. The latter part of this chapter explores some of these issues through a case study of the region around Chongqing and Chengdu, in China's south-west.

These issues relate to wider questions of China's economic and political geography: how the geography of the country's political economy can be mapped, where its balance lies, how it is changing and why, and what are the implications of the differing trajectories of various parts of this vast country. For example, from the late 1970s to the early part of this century, the fastest growing areas of the PRC were on the coast, but since around 2007 this pattern has begun to change. In 2009 – partly as a result of the global economic and financial crisis which erupted in 2008 – five of the PRC's seven fastest-growing provinces were to be found in western China and eight of the top ten in the central and western regions. This raises the question of whether the pattern of GDP growth is gradually shifting inland from China's coast.

There are other reasons why examining this part of the country is important. The western regions constitute over a quarter of the PRC's population, and the fate of these regions is therefore relevant not only to the people who live there, but to broader issues of development across the

PRC. They also have particular relationships with other parts of the globe, which are different from those of China's coastal areas. Furthermore, any major problems with development or stability in the country's west could undermine the PRC's development, and have knock-on implications for global political economy. These western regions therefore need to be taken seriously in any overall understanding of the PRC's current development situation and its possible future direction.

What are China's western regions?

What might we mean when talking about China's western regions? This chapter will take as its focus a developmentally based understanding of the western regions as consisting of twelve provinces (see below). But it begins by showing that 'China's west' can be conceptualised in different ways and is far from monolithic in nature, and that there are a wide range of issues which are relevant to understanding these regions, not all of which are directly related to issues of development.

Comments on a new textbook made by Chinese Premier Wen Jiabao during an apparently routine visit to the Beijing No. 35 Middle School on 4 September 2009 prompted a flurry of media reports on regional demarcations with the PRC. A geology teacher at the school was quoted as saying that 'Premier Wen believes the demarcation of China's regions in the new textbook is problematic, as Shaanxi and Gansu provinces should not be regarded as part of northern China [but as part of western China]'.[1] The textbook's publishers justified the inclusion of these provinces within northern China on geological grounds, and later reports suggested that the State Bureau of Surveying and Mapping would resolve the dispute by redefining China's regions, 'taking into account natural, economic and administrative factors'.[2] Indeed, a loose division of the country into north and south has long been a feature both of scholarship on China[3] and of popular discourse. In his account of wartime China, for example, the US writer Graham Peck describes the substantial changes in landscape and geography when crossing the Qinling mountains which divide Sichuan (in the south) from Shaanxi (in the north),[4] and these differences were just as apparent when I took the same route in 2006.

The media comment on Premier Wen's remarks focused on the political implications of a public disagreement between the Premier and a publisher, as well as on the quality of school textbooks. But what this episode also showed is the numerous ways in which the PRC can be divided regionally, and that different criteria produce varying conceptualisations. This approach is supported by theories which emphasise the 'constructed' nature of regions in general; in other words, that any regional definition is not an objective given, but a contingent result of a range of political, social, economic or cultural factors.[5]

Historically, ideas of what has been meant by China's western regions have also changed, not least because of the changing geography of the various imperial dynasties which preceded today's Chinese state. During these periods, notions of sovereignty were different from those under the present nation-state system; for example, when Han dynasty writers talked two thousand years ago of 'western regions' (*xiyu*), they were referring to the areas at the frontiers of the empire, rather than a geographical region within a nation-state. These are not just questions of academic interest to historians: controversy around Tibet and Xinjiang (both in Western China) is today fed by differing views of their historical relationships to Chinese imperial centres.

When the Chinese Communist Party (CCP) gained power in 1949, it divided the country into six major administrative regions, including regions covering the south-west and north-west.[6] These were subsequently abolished in 1954 after achieving their main objective of hastening the political and administrative integration of the new People's Republic, though seven economic planning regions were later devised in 1958.[7] Regional consciousness has remained strong since. Mao Zedong discussed the relative roles of industry in the coastal regions and the interior in his important 1956 comments 'On the Ten Great Relationships.' The industrial defence drive which became known as the Third Front had a dramatic impact on the economic landscape of the south-west from 1964; this reflected geopolitical and strategic more than developmental imperatives, and left legacies for the economies of these areas which still inform developments today.[8] And as we will see below, giving developmental priority to the coastal regions was an important part of the signature 'reform and opening up' policies instigated under Deng Xiaoping from 1978, as he cemented his hold on power in post-Mao China. Various regional groupings have emerged since; from the mid-1980s, for example, a strong grouping of south-west provinces emerged, and in the early 2000s, the Pan-Pearl River Delta forum included much of the south-west as well as the south-east.

In the early twenty-first century, there is – as Premier Wen's point suggests – a strong dominant official discourse on China's regional demarcation. This originates from the late 1990s and early 2000s, with the announcement of a new policy framework to 'Develop the West',[9] covering a vast area of the PRC which essentially equates to the territory of twelve provincial-level administrative units covering over two-thirds of the country's land mass, though with under one-third of the national population and less than one-fifth of GDP. These twelve are the (province-level) municipality of Chongqing,[10] the provinces of Gansu, Guizhou, Qinghai, Shaanxi, Sichuan and Yunnan, and the autonomous regions of Guangxi, Inner Mongolia, Ningxia, Tibet and Xinjiang,[11] though it was only in the autumn of 2000 that the definition became clear. This list also differed from prominent understandings of the western regions earlier in the reform era, for example in the ninth Five-Year Plan (1996–2000), which did not include Inner Mongolia or Guangxi;[12] even today, these two are often described as belonging to northern and southern China respectively.[13] Subsequent policy frameworks to 'revive the north-east' from 2003,[14] and then to 'boost the central regions', along with the classification of the remaining coastal areas as the 'east', have effectively led to a contemporary division of the PRC into four mega-regions, the western, central, eastern and north-east, though in some contexts a division into east, central and west is still used.[15]

As scholars such as Barry Naughton and David Goodman have argued, however, the construction of a vast region called 'western China' risks masking substantial differences between and within these twelve provinces.[16] Naughton divides this into the north-west and south-west, which have followed 'different trajectories'; the former is arid and sparsely-settled, with poor water resources, and the latter rugged and more densely settled. The north-west was relatively prosperous in 1978, but its economy subsequently declined; however, the south-west was more consistently economically weaker, at a level of little over half the national average in terms of income per person, and this contributed to the formation of the association of south-west provinces in the 1980s to lobby for preferential policies. These trajectories can be traced further back into history, and the huge contrasts between the twelve western provinces in their historical relationships to successive Chinese empires and the modern nation-state, as well as some changes in provincial boundaries,[17] have left legacies which are still relevant to their political, social and economic make-up today. It is these major differences within China's west, combined with the potential for different regional constructions, which lie behind the use in this chapter of the plural English term 'western regions' (the Chinese term *xibu* is not explicitly singular or plural, though it is usually rendered into English as 'western region' or simply 'the west', including by the PRC authorities).

Issues raised by the western regions

In general, contemporary discussions of these regions either approach the issues through an analysis of the Develop the West policy framework, or by focusing on particular provinces or problems within the western regions, such as policy towards ethnic minorities. Others effectively equate the western regions with Tibet and Xinjiang (see below), though as we have already seen, this is not the mainstream view in China itself. Although the bulk of this chapter is taken up with an examination of development, its conceptual premise is that there are a large number of relevant issues which are not directly development-related, and that the Develop the West framework does not cover all the issues which are pertinent to the western regions. A further premise of this chapter is that putting the study of the western regions in a global, not just a national, context can also shed different light on these issues. Understanding the dialectics between global forces, national development, the Develop the West framework, and wider issues of politics, economy and society in the western regions can therefore help explain developments in the western regions.

The range of issues pertinent to China's western regions can be broadly categorised as follows. Firstly, there are a number of security issues, both traditional and non-traditional in nature. The twelve provinces which make up the western regions adjoin thirteen of China's neighbours,[18] with international land borders some 22,000 kilometres long. The variation here is extensive too, from the lengthy border which separates the PRC's Inner Mongolian Autonomous Region from the country of Mongolia, around Xinjiang's borders with Russia and central Asia, through the Tibet–India border, to the tropical zones between China's south-west and what we call South-east Asia. Not only does this bring a range of different military and political relationships, but also varied problems in the trafficking of drugs or people, or the spread of infectious diseases. It also has a developmental angle, as many of the PRC's border provinces seek to develop economic cooperation across their borders in order to stimulate growth and prosperity. These aspects are particularly important, and I will return to them later.

Secondly, there are social and demographic issues within the PRC. The most widely studied of these relate to the role of ethnic minority groups, and these issues have come to particular prominence in the cases of Tibet and Xinjiang. Many of these minority populations (though not all) are located in the western regions, and moreover near the PRC's borders, and some have historical, social and economic links to populations of similar ethnicity in neighbouring countries.[19] Ethnic issues are clearly important to understanding the western regions, including in their relationships to official approaches to development. But there is also a huge diversity within the western regions when it comes to ethnic minorities, and it should be remembered that, although 'ethnic minorities' may be the majority in specific areas, the vast majority of the aggregate population of the western regions is Han; attempts to portray the development of western regions as *primarily* about further integration of these minority groups therefore often miss a number of important issues. Among the Han populations themselves, there is also substantial diversity, as well as social dislocations along lines other than ethnicity. The strength of provincial and other identities also needs to be borne in mind when looking at the western regions.

Thirdly, many of the urban–rural divisions which characterise the contemporary PRC more widely are more stark in the western regions. For example, in Gansu in 2003, rural incomes were only 25 per cent of urban incomes; the equivalent figure for Ningxia was 31 per cent.[20] These are not just issues of development, but relate to land use, agriculture and food security, forest cover and the environment. In the context of development, the urban–rural split is another way of looking at wealth gaps, one which creates a very different developmental map from the regional approach. This led one pair of Chinese scholars, for example, to argue that 'narrowing the urban–rural gap in West China should be a key step to reach the goal of western region development.'[21] These issues also relate to other social concerns over education and health provision across vast areas of territory, income gaps between social groups and industries, and concerns about governance or corruption.

Fourthly, there are a number of environmental and resource challenges, substantially different in nature across the western regions. As well as the local-level environmental challenges such as providing clean drinking water and good-quality air, which are general features of the contemporary PRC and tend to be exacerbated by fast economic growth, there are a number of macro-environmental issues that are particular to various parts of the western regions. In Inner Mongolia, for example, these include problems arising from deforestation, desertification and the shifts from nomadic to sedentary agriculture as the dominant model. Water resources in the north-west are among the lowest in the country, with serious consequences for the irrigation of agriculture and local populations. In the south-west, the development of hydropower as an alternative source of energy may reduce carbon emissions, but it also creates new environmental challenges such as the management of massive reservoirs, and preventing landslides and soil erosion. It is fair to say that official environmental protection departments at both central and provincial levels are well aware of these problems, and are engaged in designing policies to respond to them, though the efficacy of these responses can depend on the priority attached to these issues by provincial leaders, and – as elsewhere in the country – environmental protection efforts are in tension with more immediate imperatives of economic development. The management of water resources, which are generally most plentiful in the south-west (in spite of the drought in early 2010), is further complicated by the fact that China's – and many of Asia's – major river systems have their sources in the western Tibetan plateau. Other resources, such as minerals and natural gas, are plentiful in the country's western regions, and their developmental potential informs relations between the east and the west.

Many of these issues come together in Tibet and Xinjiang, the parts of western China with the highest name recognition in much of the world, and where increased attention has been focused since disturbances – alternatively presented as 'riots' or 'protests' – in the two regions in 2008 and 2009 respectively.[22] There is a growing tendency to lump these two regions together in public discourse, and while they share certain structural similarities, there are also important historical, political and economic differences between the situations in Tibet and Xinjiang which need drawing out in detail; nonetheless, for reasons of space, and because plenty has been written on both issues elsewhere, I here limit myself to a few brief comments on both regions together, and will highlight some of these points further in the rest of this chapter.[23]

The structural similarities arise from the conjunction of issues of development, security and sovereignty, albeit in different ways in Tibet and Xinjiang. While there are separatist tendencies in both regions, Chinese sovereignty over both is a fundamental plank of PRC policy (and indeed recognised by other countries). The tensions this creates find expression in official efforts at further cultural and political integration of the local populations, but also spill over into security clashes, including the major disturbances of 2008 and 2009, which have resulted in a notable military and paramilitary presence in both regions. Another important part of the Party's approach to these regions is to promote their economic development, in the belief that this will help resolve security issues and enhance a sense of national belonging. There are clearly development challenges in both places: as will be mentioned later in this chapter, levels of human development in Tibet are the lowest among PRC provinces (though it is the second poorest province in terms of GDP per capita), and in Xinjiang human development indicators have remained stagnant for the last ten years, though its GDP ranking is somewhat better. However, what the recent notable rises in aggregate GDP figures disguise is the extent of the disparities within both regions, both between urban and rural residents, and between the Han populations (which in large part date from migrations since the 1950s and are mainly urban) and groups of other ethnicities.

This wide range of issues around China's western regions means that a number of approaches to understanding these regions would be valid. Since Deng Xiaoping's dictum that 'it's development that counts' (*fazhan cai shi ying daoli*),[24] issues of development have been placed at the centre of the PRC's political economy over the last thirty years, even though the ideal nature of such development may have shifted over time towards the current emphasis on 'sustainable' or 'coordinated' development. This chapter therefore adopts the developmentally focused geographical understanding of the western regions as set out under the Develop the West policy rubric and which is dominant in the PRC today. This definition of western regions cannot really be described as administrative in nature, as there are no overarching regional administrative or institutional structures which manage each region, even though there are some institutions within the central government's structures with a regional focus (see below). In terms of political economy, it is the province or its equivalent, and below it the city, prefecture or county, rather than these mega-regions, which remain the most important 'power containers', and are the formal structures of government recognised in the 1982 State Constitution. These points are important for the subsequent analysis of prospects for the western regions and particularly the implementation of Develop the West, to which we now turn.

Development and Develop the West

An important component of the 'reform and opening up' policy rubric instigated by Deng Xiaoping in late 1978 was the idea that 'some people and some regions should be allowed to get rich first and in the end everyone will get rich.'[25] Much of the subsequent economic development was geographically concentrated in coastal provinces, and its scale in large part due to flows of foreign investment from overseas Chinese (including Hong Kong and Taiwanese) and foreign corporations. This coastal concentration should not be seen simply as a result of PRC policy preferences. It also reflected the nature of China's relationships to the global economy, which was being transformed from the 1980s, increasingly dominated by fast-moving transnational capital ('globalisation'), and with a revolution in the operation of multinational corporations and in the structures of supply chain management; specifically, manufacturing and assembly for export operations took advantage of the special economic zones and other areas along the PRC's coast, where access to shipping routes, as well as land and labour, was vital. At the same time, much of the labour migrated from western and central provinces to factories along the coast. This can explain much of the nature and scope of the subsequent incorporation of the coastal regions of the PRC into the global economy, and the fact that this integration primarily involved parts of the coastal provinces,[26] as well as the structural regional inequalities which were a legacy of this period.

It is therefore a key argument of this chapter that the nature of China's relations to the global economy in the 1990s and beyond has contributed to the nature of economic development in the western – and indeed the central – regions being substantially different from the coastal provinces;[27] this cannot be attributed solely to the historical legacies of lower economic development in the western regions. This perspective helps to explain the development of the political economy of the PRC's western regions after 1992, when the extension to many interior areas of the 'coastal opening policies' was expected by some in the PRC to lead to similar levels of growth to those seen on the coast in the 1980s, but did not do so. Their exposure to external trade and investment remained relatively small, as shown by low levels of foreign direct investment and minimal contribution of exports to local economic growth (see below for figures). Rather, these interior provinces have seen their growth – lower than the coastal regions over the last three decades – boosted mainly by fixed asset investment.

These developments, and the increased industrial agglomeration in the eastern provinces which accompanied them, contributed to a growing gap between the coastal regions and the interior provinces. As the 1990s progressed, both central and local policymakers became increasingly concerned about the implications of this gap,[28] and interior provinces increased their lobbying for preferential policies to aid their development. Combined with earlier comments from Deng Xiaoping that, once the coastal regions had developed, growth should start to move inland (as it turned out, this went against the grain of the nature of the PRC's integration into global capitalism), these developments led to the announcement in June 1999 of the Develop the West programme by then

Party General Secretary, Jiang Zemin. The programme was formally launched in March 2000, and a coordinating central Leading Group of very senior cadres established in January 2001. Key documents setting out the programme's content included State Council circulars in October 2000 and September 2001, and most importantly, the 'Overall plan of western region development during the Tenth Five-Year Plan period [2001–2005]', which was issued in February 2002. The initial timeframe was ten years, but there was a clear understanding that radical change would take much longer, and many commentators had a fifty-year timescale in mind.

The most prominent focus of Develop the West was infrastructure development, both to ease bottlenecks and to act as a stimulus for future economic growth. Alongside infrastructure development was a strong emphasis on ecological protection, the development of energy resources and the other 'plentiful' natural resources of the western regions, adjusting the industrial structure by increasing the contribution of tertiary (service) industries to local GDP, reforming state-owned enterprises, improving conditions for the development of a market economy, attracting foreign direct investment (the forthcoming WTO accession in 2001 gave additional hope that this would increase dramatically in the western regions), and raising both the quality of human resources and utilisation of science and technology. The delivery was to be through a combination of tax concessions for economic activity in the western regions, fiscal transfers from the centre, and new investment in specific projects through government funds and bank loans, all made much more feasible by national fiscal reforms in 1994 which strengthened central finances. A number of key projects were identified in 2000, though the list evolved, and some projects may have taken place anyway over longer timeframes.[29]

Develop the West is therefore best seen as an omnibus programme, with a number of different elements, reflecting a range of policy objectives in developing the western regions, including a quest for equality, foreign investment, infrastructure investment, dealing with ethnic minority issues, and sustainable development.[30] These built on earlier efforts, and arguably reflected more of a realignment than a sudden shift.[31] Certain elements of the programme were contested between parts of the system which focused on economic development, security and national integrity or those which saw the programme as an opportunity for a greater emphasis on ethnic minority areas (this led to the later inclusion within the geographical scope of Develop the West of several minority prefectures in provinces neighbouring the twelve outlined above).[32]

Any attempt, therefore, to reduce the multi-faceted programme to one overarching objective or theme is problematic, though the themes of development and national integration or territorial integrity are the strongest. More widely, both at its instigation, and in subsequent treatment of Develop the West, the programme has been subject to a range of differing interpretations. And what is also clear from reading PRC scholarship or government documents which talk about Develop the West, is that – whatever Jiang Zemin's own intentions might have been when the programme was announced in 1999 – it has subsequently been utilised to support a range of policy and practice by provincial governments and others with interests in western China; these included provincial lobbying for more resources and funds or energy companies looking to exploit the abundant hydropower potential of the south-west. Both among practitioners and commentators in the western regions themselves, and in subsequent scholarship, it has been suggested that, in addition to the objectives of closing the wealth gap with the coast and increasing the western regions' GDP, the programme has been aimed as much as anything at making use of the resources of the western regions to support the continued growth of the eastern regions (and therefore the aggregate national economy),[33] a view given sustenance by national programmes such as 'sending the west's power to the eastern regions' (*xidian dongsong*). Another view stresses the more political goals of national integrity, presenting Develop the West as the 'centrepiece of the Chinese government's effort to strengthen national unity and integration'.[34] Looking at Tibet, Susette Cooke sees Develop the West in primarily 'cultural' terms, and argues that the programme's effects 'are likely to be more profound [in the Tibet Autonomous Region] than for any other provincial-level constituent of the PRC.'[35]

The evolving reality of Develop the West, therefore, is not only broad, perhaps ambiguous, but has shifted over time and space. Some of these ambiguities are reflected in institutional and political structures, both those set up to manage Develop the West and those which would anyway interact with issues of development in the western regions. Gregory Chin's comprehensive analysis of this aspect[36] suggests that the 'organizational framework for decision-making . . . is largely an extension of standard Party and bureaucratic processes', representing a 'complex matrix' of elites, institutions and interests, though a permanent office in the central government was also established to help coordinate western development activity. One consequence of the cross-thematic nature of Develop the West is that pre-existing ministries and institutions – those dealing with infrastructure, environment, energy, agriculture, poverty and so on –

remain powerful players in forming and delivering policies in the western regions, and that as such authority is 'fragmented' and decision-making at the centre relies on consensus. When the important roles of the provincial administrations, and their substantially devolved economic powers, are also taken into account, the impact of Develop the West per se becomes difficult to evaluate.

An important consequence of this is that issues of development in the western regions are far from reducible to Develop the West, which may represent more of a symbolic statement of intent and of the importance attached to development in the western regions than a specific policy programme. In fact, it may be the case that, although the high-level message 'Develop the West' sends is important, the majority of development in the western regions over the last ten years can be traced more closely to other institutional, economic or even international factors than directly to the policy rubric of Develop the West. And as the Hu Jintao and Wen Jiabao administration has increasingly emphasised sustainable and balanced development at a national level, the particular features of Develop the West have become absorbed into wider policymaking priorities, and the programme arguably diluted into a broader agenda, though not dissolved; it could also be argued that the increased role of the state over the market on display in Develop the West prefigured some of the other policy shifts of the 2000s. A dialectic relationship may be the most productive way of understanding this: mega-region development strategies are not only informed by the evolving 'national' development model, but in turn inform changes in that model as regional development strategies have increasingly been integrated into the mainstream policy process; the evolving product is a different approach to both national development and regional development from that prior to the launch of Develop the West.

This political focus on balanced development also has implications for the development of officials' careers. Over recent years it has been noted by a number of commentators that time spent working in the western regions has been an important part of the careers of a number of the PRC's top leaders. It may be overstating the case to suggest that western provinces are incubators for future leaders, but what this point does bring out is that the western regions and other interior provinces have been rising in relative importance on a national level as the 1990s focus on development in the coastal regions has given way to a broader and more balanced national picture.

The year 2009 saw a renewed interest in Develop the West, as its tenth anniversary approached, and there was a sense that provincial governments used the anniversary to push the centre for further favourable policies or the announcement of new initiatives. In July 2010 a 'work meeting' convened by Hu Jintao and attended by the Politburo Standing Committee and other key officials reaffirmed the importance the leadership attached to developing the western regions. Hu stated that this was important for achieving a number of national goals, including the establishment of a 'moderately well-off society' (*xiaokang shehui*), prosperity, the development of reform and opening up and socialist modernisation, and the 'great renaissance of the Chinese people'. The more detailed focal points were largely familiar both from earlier statements of Develop the West and wider national priorities, and included infrastructure development (railways, road, airports, energy, water and environment) and the development of minority areas. There was a greater emphasis on livelihood issues than in 2000, a shift which has taken place at a national level during the Hu and Wen administration too. Separately, a new list of priority projects was announced, complementing earlier plans promulgated by the Ministry of Railways and other parts of the government to increase investment in the western regions.

Popular perceptions of the Develop the West programme are also important. One of its implications has been to reinforce the long-held perception that the western regions are 'backward', and with it the idea that the western regions are primarily regions of ethnic minorities.[37] As the 'revive the north-east' programme shows, however, this is too simplistic: discourse on the north-east also emphasises the sizeable ethnic minority populations there. And while a simple comparison of aggregate GDP per capita between the western and eastern regions appears to bear out the judgement that 'the west is less developed than the east', it also masks huge differences in income and development levels within each of these mega-regions. As noted at the beginning of this chapter, dissecting Chinese society into urban and rural (or by industry, position in society or economic role) would create different wealth profiles; a 2009 World Bank report suggested that the greatest indicators of inequality within the PRC have increasingly been apparent *within* regions, rather than between them, and that rural–urban inequality was a greater challenge than regional inequality.[38] As I will demonstrate later in discussion of Chongqing and Chengdu, there are substantial pools (or nodes) of wealth and development within the western regions which make the 'backward' designation too simplistic to be useful analytically, even if the impression it creates has helped to build political support for attention on development in these regions.

Economic growth and human development in the western regions

Against this background, this next section gives an overview of development in the western regions over the last decade. This is primarily done through quantitative analysis of GDP and human development indicators, complemented by reference to a number of existing studies on these regions. It should be stressed that this is an overview; given the scale of the western regions, it is not feasible to offer in-depth analysis of every aspect of their development.[39]

In terms both of overall GDP and per capita GDP, the western regions have in recent decades consistently lagged behind the national average. This generalisation has not necessarily always been valid. As noted above, the north-west was considered relatively prosperous in 1978. At that point, for example, the north-west province of Qinghai, where a major earthquake occured in April 2010, 'had been a wealthy (in relative terms) middle-income province, with annual GDP per capita well in excess of the national average (112.9 per cent). By 1994 it had become one of the lowest income provincial-level jurisdictions'.[40] But by the end of 1999, the 29 per cent of the PRC's population in the western regions[41] accounted for around 18 per cent of national GDP, with GDP per capita levels around two-fifths of those in the east. Moreover, the incidence of poverty was relatively high, with 62 per cent of the country's designated 'poor counties' located in the western regions. This broad pattern is reflected when the focus is shifted to individual provinces.

The substantial growth in GDP across the PRC during the first decade of this century has included the western regions, whose GDP increased from $185bn in 1999 to US$979bn in 2009, an average yearly growth rate of nearly 12 per cent, around two percentage points higher than the national average growth rate. However, given the size of the rest of the national economy, this increase had only a minimal impact on the western regions' proportion of national GDP.[42] The story is similar with respect to GDP per capita. Again the increase, according to official statistics, has been slightly faster in the western regions than at a national level, but without fundamentally altering the imbalances in income and wealth between the populations of the different mega-regions. When looking at GDP per capita, however, the statistics become more difficult to interpret sensibly, partly due to the ambiguities introduced by large levels of internal migration within the PRC, flows which result in substantial net migration out of western regions towards the coast, as well as within provinces and regions from rural to urban areas. For example, academics in Chongqing have in the past reported that, of the municipality's official population of around 31 million, perhaps only some 27 million are actually living in the municipality; Guangdong's population statistics display a similar trend in reverse. The scale of this migration, and the uncertainties in its measurement, makes precise comparisons of provincial per capita GDP figures difficult.

Although over the last decade the relative GDP growth of the western regions may not have been that spectacular, data from the late 2000s suggests that the growth rates of parts of the western regions have consistently and more obviously surpassed that of the eastern coast and the national average. In 2009, GDP in the western regions grew by 13.4 per cent year-on-year, compared to the 8.7 per cent average for the country as a whole.[43] This must partly be attributed to the rapid fall-off in economic growth in many of the most externally-exposed coastal provinces prompted by the global financial and economic crisis from 2008, as well as the relative focus of the PRC's stimulus package – introduced in response to that crisis – on infrastructure development (and reconstruction in Sichuan after the May 2008 earthquake), which has had a strong impact on GDP figures in the western regions. The question is whether this relatively good performance is sustainable, and when export growth resumes whether the coastal provinces will resume their role as the major engines of Chinese economic growth.

What the statistics also reveal about the western regions, both before and during the recent global crisis, is the extent to which fixed-asset investment has acted as a driver of growth in the western regions, even more so than for the PRC on a national level, given their lower exposure to international trade and investment. Fixed-asset investment in the western regions increased from 18.7 per cent of the national total in 1999 to 23.2 per cent in 2009. Much of this has gone into the development of transport infrastructure, in particular airports, roads, and more recently increasingly into the development of the rail network: this grew from 20,000 km to 30,000 km between 2000 and 2008, and the Ministry of Railways' aim is for 50,000 km by 2020. As set out in the Develop the West plans, this is seen as important not just in its contribution to development, but in providing the basis for future growth, and in linking the western regions better with other parts of the PRC, as well as with neighbouring countries. These projects are too numerous to list here, but examples include major highways from coastal cities such as Shanghai to western centres such as Kunming or Chongqing; the upgrading of railways such as that between Xi'an and Zhengzhou (in eastern central

China), which from February 2010 reduced the 505km journey from six hours to less than two hours, or the approval in early 2010 of a high-speed line between Chengdu and Xi'an. Other examples include developing routes to port cities in the south, such as the highway from Chongqing to Zhanjiang in the southern province of Guangdong. The railway from Qinghai to Tibet, which opened in 2006, is one of the more spectacular and influential of these projects.

It can therefore be argued that at least the gap between the regions shows signs of beginning to shrink, and that this is partly attributable to the greater policy emphasis on these regions and the gradual accumulation of investment over this period. The preferential policies of western regions may not have attracted as much foreign investment as hoped for, but its absolute value has increased substantially, and its proportion of total foreign direct investment into the PRC has doubled and is approaching double figures. The efforts that western regions have made to learn from the coastal regions by establishing preferential policy frameworks, and to promote themselves as favourable locations for foreign investment by advertising their lower labour costs or land prices, have anyway created an improved investment environment. Over recent years this has increasingly drawn domestic Chinese capital (though the inflow of non-state funds to the western regions from 2000 to 2003 declined),[44] which may increasingly play the sort of role in developing the western regions that foreign (and overseas Chinese) capital played in the earlier coastal development. Nonetheless, as suggested above, the PRC's global economic interactions have not been substantial drivers of growth for most of this period, although I return to structural comments on this below in discussion of some recent developments.

The diversity of the western regions also needs taking into account, and here – as within other regions too – there is substantial variation, both in terms of the situation in 1999 and the change over the following decade; the material below on Chongqing and Chengdu will look at some of the disaggregation below provincial level. At this level, Inner Mongolia not only displayed the fastest growth of any western province between 2000 and 2009, with average annual GDP growth of 16.8 per cent, but its growth was ranked highest of any province in the country for each year from 2002 to 2009.[45] The slowest growth was registered by Yunnan, followed by Xinjiang, Guizhou and Gansu, though their average growth rates are still reported at around 10 per cent. Most of the other western provinces grew between 11 per cent and 12 per cent on average.

This analysis of GDP growth is helpful, but only reveals part of the development picture. Particularly in a country the size of China, there are plenty of reasons why it is problematic to reduce understandings of development to aggregate GDP, which masks disparities (not just regional ones) within the country and within regions. Although GDP remains the dominant indicator of development in the PRC, official pronouncements have increasingly moved towards talk of more balanced development, and officials' scorecards are also marked by their performance with respect to industrial safety, social stability, and perhaps even the environment (there have always been other priorities in appraising local performance too, such as implementing the 'one child' policy). To help paint a broader picture of development than that provided by GDP data, it is helpful to look at the human development index (HDI) scores for the western regions, using data for 1999 and 2006.[46] HDI combines three elements: life expectancy at birth, education levels measured by a combination of literacy rates and school enrolment ratios, and level of economic development as indicated by GDP per capita. As such, it gives a broader picture of levels of development than a simple focus on aggregate GDP or GDP per capita.

Over the period in question, all of the western provinces saw an increase in HDI, on average 12 per cent. The scores across the PRC also increased over the same period, though the ratings for Shanghai and Beijing – which top the table – remained little changed. In general, the magnitude of increases was similar across the western provinces, and the ranking of PRC provinces by HDI stayed relatively stable. There were, however, a few exceptions to this. Inner Mongolia rose up the rankings from 22nd place to 14th, with its score rising from 0.679 to 0.790, the highest of the western provinces, and on a par with the lowest of the east coast. At the same time, Xinjiang dropped from 15th place to 22nd, with its HDI rating staying the same (to three decimal places). The Tibet Autonomous Region's HDI score increased the most of any province, from 0.521 to 0.656, but it still remained lowest of all the PRC provinces.

Further insights into aggregate provincial development levels can be gained by looking at the life expectancy and education indicators which contribute to HDI. All the western provinces – with the exception of Tibet – showed increases between 1999 and 2006, mostly quite substantial, in their life expectancy. This, however, disguises urban–rural differences in these provinces, with life expectancy for those in the countryside often many years less than for those living in cities.

However, the performance of western provinces in education is much less promising. Tibet and Qinghai (just) increased their scores on education, but all of the other western provinces saw a decline in educational rating between 1999 and 2006. In some cases, such as the fall in Guizhou's score from 0.706 to 0.554, these declines were substantial. To put this in context, though, the western regions were not peculiar in this. Falls in the educational index were also recorded in the north-east and in many central provinces, and in separate research, Min-dong Paul Lee has identified widening gaps of educational opportunity in the PRC. Lee's analysis – using different indicators from those in HDI – suggests that educational opportunity is notably lower in most western provinces, and highest along the east coast (Zhejiang and Fujian score best), and that '[s]tudents from inland provinces continue to face considerable structural inequality in educational opportunity'.[47] He shows that differences between urban and rural populations account for some of the differentials ('over 36% of the variance'), but that this is not the main reason for inter-provincial differences in educational opportunity. He cites as possible explanations difference in income and marketisation levels, as well as the proportion of minorities in each province.[48]

Changes in the domestic PRC economy, including as a consequence of global trends, will also have implications for the western regions. The desire to boost domestic demand has been a prominent theme in discussions of the PRC economy for some years, but has grown in volume in the context of responses to the 2008 global economic and financial crisis. Delivering on this has so far proved more difficult, but if domestic demand does become an increasingly important driver of the PRC economy, the western and central regions, especially those areas with large population concentrations, will become relatively more important developmentally. In this context, a city such as Chongqing, centrally located within the PRC, and with fast-improving logistics and transport links to a large number of other heavily populated domestic markets, could take on a much more important national role.

Western regions in global perspective

The picture painted so far in this analysis of economic and human development is largely a domestic one, which looks at the western regions in the context of the PRC, and compares them with national indicators. As suggested earlier in this chapter, however, at least some of the development differential between the western regions and the coast is a reflection of the way that the PRC's economic growth in the reform era, especially since 1992, has resulted from the incorporation of its eastern coastal regions into the (changing) structures of a global economy during this current phase of 'globalisation'. This has left the western regions relatively much less engaged with the global economy.

At the time of writing, however, there are a number of factors in play which could have important implications for the structural global relationships of China's western regions over the next decade, and though it may not seem likely that the western regions of the PRC will play a significant part in the evolving structures of the global economy, some shifts may already be under way at the margins. Firstly, there is the changing nature of the PRC's overall economic and political interactions with the rest of the world. The strong priority given by Beijing to the developed triad economies (North America, Europe and Japan) after 1978 is being diversified into an increased emphasis on political and commercial relationships with countries in the developing world, a trend which the recent global financial and economic crisis has hastened. Concurrently, greater priority in Beijing to good relations with China's neighbours has brought new dynamics to economic interactions across most of China's land borders, the bulk of which lie in what have been defined as its western regions, and the PRC has now resolved its land borders with all neighbours except India (maritime boundaries are a different matter).

This is in turn related to the PRC's increased engagement with regional organisations, and these institutions' greater influence over issues of development. The most obvious examples are ASEAN and the Shanghai Cooperation Organisation (SCO), both of which border China's western regions.[49] Diplomacy with ASEAN has already resulted in the establishment of a free trade area, and Chinese leaders have spoken about a similar idea with central Asia, diversifying away from the security focus of the SCO to date. There are other subregional structures which bring together territory in China's western regions with neighbouring countries. The longest-established of these is the Greater Mekong Subregion, whose geographical coverage includes the provinces of Yunnan and Guangxi, as well as the South-east Asian countries of Cambodia, Laos, Myanmar, Thailand and Vietnam.[50] There has even been some talk of developing local cross-border economic zones between Xinjiang and central Asia.

All of these interactions are being supported by substantial developments in road and rail infrastructure which will facilitate trans-border interactions between the PRC and its western neighbours, ranging from local cross-border trade zones to plans for a fast 'Eurasian land bridge' from Jiangsu province (near Shanghai) through central China, the western region of Xinjiang, central Asia, and eventually on to Europe, with a separate similar route through southern China and south Asia also mooted by some in the PRC. These complement the existing trans-Siberian route. These links have also been complemented by outward investment – and aid – from the PRC into central Asia (including Afghanistan) and bordering countries in South-east Asia, especially Myanmar and Laos. Hydropower, energy and resources have featured prominently in these investments. A further angle to this is the export of Chinese labour, often to work on these major projects. This may also have been affected by the recent economic crisis, which saw millions of migrants return to their original homes in western provinces after the sudden fall-off in demand for coastal exports: in one south-west Chinese border town, I saw an advertisement for officially sponsored Vietnamese language training for migrants who had been obliged to return home due to the crisis; their next destination was envisaged as across the national border to the south, not back in Guangdong (at the same time as there were other reports of Guangdong factories importing cheaper Vietnamese labour).

It is in these areas that these shifting global dynamics are, at present, most evident. Due to broader security concerns, in particular a sense of vulnerability to reliance on oil imports passing through the Malacca Straits, the PRC has been developing alternative routes for the import of energy. These include the north-east (from Russia), but the western regions play a crucial role as the receiving points for oil pipelines from Kazakhstan and Turkmenistan into Xinjiang, which then go on to Lanzhou, Chengdu and Chongqing, and the oil and gas pipelines from Myanmar into Yunnan province. With links to the eastern coast (such as the planned gas pipeline from Sichuan's Puguang gas field to Chongqing and on to Shanghai), the region around Chongqing and Chengdu is set to become an important energy hub not just within western China, but nationally. In turn, this will support the emergence of this region as a growth pole (see below); plans to develop the railway network further reinforce this trend, with both Chongqing and Chengdu developing roles as rail hubs.

Certain parts of western China could also become hubs or nodes of commerce and development between the PRC and other economies. Kunming airport in the south-west is one of the top four in China, and performs a hub role in tourism and cargo traffic between the PRC and south-east (and even south) Asia. The presence in Chengdu of Intel, which has its major manufacturing centre for semiconductor chips in the city, and Chengdu's strong air cargo and logistics services, brings an interior Chinese city into the global supply chain for a major transnational corporation in a way that has so far almost exclusively been limited to the coastal regions which lie closer to shipping routes. No doubt the attraction – as for other foreign companies setting up in Chengdu – is partly the highly favourable deals on land or taxation which the municipal government offers; as such, it is perhaps too early to claim this as a sustainable shift, though it is precisely this sort of preferential policy which contributed to earlier shifts of supply chain activity to coastal China, Vietnam and elsewhere.

The picture which emerged from the 1990s and early 2000s, where effectively only eastern regions of the PRC participated in Asian – and global – regional integration, is therefore already changing.[51] All of these trends have important implications for economic interactions between China's western regions and neighbouring territories, implications which could result in a shift in the balance of China's international commercial interactions, with a consequent positive boost to the economic importance of the western regions both nationally and globally.

Chongqing and Chengdu – growth pole(s) for the western regions?

Some of the issues around China's western regions can be further illuminated by looking at a specific geographical area within western China, that encompassing Chongqing and Chengdu, the area which is probably the most important subregion within the western regions. As will become apparent in the section below, understandings of this geographical area take on a number of permutations in different contexts: the area could be constituted as the two cities of Chongqing and Chengdu, an economic belt between the two cities encompassing other administrative districts, wider institutional arrangements between Chongqing municipality and Sichuan province, or – in some of the most recent iterations of what is an ongoing debate – a 'western triangle' covering Chongqing, Sichuan and Shaanxi province. These various permutations raise a number of questions of administrative and political structures and economic interactions. They also highlight some of the diversity within the western regions, and the changes in global interactions of these parts of the PRC.

Early statements of Develop the West included specific geographical focal areas in which development should be prioritised. These were the Xi'an–Lanzhou–Xinjiang belt in the north-west; the Upper Yangtze River economic belt (around Chongqing and Chengdu); the Nanning–Guiyang–Kunming region further to the south-west; and ethnic minority areas, especially Tibet and Xinjiang.[52] These areas benefited particularly from the major projects promoted in the early years of Develop the West and from the communication and transport arteries outlined in the tenth and eleventh Five-Year Plans (2001 to 2005 and 2006 to 2010),[53] and more generally from infrastructure development since then. However, the early attempts to give broader development priority to these trans-provincial belts (rather than provinces or cities) also met political and administrative resistance, reflecting the continued strength of provincial administrations in issues of political economy, and differing priorities for government at the provincial level and below.[54] In terms of the economic potential for cities within the western regions, Chongqing, Chengdu and Xi'an are generally seen as the strongest, followed by a second rank which includes locations such as Lanzhou, Urumqi and Kunming.

The idea of nurturing areas which have the potential to grow more quickly, and in doing so spurring development across the western regions, has remained a potent one in some quarters, particularly at the central planning level, where the interest is in the aggregate western regions, and policymakers are looking for drivers of growth for this mega-region, not just within particular provinces. An example of this was some talk of the inclusion of a Chengdu–Chongqing economic region or belt (*Cheng-yu jingji qu/dai*) in the Eleventh Five-Year Programme (covering 2006 to 2010), and although this did not happen, research into the idea continued at both a central and provincial level. To explore these issues in more detail, I will first set out some of the historical background to the relationships between Chongqing and Chengdu, then examine thinking on the Chengdu–Chongqing economic belt in more detail, and finally outline some other regional concepts.

The general challenges faced in attempts to concentrate developmental efforts in trans-provincial belts have been noted above. In the specific case of Chongqing and Chengdu there are also complicated political and economic relationships which reflect various historical legacies of the changes in political status and economic management of the two cities throughout the twentieth century. The structures of the relationships between the two have continued to change in recent years, most recently under the impact of Chongqing's upgrading to municipality status (1997) and Develop the West (2000). Lijian Hong has set the historical background out comprehensively,[55] arguing that the political relationships between the two cities, and between them and Sichuan province and the centre, have been key variables in the development paths of both Chongqing and Chengdu. He traces Chongqing's path from its political elevation as wartime capital of China in the 1940s, through various changes between sub-provincial status and a designation as a city within Sichuan with direct economic planning status under the centre, to its political promotion to province-level municipality status in 1997. As well as these institutional changes, personalities were also important, particularly during Li Jingquan's 17-year tenure as top official in Sichuan from 1952,[56] a period which saw Chengdu's industrial and economic performance gradually catch up with that of Chongqing; this had not been expected at the end of the 1940s when Chongqing's economy was much stronger, even after the departure of wartime enterprises from 1945 onwards. However, Chongqing continued to enjoy preferential policy treatment from the centre, and benefited from some provincial-level reforms enacted after 1978 by Zhao Ziyang during his time running Sichuan, as well as the advantages of its location on the Yangtze River and being in greater proximity to the central and eastern regions of the country than Chengdu. However, Hong argues that the first of these points has led the city to be too dependent on the centre, while Chengdu – at least in the late 1990s – 'seems to have restored its pre-1949 tradition as a trade centre for the entire western region'.[57]

The other important historical legacy is the Third Front (1964–1971). It was this that gave Chongqing, and to a lesser extent Sichuan, the heavy industrial and military bases to their economies. From the perspective of economic efficiency, this legacy has proved to be a challenging one, as many of the enterprises have continued to require outside support to ensure profitability, and their high levels of employment add complicated social challenges to the economic and financial ones. However, it could also be argued that this investment has benefited these areas both in terms of infrastructure development, especially railway networks in the south-west, and in some positive industrial legacies.[58] Today, for example, nationally competitive enterprises such as automotive manufacturer ChangAn in Chongqing owe a certain amount to the heavy industry concentrations which date from the Third Front period.

With this in mind, let us look further at the recent development of each of the two cities in turn, including placing Chengdu in its provincial Sichuan context, before looking at the ideas of the formation of an economic region encompassing both cities. Chongqing's development between the end of the war in 1945 and the late 1990s was less than spectacular. However, after its elevation to municipality status in 1997, this began to change. The increased attention from the central authorities that this political change brought was manifest most concretely in financial support for a range of infrastructure projects. Fixed-asset investment in the city (in industry as well as infrastructure) increased substantially, though it was a number of years before this was reflected in rates of GDP growth which were higher than those in the other western regions or nationally, such as the 14.9 per cent growth in 2009 which ranked it third among China's province-level units. Alongside this came substantial urbanisation, part of which was the result of resettlement of residents within Chongqing's municipal boundaries as a result of the Three Gorges Dam project.[59] Foreign consulates opened in the city,[60] and overseas investment began to increase too, with BP, Ford, ABB and others taking advantage of the city's industrial base, though domestic PRC and Taiwanese investment remains more significant overall.

Chengdu's performance in the decades after 1949 was relatively stronger, and at the time Chongqing was carved out of Sichuan, Chengdu was clearly the more developed of the two. It has continued to grow fast, again through substantial fixed-asset investment, and supported by investment from foreign corporations such as Intel, though in general terms the lead over Chongqing has probably narrowed over the last decade. While Chongqing has promoted its logistics strengths from its position on the Yangtze River, Chengdu's potential as an air cargo hub has continued to grow.[61] Both cities have substantial rural hinterlands. In Chongqing's case (an urban core population of maybe six million in an overall population of 31 million) this is managed within the same bureaucratic structure by the municipal government. Chengdu's hinterland is larger (the municipal core has over four million), and the city remains under the close watch of the Sichuan provincial authorities; within the province (population 84 million), the urban–rural gaps are particularly stark, and the mountainous region in the west of the province (the earlier Xikang province) is remote physically, culturally and in terms of development. This brings greater challenges for Sichuan than Chongqing, and is seen by some in Chengdu as diluting the potential for the city's development.

So far, this analysis has treated the administrative and political entities (municipalities and provinces) as the key actors, without introducing the nature and influence of leadership. There is not space to cover this in detail here (Lijian Hong's work looks at these questions in both Chongqing and Sichuan).[62] Chengdu, for example, has benefited from consistency in its mayor for a number of years: Ge Honglin's reputation is as a pragmatic and efficient operator. It is also worth noting that, from 2005, Chongqing has seen two successive Party Secretaries with strong political clout at a national level. Wang Yang (Party Secretary 2005–2007) is a close ally of Hu Jintao; during his time, Hu Jintao made a high-profile statement about Chongqing's growth pole potential (see below). Wang's successor, Bo Xilai (appointed in late 2007) is of a different political hue. His influence has been seen in a number of ways (the most high-profile being his 2009 crackdown on organised crime in the municipality); he too has talked about pushing Chongqing's cooperation and engagement with neighbouring territories, including the idea of a triangle between Chongqing, Sichuan and Shaanxi.

These local perspectives are somewhat different from those at the centre, and this leads us on to discussion of an economic region or belt encompassing the two cities. In April 2006, for example, a research paper under the State Council's Development and Research Centre (DRC) set out to address the question of 'growth poles' in the western regions and the Chengdu–Chongqing economic region (elsewhere this is also described as an 'economic belt').[63] It started by noting that, from the 1990s, the phenomenon of 'the regionalisation of economic growth' had become more evident, and that this had been accompanied by academics putting forward 'five major growth poles', namely the Yangtze River Delta region, the Pan-Pearl River Delta region, the Bohai Bay region, the Northeast Economic Region, and the Chengdu–Chongqing region in the west.[64] The concept of a growth pole this paper sets out is a location which is its own sustainable motor for growth, and contains core industries that have internal economies of scale, acting on other industries and delivering positive benefits for surrounding areas.[65] The paper argues that the Chengdu–Chongqing region meets these criteria for a number of reasons: its defence industries occupy the most important strategic position nationally; Sichuan had ten industries in the top national rankings (including mining, food and medicine) and Chongqing three; and the region has competitive or comparative advantages within China in automotive, motorcycle, heavy machinery, natural gas and a number of other sectors. Another important facet of the Chengdu–Chongqing region, which makes it a valid growth pole, is the density of its population, levels of urbanisation, and high level of productivity relative to its land area. The paper defines this region as containing a population of 99.56 million, in an area of over 200,000 square kilometres; the population density of 490 people per square kilometre is therefore higher than the east (456 per km^2), central regions (260 per km^2), the western regions (53 per km^2) or the national average (134 per km^2). The paper goes on to describe the region as the 'most developed' in the western regions; it should strive for unification of its regional economy and of its urban and rural areas within a 15- to 20-year timeframe, and spread its strength to the south-west and north-west regions, in order to become a real economic growth pole for the western regions. The paper adds that this region also has the potential to become a pole for ecological and environmental protection, as well as for economic growth.

However, there are at least two elements which challenge the viability of the 'belt as pole' idea. Looking at both Chongqing and Chengdu in the context of this discussion raises the question as to whether either might act on its own as a sufficient driver for growth in the wider western or south-western regions of the PRC. Some of the discourse about Chongqing's role in Develop the West, launched just a few years after Chongqing's own elevation to municipality status, suggests that this was in the minds of at least some policymakers. Examples include references to Chongqing driving western development, or acting as a 'gateway to the west'. More recently, remarks by Hu Jintao in the spring of 2007 were seen by many in Chongqing as further support for that view. Hu said the aim should be to 'accelerate development of Chongqing as a key growth pole in the west, the key economic centre of the upper reaches of the Yangtze River, a demonstration municipality of urban–rural development, and the first to achieve a comprehensive well-off society (*xiaokang*) in the west'. Sichuan leaders have utilised their own discursive concepts in a structurally similar way, with references to the province as a 'high plain' (*gaoyuan*) of growth.

Secondly in this context, and more generally, the relationship between the two cities seems to reflect some of the wider characteristics of devolved economic development in the PRC's reform era. Dali Yang has talked about 'competitive liberalisation' between provinces,[66] and this phrase aptly characterises much of the relationship between Chongqing and Chengdu. Hong concludes his analysis by noting the interest in cooperation between the two cities, but his account is mainly one of a competitive relationship. The institutional arrangements reinforce this: with economic and political planning and responsibility clearly the remit of the municipal (or provincial) governments, these (national) structures of political economy reinforce independent approaches to development issues, another aspect of the institutional constraints mentioned above. These factors therefore complicate the practical application of ideas such as the Chengdu–Chongqing economic belt which, when seen from a central perspective, appear obvious ways of stimulating growth not just in the areas covered by the region, but in their hinterland too.

Nonetheless, partly as a result of prompting by the centre, there have been some positive responses within both Chongqing and Chengdu to the belt idea, probably stronger in Chongqing than in Chengdu. In Chengdu's case, there may be some residual reluctance as a result of the city's historical status as the senior of the two. There are also other pressures for Chengdu in integrating its development planning with neighbouring areas; some officials in Chengdu have suggested that developing closer ties with Sichuan cities to Chengdu's north (Mianyang and Deyang) might be a higher priority, and others have suggested that Chengdu's priority is not to face towards Chongqing, but to its west.[67]

At the provincial level, the reluctance is less apparent. But there is also a problem of bureaucratic protocol, in that Chengdu has 'deputy provincial' status, whereas Chongqing is a provincial-level municipality – the two levels do not quite match. In April 2007, therefore, it was agreements between the (same-level) governments of Chongqing municipality and Sichuan province which made progress towards the establishment of a Chengdu–Chongqing economic region. These put forward shared visions of the development of the two cities and surrounding regions, in the process identifying the geographic scope of the Chengdu–Chongqing economic region (along the lines of earlier work referred to above),[68] and establishing regular coordination mechanisms in the areas of infrastructure, industry and the environment. Subsequent meetings and announcements developed these ideas further, though issues within each of the administrative jurisdictions still took priority for the local governments. In November 2009, the Sichuan Governor, Jiang Jufeng, said that six cities in the east of the province would be encouraged to develop their economic planning in a way that linked them more closely with Chongqing's 'economic circle', and at the Second Sichuan–Chongqing Cooperation Forum in November 2009, the Vice Chair of Chongqing's People's Consultative Congress, Yu Xuexin, said that western Chongqing could merge into the Sichuan 'development circle'.[69]

Whatever the outcome of these high-level policy debates, the rapid development of infrastructure between the two cities, symbolised by the new high-speed train, which only takes two hours to cover the few hundred kilometres between the two cities, is in practice creating a strong 'belt' along which people, goods and services can travel quickly and conveniently. And the potential for further industrial agglomeration in the Chengdu–Chongqing region, reflecting the nature of the current capitalistic development in the PRC, will reinforce the policy focus on these areas. Market-driven migration to the cities will similarly reinforce government efforts to reshape the social and demographic make-up of these areas.

Another idea which has been suggested in the Chongqing media, and which may also gain national approval, is constructing a growth triangle that also includes the province Shaanxi to the north, forming a region of 140 million population covering 61 cities. The scale here is different – it could account for 45 per cent of the western regions' GDP in 2015 (in this version this is the 'fourth pole').[70] The geomorphology is important too. While Chongqing and Chengdu lie at opposite ends of the Sichuan basin, and therefore travel between the two cities is relatively easy to facilitate, Shaanxi lies to the north of the Qinling mountains. Developing transport infrastructure therefore becomes much more challenging and expensive (as it was in integrating the south-west for an earlier generation of PRC planners), but has already received several boosts, including the approval in early 2010 of a high-speed rail line between Chengdu and Xi'an, cutting the journey time from 13 hours to three hours by 2014.

The development of infrastructure between the three cities of Chongqing, Chengdu and Xi'an is likely to enhance the economic interactions between these three nodes, whatever the bureaucratic fate of the plans for a triangular region. At the time of writing, the expectation is that a new plan for cooperation will be propagated some time in the early 2010s, and that some sort of reference to Chengdu–Chongqing regional cooperation might be included in the Twelfth Five Year Programme (2011–2015).[71]

This discussion of Chongqing and Chengdu has focused on the geographical and administrative structures of a possible 'growth pole' within the western regions, and has implicitly assumed that the potential for such a growth pole exists in this area of the PRC. The improvements in economic indicators over recent years, along with the coming together in this area of a number of important national policies,[72] certainly suggest that a clear positive trend has developed over recent years. However, it should be remembered that this assumption is subject to many of the challenges that the wider issues of the sustainability of PRC growth face, with the added complication of a weaker track record in the south-west on which to base confidence. A lack of developmental success in the south-west could undermine wider optimism about the PRC's economic future, and therefore there is a need for the national leadership – not just the provincial ones – to deliver substantial development in the Chongqing–Chengdu area. A failure to do so would constitute a major problem at a national, not just regional, level.

Prospects to 2020 and policy implications

This examination of Chongqing and Chengdu underlines the diversity of the western regions, and shows the potential for urban areas in the west to deliver economic growth at rates above the national average. But this upbeat tone needs balancing with a reminder of the substantial development challenges that remain, such as in human development or industrial productivity.[73] These are legacies of the size, scale and histories of these regions, in some cases compounded by earlier regional strategies which planted inefficient industrial development in central and western regions. A focus on developmental and economic issues also risks marginalising questions of national territorial integrity and security, which the first part of this paper suggested were important to the PRC authorities' considerations of the country's western regions. Analysis of this nexus reminds us that the western regions can also act as a security buffer, and this element will no doubt remain important in PRC thinking.[74]

There are therefore likely to be some contradictory elements in future handling of the western regions, produced by the interactions between various security concerns and the imperatives of development, and played out through the complex institutional arrangements through which these various interests are refracted within the PRC. These developmental imperatives draw on the potential for greater regional and neighbourly economic cooperation, and might suggest a characterisation of the western regions as bridges rather than buffers. Non-traditional security challenges – such as the transmission of infectious diseases or illicit flows of drugs or people – can also be increased by greater integration across land borders in the PRC's west, while the logic of energy security requires the development of trans-border infrastructure, reinforcing the developmental imperatives for these western regions to act as bridges.

If in general terms understanding China's western regions is important in gaining a full picture of prospects for the PRC over the next decade, there are numerous more specific policy implications of this analysis. These will differ for actors depending on their interests and geographical origin. In mainland south-east Asia, for example, the implications of the rapid development of China's south-west, including the increasing tendency of enterprises there to 'go out' into South-east Asian markets, is already an important consideration in governments' strategic planning, and creates some nervousness. This analysis hopefully shows some of the diversity of China; it therefore underlines that approaches from the outside need to be differentiated across the country, and a presence on the ground in the western regions is probably needed for particular organisations to understand the implications for their operations. Furthermore, the emergence of urban centres of growth within western China creates new opportunities for engagement, whether in trade and investment or 'softer' areas such as cultural diplomacy.

In sum, the regional differences between the western regions and the coastal areas are likely to remain significant for at least the next decade, even if the inequalities in development which the PRC faces after thirty years of 'reform and opening up' are far from reducible to these regional gaps. However, these differences look to be reducing in magnitude as we enter the 2010s. This chapter has sought to show how a combination of structural shifts in the domestic features of the PRC's development, and the beginnings of more important and more substantive roles for the western regions in China's global interactions, could produce a further closing of regional development gaps over the next decade. As we focus on the overall trends in the PRC in the years to 2020, we therefore also need to be mindful of the economic geography of development within the country: this too has implications for the PRC, and for the nature of global interactions with China.

Notes

1. 'Premier and publisher locked in war of words', *South China Morning Post*, 23 September 2009.
2. 'Surveyors called in to decide on Wen's north-west divide', *South China Morning Post*, 15 October 2009.
3. See for example Edward Friedman, 'Reconstructing China's National identity: a southern alternative to Mao-era anti-imperialist nationalism', *Journal of Asian Studies*, 53(1) (February 1994), 67–91.
4. Graham Peck, *Two Kinds of Time*, Boston, Houghton, 1950.
5. See, for example, Michael Keating, 'The invention of regions: political restructuring and territorial government in Western Europe', in Neil Brenner, Bob Jessop, Martin Jones and Gordon Maclead (eds), *State/Space: A Reader*, Oxford, Blackwell, 2003.
6. Dorothy Solinger, *Regional Government and Political Integration in Southwest China 1949–1954*, Berkeley, University of California Press, 1977.
7. Zheng Yongnian, *De facto federalism in China: reforms and dynamics of central-local relations*, Hackensack, NJ, World Scientific Press, 2007.
8. Barry Naughton, 'The third front: defence industrialization in the Chinese interior', *China Quarterly*, 115 (September 1988), 351–86.
9. In Chinese this is *Xibu da kaifa*, variously rendered into English as 'Great Western Development', 'Western Development Project', etc. In this chapter, 'Develop the West' (henceforth without quotation marks) will be used. I also use the shorthand 'twelve provinces' to refer to the twelve provincial-level units (municipality, province and region) which make up the western regions.
10. Chongqing was separated out of Sichuan province in 1997 and elevated to a municipality reporting directly to the central authorities (giving it the same status as Beijing, Shanghai and Tianjin). It is no longer part of Sichuan province (though even some reputable publications continue to refer to it in these terms).
11. These are short names. The full names of the autonomous regions are the Guangxi Zhuang Autonomous Region, the Inner Mongolian Autonomous Region, the Ningxia Hui Autonomous Region, the Tibet Autonomous Region and the Xinjiang Uyghur Autonomous Region. There are important issues of politics and administration in defining Tibet: the Tibet Autonomous Region (TAR) is the province-equivalent administrative unit in the PRC, though a broader conception of Tibet, sometimes called 'ethnographic Tibet', includes other areas where there are majority Tibetan communities.

12. David Goodman, 'The campaign to "open up the west": national, provincial-level and local perspectives', *China Quarterly*, March 2004, 317–34.
13. For example, 'Business Guide to West China' by the consultancy *China Briefing* (Hong Kong, Asia Briefing Ltd, 2008) excludes Inner Mongolia and Guangxi from its definition. Some writing on Inner Mongolia describes it as part of northern China (e.g. Suzhen Zhou, 'Study on the management factors of the sustainable development environmental governance mechanism in Inner Mongolia', *Journal of Sustainable Development*, 2(2), July 2009). There has long been debate over whether or not to see Guangxi as part of the south-west; see Katherine Palmer Kaup, *Creating the Zhuang: Ethnic Politics in China*, Colorado and London, Lynne Rienner, 2000, p. 164. Chongqing is often described as central-western or central. These are not purely academic issues, but have implications for understandings and perceptions of these areas.
14. See Jae Ho Chung, Hongyi Lai and Jang-Hwan Joo, 'Assessing the "Revive the Northeast" (*zhenxing dongbei*) programme: origins, policies and implementation', *China Quarterly*, 197, March 2009, 108–25, which includes some comparisons with Develop the West. For example, foreign direct investment has been more important in the north-east, though Chung et al. do not highlight the link to the global economy to explain why.
15. The military has its own regional structures, not covered here.
16. Barry Naughton, 'The Western Development Programme', in Naughton and Dali Yang (eds), *Holding China Together*, Cambridge, Cambridge University Press, 2004.
17. The most substantial example is Sichuan, whose western regions were until 1955 part of the Republican era (1912–1949) province of Xikang.
18. The fourteenth country which shares a land border with the PRC is North Korea.
19. This also brings to the fore some ambiguity in what is meant by border areas. In one sense this refers to borders with a neighbouring country, but it can also be used to refer to the periphery to the core state. For example, Goodman talks about Qinghai as 'essentially a border region', though it is not adjacent to an international border; 'Qinghai and the emergence of the west: nationalities, communal interaction and national integration', *China Quarterly*, 178 (2004), 383. In neither sense are all of the western regions border regions.
20. Cited in David Kerr and Laura Swinton, 'China, Xinjiang, and the transnational security of Central Asia', *Critical Asian Studies*, 40(1) (2008), 113–42 (p. 122).
21. Shi Yulong and Du Ping, 'On the urban-rural relationship in Western Region Development Program', in Ding Lu and William Neilson (eds), *China's West Region Development: Domestic Strategies and Global Implications*, World Scientific, 2004, pp. 219–38.
22. For an excellent analysis of the disturbances in Tibet, see Robert Barnett, 'The Tibet Protests of spring, 2008: conflict between the nation and the state', *China Perspectives* 3, (2009), 6–23.
23. There are also international implications of these issues for the PRC, as a result of concerns over human rights in Europe, the US and elsewhere. The

Tibetan issue complicates relations with India, and problems in Xinjiang have also affected diplomacy with Turkey, as well as with the central Asian republics.

24. My translation.
25. Quoted by Justin Yifu Lin and Peilin Liu, 'Development strategies and regional income disparity in China', in Guanghua Wan (ed.), *Inequality and Growth in Modern China*, Oxford, Oxford University Press, 2008, p. 61.
26. Before 1978 Guangdong was one of the poorer provinces, but shot up the rankings during the reform era. There have been subsequent variations within and among coastal provinces as 'not all Eastern provinces performed well during the 1999–2003 period'; Jane Golley, 'China's Western Development Strategy and nature versus nurture', *Journal of Chinese Economic and Business Studies*, 5(2), (2007), 115–29.
27. Historically, a global perspective also helps explain the Third Front as a response to Mao's geopolitical concerns over threats from the US and USSR.
28. A key piece of research in influencing policy thinking was Wang Shaoguang and Hu Angang, *The Political Economy of Uneven Development: The Case of China*, Armonk, NY, M. E. Sharpe, 1999.
29. Naughton, 'The Western Development Programme', notes that the first twenty large projects had a total value of RMB 400 billion, or around 5 per cent of national GDP. But his analysis suggests that the actual investment was RMB130bn, and he estimates the incremental (new) cost of Develop the West as RMB114bn in 2001 (or 1.2 per cent of national GDP).
30. Heike Holbig, 'The emergence of the campaign to open up the west: ideological formation, central decision-making and the role of the provinces', *The China Quarterly*, 2004, 335–7.
31. Naughton, 'The Western Development Programme'.
32. These were the Xiangxi Tujia-Miao Autonomous Prefecture in Hunan, the Enshi Tujia-Miao Autonomous Prefecture in Hubei, and the Yanbian Korean Autonomous Prefecture in Jilin; see Goodman, 'The campaign', p. 320. As noted above, the definition of the western regions expanded from that of the ninth five-year plan to include Inner Mongolia and Guangxi from the early 2000s.
33. See, for example, Goodman, 'Qinghai', p. 395.
34. Naughton, 'The Western Development Programme', p. 253.
35. Susette Cooke, 'Merging Tibetan culture into the Chinese economic fast lane', *China Perspectives*, November–December 2003, 1–20.
36. Gregory T. Chin, 'The politics of China's Western Development Initiative', in Lu and Neilson *China's West Region Development*, pp. 137–74.
37. This point is argued by Elena Barabantseva, 'Development as localization: ethnic minorities in China's official discourse on the Western Development Project', *Critical Asian Studies*, 31(2), 2009, 225–54.
38. World Bank, 'From Poor Areas to Poor People', 2009 (downloaded from *www.worldbank.org* July 2009).
39. Some earlier work on this was published in a paper I co-authored with Doris Ma, 'Is China's development moving inland? A decade of "Develop the West"', Chatham House Asia Programme Paper 2009/02, October 2009. I

am most grateful to Doris, and to Chatham House, for allowing me to reuse some material from that paper in this chapter.

40. Goodman, 'Qinghai', p. 379.
41. There was a slight fall in this proportion to 27.5 per cent in 2009, though the total increased in line with population growth across the country.
42. There are difficulties with the statistics here. Provincial statistics (on which regional aggregates are based) do not add up to national totals. Nonetheless, they can still give us some idea of the trends and major shifts.
43. See the previous note.
44. Golley, 'China's Western Development Strategy'.
45. Inner Mongolia is a clear outlier among western provinces. If it were not included in the western regions, then the overall rate of growth in this mega-region would be marginally lower.
46. This choice of years reflects the availability of data. See *United Nations Development Report, China Human Development Report 2002* (Beijing: China Financial and Economic Publishing House, 2002) and *China Human Development Report 2008* (Beijing: China Translation and Publishing Corporation, 2008).
47. Min-dong Paul Lee, 'Widening gap of educational opportunity? A study of the changing patterns of educational attainment in China', in Wan, *Inequality and Growth*, p. 179.
48. There have been questions raised about the effectiveness of the education system on a national level in recent years.
49. For the PRC, one aspect of its agenda in the SCO has been to gain cooperation from neighbouring central Asian republics in managing the separatism among the Uyghur population of Xinjiang mentioned near the start of this chapter.
50. See Tim Summers, 'China and the Mekong Region', *China Perspectives*, 3, 2008, 68–77.
51. For a statement of this earlier perspective see Chen Zhilong, 'The significance of West China development to Asian economic integration', in Lu and Neilson, *China's West Region Development*, pp. 439–63.
52. See, for example, Yue-man Yeung and Xiaojin Li, 'China's Western Development: the role of the state in historical and regional perspective', Shanghai-Hong Kong Development Institute Occasional Paper No.10, April 2004.
53. Holbig, 'Emergence of the campaign', p. 349.
54. Chin, 'The politics of China's Western Development Initiative', p. 157.
55. Hong Lijian, 'A tale of two cities: A comparative study of the political and economic development of Chengdu and Chongqing', in Jae Ho Chung (ed.), *Cities in China: Recipes for economic development in the reform era*, London, Routledge, 1999, pp. 183–214.
56. Li's wider political and social legacy is, however, a mixed one.
57. Hong, 'Chengdu and Chongqing', p. 203.
58. Naughton, 'The third front', makes clear that the speed with which rail networks were developed was a result of the Third Front. He also suggests that the Third Front did more damage to the national economy than the Cultural Revolution itself.

59. Contrary to many references, the Dam itself does not lie within Chongqing's municipal boundaries, but in Hubei province. However, some 80 per cent of these relocated to make way for the dam were in Chongqing.
60. From March 2000, this included the British Consulate-General, which I ran from 2004 to 2007. Its geographical coverage is Chongqing and the provinces of Sichuan, Yunnan and Guizhou.
61. For example, the Shenzhen-based Jade Cargo launched a twice-weekly service between Chengdu and Amsterdam and Vienna in late 2009.
62. For example, Hong, 'Chengdu and Chongqing', p. 458, notes that then Chongqing Mayor Bao Xuding was keen to develop a western corridor out towards Chengdu.
63. Liu Zhaoming, Dong Hui and Han Bin, 'Xibu zengzhangji yu Chengyu jingjiqu zhanlue mubiao dingwei yanjiu' ('Research on western region growth pole and the Chengdu-Chongqing Economic Zone'), *Jingji Xuejia*, 2006, Vol. 2.
64. Note that these vary over time. Many earlier, and some later, accounts omit the north-east, whose inclusion probably results from increased focus on northeast from around 2003 (Chung et al, 'Assessing the "Revive the Northeast" programme'). The Chengdu–Chongqing area is also referred to as the Upper Reaches of Yangtze River, especially when viewed from the Chongqing angle. When this region is described as the 'fifth [in other contexts, fourth] growth pole', it should be made clear that this ordinal refers to the (fifth) geographic region, rather than to the absolute strength of the economy in a national context. As the breakdown of GDP and industrial value added in the 2006 paper makes clear, the per capita levels of development in this Chengdu–Chongqing belt remain low in comparison to the other 'poles', and there are a number of regions or cities in the eastern regions which, although smaller in scale than Chengdu-Chongqing, clearly outrank the latter in terms of existing development and the potential for growth.
65. The paper cites F. Perroux, 'Note sur la notion de pole de croissance', *Economic appliqué*, 7, 1995, 307–20 and M. Porter, 'Competitive advantage of nations', *Harvard Business Review*, 68(2), 1991, 82.
66. Yang, Dali, *Beyond Beijing: Liberalisation and the Regions in China*, London, Routledge, 1997. The dynamics may have shifted somewhat in the 2000s, with the centre taking a stronger role; nonetheless the concept remains valid.
67. Susan Walcott, 'The dragon's tail: utilizing Chengdu and Chongqing technology development zones to anchor west China economic advancement', *Journal of Chinese Economic and Business Studies*, 5(2), 2007, 131–45, suggests Chengdu's priority is not to face to Chongqing, but to its west, and also highlights the competitive nature of the relationship.
68. This would be an area containing 37 cities and counties, and accounting for over 5 per cent of national GDP. Its urbanisation density would be 1.73, compared to a national average of 0.7 and 0.24 for western China. Output per square kilometre would be RMB 3.5 million, compared to the national average of RMB 1.23 million and RMB 0.34 million for the western regions.
69. 'Yuxi ke rongru Sichuan fazhan quan' ('Western Chongqing can integrate with Sichuan's development circle'), *Chongqing Morning Post*, 28 November

2009. The same reports suggested that cooperation between Sichuan and Chongqing could become the engine for the western regions' economy within 15 years. The range of different economic belts under discussion at this and other meetings is broad, and their analysis lies outside the scope of this chapter.

70. *Chongqing Daily*, 2 December 2009.
71. *Chongqing Daily*, 17 November 2009.
72. These policies include Chongqing's municipality status, the Develop the West programme, the emphasis on Sichuan in post-earthquake reconstruction and the stimulus package, infrastructure development, the benefits as well as drawbacks of industrial legacies, and the high levels of population and population density.
73. Ke Zhang, 'The industrial development of Western China in the first five years of the Western Development Program', *Journal of the Washington Institute of China Studies*, 3(1), Spring 2008, 63–74, argues that raising industrial productivity is the most important challenge for western regions.
74. Robert Bedeski, 'Western China: Human Security and National Security', in Lu and Neilson, *China's West Region Development*, p. 43.

7

China's rule of law

Elizabeth Corrin

In the last few decades, since starting its reform and policy of opening up, interest in China has been reawakened in the popular consciousness of the West and has become a staple in the diet of western media. China's emergent form is that of a growing economic power set to occupy centre stage in the near future. The relatively sudden attentiveness of the mainstream media in the West is perhaps not so remarkable as its previous absence, given that the people of China make up one-fifth of the world's population. This third of humanity is under the de facto control of – and has its destiny shaped by – the Communist Party of China.

Perhaps the reason for past inattentiveness is that China has been perceived as both isolated and distant. This was certainly true in the Maoist period from 1949 to 1976. However, China's rapid economic growth since then is increasing its sphere of influence considerably. By virtue of its economic success alone, it can be expected that other countries of the world will seek to emulate China in an attempt to reproduce such success. Emulation will likely extend to its legal system and the rule of law model it has adopted (see also Vicky Tuke's contribution to this collection on the reach of China's global influence through soft power).

Provided it can maintain its economic growth, China's version of the rule of law is therefore set to gain currency, and the West will see increased challenges to its own rule of law model. Because of this, it is worth enquiring into the rule of law approach China advocates and examining how such an approach might develop in the next decade and beyond.

Calls for China to bolster its rule of law and improve its human rights record are familiar to both western and Chinese audiences alike. In the West, the need for improvement with regard to its human rights record is a typical comment made when considering China. In the US Department of State 2008 Human Rights Report on China, the government structure is described as 'an authoritarian state in which the Chinese Communist

Party (CCP) constitutionally is the paramount source of power'. A significant section of people in the West believe the implementation of a western liberal style rule of law in China, with its concomitant protection of human rights, is an urgent task that cannot take place soon enough.

This attitude has its roots in western Enlightenment thinking, which proposed that there are certain basic universal rights. It follows that, where it is found that these rights are not freely exercisable, the situation is one that should be rectified. The state is primarily viewed as obstructive. A convenient truth for those urging reforms in these areas used to be that a prerequisite for sustained economic development in a country was the implementation of a western liberal style of rule of law. This was the spoonful of sugar that helped the medicine go down. China seems to offer a challenge to this assumption and gives short shrift to calls for it to accelerate its pace of legal reform.

It might be easy to assume that such curt responses are the calculated actions of a one-party state that relies on the curtailment of rights in order to maintain its grip on power. Certainly, this would chime with a view of the state as wilfully obstructive. However, recent research has suggested that the pace at which the rule of law develops relative to economic development influences the ultimate sustainability of both.[1] A model of stable development has been formulated by analysing countries in the modern era that have managed successfully to negotiate the path from relatively low-income countries into high- or upper-middle-income countries with some form of democratic rule of law. This model sets out the common steps and sequences followed by those countries that have managed to maintain stability and build a country with a relatively good economy (that is to say, high- or upper-middle-income status, as this is currently described) and the rule of law.

A common pattern emerges. Economic development takes place initially within a relatively weak rule of law setting. Furthermore, even as the rule of law is being gradually strengthened, the granting of civil and political rights is a late-stage occurrence for these countries. This would suggest that, at least from the perspective of a country which desires to develop into a high- or upper-middle-income country with some form of democratic rule of law, the early implementation of a full-blown version of western liberal rule of law can actually be counter-productive and certainly does not give a reliable and stable path to development. If this is accepted, then China's resistance to calls for urgent reform in the area of civil and political rights seems more akin to steady statesmanship with the ultimate objective of national betterment, rather than the knee-jerk reactions of an authoritarian state seeking to retain its power.

Chinese and foreigners

The prevailing western assumption that its own political and legal structure is evidently superior can come across as arrogant. It is one thing to reach your own cultural epiphany, quite another to demand it be accepted wholesale by another culture. As one writer put it: 'It's almost impossible for people in the West not to see the West as the God-given gift to the world.'[2] The West has had the time for its thought on subjects such as human rights and rule of law to mature gradually. The ideas we have developed are part of a continuum of philosophical thinking in our culture that has developed over hundreds of years. Human rights philosophy is generally thought to have developed from the Enlightenment onwards and has over 300 years of history. Rule of law philosophy predates even this.

China, on the other hand, feels itself to be a nation that has played a very grand role in the history of mankind. From the tenth to the fifteenth century, China was the leading economy in the world in terms of per capita income.[3] Even in the early nineteenth century, the idea that China was the founding nation of the world was an unremarkable one.[4] As a modern nation, it is conscious of this past grandeur and also of the fact it has fallen behind and on hard times. For a time, from the latter stage of the Qing dynasty (which ended in 1911) until the founding of the PRC in 1949, the country was in such a weakened state it could no longer be run as a single unified state; a situation only turned around by the Communist victory. One academic made the astute observation that the determination to restore China's national grandeur is the crux of Chinese nationalism.[5]

If China believes it has fallen on hard times, then one of the oft-cited causes is foreign aggression and willingness to infringe on Chinese sovereignty. In terms of historical perspective, China and the West seem to view history through different ends of the telescope. While the Second World War and the Opium Wars (between 1839 and 1860) may seem ancient history in the West, in China the Opium Wars and the war with Japan (1937 to 1945) are experienced as fresh memories and humiliations.

When the West enthusiastically suggests the ways in which China should reform its political and legal system, this is felt as a humiliation – to be preached at by the West on how to run itself – and viewed in the context of historical western strategies to undermine Chinese rule and sovereignty: with suspicion.

It is apparent that the seemingly static position of demands for reform and resistance to this becomes more complex when a notion such as stable and sustainable development is introduced. It is also clear there is the strong potential for engagement to be a negative process, given the historical context in which it occurs. It might be concluded that China should resist the suggestion that it introduce immediate reform and, instead, pursue its own path. At this point, I would like to turn to the suggestion at the other end of the spectrum: that western liberal ideas are ultimately incompatible with what has been termed 'Asian values' and can never be introduced into the cultures of Asia.

Asian values and the law

'Asian values' was an idea that gained currency in China, among other countries, for a brief period in the 1990s.[6] While it is now less commonly encountered as an objection to legal reform, it is worth reflecting on some of the basic ideas raised, as it was during this period of debate that the issue of compatibility between western liberal notions of human rights and Asian culture was explored in depth.

'Asian values' are generally thought to refer to the common Confucian heritage of many of the major Asian nations, which include China, Korea, Japan and Vietnam, but, below, I will consider both a narrow concept of Asian values, including only Confucian philosophy, and a broader concept of Asian values that encompasses numerous strands of Chinese philosophy.

Confucianism is a philosophy based on the teachings of Confucius, who was born in China in the sixth century BC. At its core, Confucianism emphasises the desire for social harmony. The key to achieving social harmony, it is proposed, lies with a proper observance of social mores and in particular respect for a hierarchy based on what became known in following centuries as the 'five major relationships' (see below). Confucianism therefore seeks to identify the generalisable behavioural patterns in human society that are the source of social harmony. In order to do this Confucius looked to the past and essentially saw himself as the conduit of existing knowledge from past ages of wisdom.

In establishing the social mores that are the building blocks of social harmony, certain categories of social relationship are typified by certain behavioural patterns: between parent and child there should be affection, between friends trustworthiness, between older and younger siblings an order of precedence. Each individual is at the centre of a range of different types of social relationship and should seek to act in an appropriate manner when engaging in each type of relationship. Every type of relationship will impose particular duties on an individual and will arise from one's position relative to others. When each individual knows his or her place in the social order and behaves accordingly, social harmony will result. Texts and sayings attributed to Confucius and his followers typically took a dim view of rule by law and advocated that the way to achieve social harmony was not through threat and punishment but through the individual's correct internalisation of his or her social duties to others.

A popular expression of western liberal ideas on liberty is that freedom means the individual is free to act as he or she wishes without restraints being imposed by the state. This view puts the individual at the heart of the meaning of liberty. It has been said that Asian societies have a fundamentally different world view that derives from their common Confucian heritage and, in contrast to western societies, is not centred on the individual. The individual-centric conception of liberty used in the West is fundamentally unsuited for use in Asian cultures, where the individual's rights are more commonly subordinated to the needs of the family and community. Each culture has its own valid conception of liberty and the human rights standards that should be applied to each country are therefore culturally specific. This is the argument frequently used to bat off calls for reform on the approach to rights in China.

Furthermore, such western individualism, it is said, has led to a breakdown of community and family, resulting in widespread problems of drug abuse and crime less apparent in Asian cultures where there is a strong focus on the family and the wider community. The greater emphasis on the individual, therefore, is not necessarily without its negative aspects. It is proposed that the individual-centric approach to liberty is not just invalid and unworkable for Asian societies, but undesirable.

The above might suggest there can never be a common standard of agreed basic rights an individual may enjoy irrespective of his or her culture. China can simply say 'This is our culture, not yours.'[7] However, to what extent is it correct to say that Confucianism places the individual and his or her rights in a subordinate position to the interests of the community? To what extent in traditional Confucian philosophy can we find any corollary to the fundamental rights as understood in the West?

This point has been examined by academics such as William De Bary,[8] who concluded that it is a misconception that Confucianist writings dictate that the individual should subordinate his or her interests to that of the community and that private desires are in some way selfish. References to the need to sublimate private interests to the interests of the larger community in Confucianist writings are made only in the context of the ruler. It is the ruler who has this obligation not to allow his or her individual interests to get in the way of public interests. The ruler therefore has the duty to act in the greater good; however, this is not an obligation imposed on the populace at large in their capacity as individuals.

Neither are concepts of fundamental rights of the individual alien to Confucian thought. De Bary cites the example from Mencius, one of the great Confucian philosophers, pertaining to the duty of a minister when dealing with his ruler to stand up for what is right. The positive example is given of the minister Fang Xiaoru (1357–1402) standing up for what he believed was correct, despite the disapproval of the current emperor Yongle (1360–1424), for which opposition he paid with his life. De Bary finds in this abidance to the truth, in direct opposition to the will of the ruler, a possible corollary with western notions of free speech. A Confucian text known as *Xunzi* also presents the idea that the common good is sustained by recognition of a duty to speak.[9] The writings of the Confucian philosopher Mencius (371–289 BC) confirmed that Chinese moral reasoning rejects bald attempts to appeal to tradition.[10]

If 'Asian values' are construed more widely to include non-Confucian strands within the Chinese philosophical tradition, there are elements in various philosophical traditions that would run counter to any idea that Chinese society is constrained by its past tradition and has a more community-focused viewpoint that negates individualism.

Mohism was a leading school of philosophy founded by Mozi (479–391 BC). The Mohists were a group of warriors whose ethics were based on the professional code of the warrior. They criticised Confucianism on the grounds it was non-utilitarian; for example, music was viewed as socially useless. Unlike other groups, the Mohists were ready to break from past tradition and they explicitly rejected the need to follow tradition for its own sake. The Mohists therefore present a further example of how Chinese philosophy contains within itself the permission to abandon tradition viewed as redundant.

Daoist thought is also a major element of Classical Chinese philosophy. The ideas of Yang Chu (sometime between 479 and 289 BC), the first Daoist, embody a radical individualism that seeks to disengage from the community. A retreat from the community and solitary living are also aspects of Daoism as it developed. The essence of Yang Chu's philosophy is stated in Mencius as being 'Each one for himself. Though he might have profited the whole world by plucking out a single hair, he would not have done it.' This negates any suggestion that Chinese philosophy is united in the acceptance of a community-focused ethic and highlights the fact that attitudes placing the community before the individual are controversial within the Chinese tradition itself.[11] As does an alternative summary of the ideas of Yang Chu found in a third-century BC text: 'There is a man whose policy it is not to enter a city which is in danger, nor to remain in the army. Even for the great profit of the whole world he would not exchange one hair of his shank.'[12]

Any assertion of entrenched community-based 'Asian values' that are in opposition to western individualistic values has several weaknesses. The first is that if a broad concept of Chinese values is used, which encompasses multiple strands of Chinese philosophical tradition, it becomes clear that Chinese tradition itself contains a lively debate on individualism versus communitarianism and this is by no means an area in which a unity of ideas is found. Whether Confucian or non-Confucian traditions are considered, it is clear there is a rejection of any entrenching of tradition for its own sake.

Even where the narrow concept of Asian values is adopted, apart from rejection within Confucianism of a mindless appeal to tradition, there is also room for debate over whether Confucianism does actually represent a more community-focused philosophy as exemplified by the Qing dynasty debates over reform.

The divide between philosophical approaches of the East and West is perhaps not as definite or impassable as suggested and any asserted opposition an artificial construct that necessarily negates aspects of Chinese philosophical heritage. It would be equally misguided to call for instant reform or to accept that there is a pan-Asian culture that can never incorporate the concepts of basic rights of the individual. Let's now move to consider the current state of rule of law in China.

Development of law in China in modern history

The first dabbling with the idea of adopting a constitution in China and implementing constitutional government took place during the Qing dynasty (1644–1911/12) – the last of the dynasties in China – and followed on from the Opium Wars (1839–1861). The effect of the Opium Wars, in which foreign military might triumphed, was that China's sense of self saw a radical transformation.

Prior to the Opium Wars, China could be confident she was morally and culturally advanced compared to other nations of the world. The

Opium Wars revealed clearly that this deep-set assumption was incorrect. China had spent the last few hundred years prizing the humanities at the expense of the sciences, and this while the Scientific Revolution was under way in the West. A gulf had opened up in the arena of scientific knowledge between China and Europe and North America. What is more, given that military technology was one aspect of this, China discovered it was now a vulnerable nation.[13] However, the realisation that it had fallen behind led to a willingness to look beyond its borders for the means by which to reinvigorate the nation. There was a natural influx of many new ideas.

This influx was manifested in a series of phases in which foreign ideas on constitutional government were discussed as possible means by which China could strengthen itself. These phases were broadly from 1860 to 1880, the early 1890s and 1895 to 1911. During the first period, from 1860 to 1880, the prosperity and power of western parliaments was ascribed to their constitutional governments, especially parliamentary government. The proposed ideas for changing the Qing system of rule became increasingly radical over the three periods, starting with the introduction of western-style politics, moving to calls for a constitutional monarchy and, eventually, for a democratic republic.

The Qing efforts to introduce a more constitutional government ultimately failed. It has been suggested that, in the end, Chinese society was not capable of accepting a bottom-up vesting of power and that those seeking to modernise China at the turn of the nineteenth century faced 'the strongest tradition of absolute monarchy and the scantiest belief in representative government'.[14] It is true that Enlightenment philosophy, which held 'that government was held in trust instead of by ordained right and that the monarch was a mere agent of society with "no will, no power but that of law" – were concepts alien in the traditional Chinese social structure of hierarchical relationship and patriarchal values'.[15] However, it is equally true that, by 1919, China could be described as a country in which there was to be found 'a plurality of competing ideas . . . and an audience ready to receive, welcome, contest and adapt these ideas'.[16] Such innovative thinking had its origins in the late Qing. With hindsight, we know China, in a relatively short space of time, managed to move from an imperial system, in which women were subordinate, to a society in which there was (at least professed) sexual equality and collective ownership of land. This was no mean feat and effectively ran a coach and horses through the established social order. A claim that Chinese society is resistant to any bottom-up vesting of power seems less convincing than the suggestion that a move to democratic reform during the Qing proved impossible because of the incumbent's reluctance to relinquish power. It therefore fell to the political challengers to offer this change and stake their claim in the new political landscape that followed in the wake of the Qing.

The constitution

After the demise of the Qing dynasty, the Nationalists (the Kuomintang) and the Communists battled for control of China. Both groups stated their intention to establish democratic elections. Five years after the Communists came to power the first constitution of new China was adopted. Liu Shaoqi, who was to become President of the PRC in 1959 and who was, in 1954, the Chairman of the Standing Committee of the National People's Congress (NPC), wrote an accompanying note to the 1954 Constitution. This set out basic rights including freedom of speech, freedom of the press, freedom of assembly and association, freedom of procession and demonstration, and freedom of religion, along with the intention to establish a universal, equal, direct and secret ballot; the idea of party dictatorship followed by constitutional government was an intrinsic part of the Nationalists' stated plans.[17]

It is clear in the explanation of the 1954 Constitution that the document was an expression of intent, with Liu Shaoqi suggesting the state would step by step extend the material conditions to guarantee enjoyment of constitutional rights. However, at some point this political process stagnated despite repeated rehashings of the constitution. The constitution in the history of new China has been rewritten four times and the last constitution of 1982 has now been revised four times. The democratic reforms anticipated by Liu Shaoqi, however, became fading hopes and it is true to say the freedoms and rights set out in these various iterations of a constitution are still not able to be relied upon directly by a citizen in a Chinese court of law.

The section of the constitution dealing with a citizen's rights saw various changes across the decades. The 1975 Constitution added to the rights mentioned above (and contained in the 1954 Constitution) the freedom to strike and the freedom of correspondence. The 1978 constitution supplemented these with the right to use big-character posters (popular ways of conveying opinions in China in the days before widespread access to newspaper and electronic communication), the right to have a free airing of views and the right to have mass debate. The 1982 Constitution removed the right to strike along with the changes made to the 1978 Constitution.

However, despite the various amendments to the constitution over the years, the courts in China will currently not allow the rights set out in the constitution to form the basis for a civil suit unless those rights have been manifested in an ordinary legal norm, which means those fundamental rights have been converted into ordinary laws and regulations. It was suggested this had changed in 2001 when the Supreme People's Court issued a document (the Official Reply)[18] which was hailed by Huang Songyou, the then Chief Judge of the First Civil Division, to be the equivalent of establishing a precedent that the courts could use the constitution as a standalone basis for a civil claim and without enquiring further into whether or not such rights were manifested as ordinary laws and regulations. However, subsequent to the issue of the Official Reply, commentators have noted that cases dealing with constitutional rights are rare and generally involve disputes of nominal societal interest, rarely challenging the actions of the government. Furthermore, in December 2008, the Official Reply was included in a list of abolished judicial interpretations.[19]

With regards to interpretation of the constitution, the Supreme People's Court is actually constitutionally precluded from performing this role (as is found in some civil law jurisdictions). If the judiciary were to extend its powers to include the power of interpretation of the constitution, this would directly contravene A67(1) and A67(4) of the 1982 Constitution, which vests that power in the Standing Committee of the National People's Congress. So, barring a fundamental change to the Chinese constitutional structure, the Chinese Supreme Court is precluded from becoming a court that is able to determine what is constitutional or unconstitutional.

Elements of the legal system in China

The lawyers

In 1978 China had only 2000 lawyers.[20] The period from 1957 until the end of Mao Zedong's rule in 1976 saw the legal profession the target of political attack. It was only when Deng Xiaoping came to power in 1978 that this changed. Deng Xiaoping initiated the development of China's modern system of legislation and was responsible for the rehabilitation of the legal profession, vital to this national construction. As of 2010, the number of lawyers in China had increased to 180 000.[21]

During the 1980s, there was an emphasis on the political credentials of lawyers and no bar examination existed. This early period of reconstruction was a time in which lawyers were viewed as workers of the state and were employed in law offices that were supported financially by the state. The national bar association was established in 1986.

By 1996, the year in which the Lawyers Law was passed, the role of the lawyer was being defined less politically. However, in the late 1990s the majority of Chinese law firms were still state-funded.

Given that the legal profession in China has historically been a tool and emanation of the state, it is a considerable psychological leap for Chinese lawyers to see themselves as independent and in opposition to the state. However, by the turn of the millennium, lawyers in China were, to a much greater extent, prepared to represent clients who were the non-state party in administrative and criminal litigation. While there is a now a greater willingness of lawyers to represent clients in these broad areas of law in which the state is the adversary, there is still reluctance to accept cases that involve representing clients in cases concerning political rights and freedoms.

This reluctance is not just a historical anachronism. In recent years, lawyers have appeared on the state's radar after becoming involved in cases where they are acting against the state in cases involving civil and political rights.[22]

Lawyers in China currently have an absence of senior role models due to the historical waves of attack on the profession and the resultant problem of a lack of continuity within the profession. The profession is in its infancy and suffers from a low standard of professional ethics, a problem exacerbated by the widespread phenomenon of corruption that exists more generally in China, in which the passing of bribes has become largely normalised.

The status of the lawyer in China is much lower than in western countries. Lawyers in China currently account for only 0.009 per cent of the population and this is a much lower figure than in countries such as the UK.[23] There is also a paucity of lawyers among the elite leadership of China, with engineers dominating the political arena.[24] This is in contrast to the position in the West, where many politicians will have legal backgrounds.

The judiciary

There is now a Judges Law, promulgated in 1995, and a Judges Code as of 2001. In 2001 it became a requirement that all new judges pass a nationwide judicial examination.

Courts are accountable to the level of people's congress that created them (and who finance them), and are supervised by the procuracy and from above by a higher-level court. The role of the court is to apply the law rather than interpret it.

In terms of overall power and authority, the courts in China are relatively weak compared to their western counterparts. There is a huge problem with judicial corruption and, although the tools exist for removing judges due to corruption, this is not done enough in practice.

The quality of the judiciary has also been called into question. Across the 1970s and 80s, it was common for judicial positions to be used as a retirement placing for military officers. This is a legacy with which the current system is now burdened. Judges of a court can be dismissed by the same-level people's congress.

Lawyers, who are generally better versed in the law, can feel their arguments are wasted on a judge who lacks basic legal knowledge. I have had lawyers comment to me that it is necessary to bribe the judge in a case 'just to win your client a level playing field'.

Judges can also lack a high standard of professional responsibility. The social position of judges is relatively low and the fact that judges are held in such low regard also hinders the ability of the judiciary to attract the best in the country. The problem with the quality of judges has been widely recognised and there are serious efforts to remove the large numbers of judges who lack knowledge of the law.

The legislative system

A brief survey of the legislation that has been introduced since Deng Xiaoping came to power reveals that huge swathes of legislation have been laid down and that these form the very framework of modern China's legal system. The Criminal Law and Criminal Procedure Law were introduced in 1979; the General Principles of the Civil Law was passed in 1986; the Administrative Procedure Law in 1989; the Civil Procedure Law in 1991; the Arbitration Law in 1994; the Lawyers Law and Judges Law in 1996 and 2001 respectively; and the Contract Law in 1999.

While the legislative system tends to draw heavily on the European civil law systems, elements of the Anglo-American common law have also been incorporated where this is deemed advantageous.

The sheer speed at which the body of Chinese legislation has been constructed is both breathtaking and brings with it inevitable problems.

While criticisms can be made of standards of legal drafting and levels of consistency within this body of legislation, these should be considered in light of the breakneck speed at which the entire project has been carried through.

Law versus the state in China

Let's now consider the extent to which the state's decisions can be challenged through the legal system in China. This area of law is traditionally known as judicial review in the West as it involves the courts, on an application by an individual or a group, scrutinising decisions made by a minister, the government or a public body. In the West, judges in the legal system are not elected by popular vote and, therefore, a balance needs to be struck between allowing government officials elected by the populace to act and preserving a mechanism by which government actions can be held to account using fairly broad notions of justice. In the West, the theory of separation of powers underpins the judicial review system. That is, the judiciary is not under the influence of the government and this independence is key to keeping the power of the administration in check and under scrutiny.

China's 1954 Constitution provided for the courts to conduct adjudication independently and subject only to the law. From the 1950s to the 1980s, there were in reality no courts in China set up for the purpose of conducting judicial review. The current judicial review system in China emerged during the course of the 1980s. This included the establishment of courts whose purpose was to hear judicial review cases, and a special procedural law for hearing these kinds of cases. This special procedural law was adopted in 1989, to much controversy, and is known as the Administrative Litigation Law (the ALL). The law on judicial review in China is a combination of the ALL as supplemented by the Civil Litigation Law and the various opinions issued by the Supreme Court.

The scope of the courts' power of review has been set narrowly and the courts are only empowered to enquire into the legality of a decision, not its merits or appropriateness. Furthermore, cases can only be accepted that challenge 'particular' administrative actions and not 'abstract' administrative action.[25] Regulations 11 and 12 of the ALL, along with Explanatory Notes of the Supreme People's Court, set out the scope of judicial review in China.

The courts have very limited powers to replace the decision of an administrative body and this extends only to a court's substitution of an administrative penalty as provided for under Article 54(4) of the ALL. In all other circumstances, the court is only empowered to quash or partially quash the administrative decision.

There is the question of whether or not the courts can use the ALL powers of review to decide on the validity of any kind of administrative regulation. The current conclusion appears to be that, while in a case before it the court can consider the quality and consistency of the regulations (that are the subject matter of the litigation) with any higher level enabling laws, disregarding regulations that conflict with higher level laws, this does not amount to a power of the court to declare the regulation invalid. The court only has the power to bring any inconsistency to the attention of the administration. Article 53(2) of the ALL requires the Supreme People's Court to refer any issue of inconsistency of lower regulations with the enabling higher-level regulations to the top administrative body in China: the State Council. It is therefore the administration itself that is responsible for the resolution of conflict between regulations at differing levels and the judicial system is not permitted to play a role in this other than that of highlighting the existence of a conflict.

Under the current formulation of the ALL, the making of laws and regulations by the administration is outside the scope of judicial review. Even within the prescribed scope of the ALL, the courts find themselves compromised in reality by the fact that local government controls the personnel appointed to the court, along with dictating the financial and economic matters of the court. The courts can be reluctant to be seen to bite the hand that feeds them. Added to this, there is an absence of pressure from the citizenry because China also lacks the legal consciousness whereby individual citizens or the courts see themselves as equals of the government.

Given the relative lack of independence of the judiciary that is determined in part from a one-party system and in part from the constitutional arrangement whereby the local government holds the strings to the purse of the court and dictates the appointment and dismissal of judges, the courts are in a weak and compromised position.

Human and civil rights

The Chinese state's espoused approach to fundamental rights differs from the liberal approach, which would hold that human rights are universal and equal rights. As mentioned above, human rights standards are seen by the Chinese state as determined by the particular culture in question based on that culture's philosophical heritage. China imposes a hierarchy of importance on the fundamental rights. In this hierarchy, economic rights take precedence over civil and political rights. This approach has been put forward clearly by China in white papers issued by the State Council Information Office variously published in 1991, 1997 and 2000.[26] These white papers maintain that the right to subsistence is the primary right from which all others derive, that the right of development must be placed ahead of civil and political rights and that the two rights of subsistence and development are together the paramount human rights. Furthermore, China's position on these fundamental rights is that they are benefits conferred by the state rather than universal rights automatically enjoyed by all. In particular, in reference to civil and political rights, China does not accept the principle of universality and makes clear the conferring of these rights by the state will take place according to the level of development of the nation.

This approach, which staggers the introduction of fundamental rights and makes such introduction conditional on having achieved a certain level of development, might be seen as in accordance with the reality of stable development of a lower-middle-income country in the modern age, as discussed previously. Once again, such evident state resistance to the granting of rights can be viewed either as an authoritarian state's attempt to resist reform on rights that would ultimately risk undermining its position of authority or as a sensible and pragmatic mode of development that follows a well-trodden path by other lower-middle-income nations. There is also the point to be made that these two are perhaps reconcilable, as widespread and deep-reaching political reform could lead to the compromising of the economic development that is a key aspect of the early-stage model of development of a state which eventually moves towards some form of democratic rule of law.

Profound changes in the arena of rights are not necessarily easy, nor changes for which the public appetite can be taken for granted. While finding its philosophical origins in the Enlightenment, Western Europe found its practical will and momentum to establish a consensus on fundamental rights in the wake of the Second World War, a time in which Europe was ready to set down a new framework for society. China's era in which the people were open to ideas that could fundamentally alter the social contract was arguably in the 1920s and followed the demise of the Qing dynasty. Since the 1930s, plurality of thought has not been supported by any controlling regime and the triple tragedies of the Great Leap Forward, the Cultural Revolution and the 1989 Tiananmen Square incident have led to a general aversion to idealism.

New developments influencing law in China

In China, the Internet has brought with it the growing phenomenon of blogging communities, who form loose groupings of citizens and a forum in which public opinion can be expressed. In a growing number of instances, such online forums have provided the environment in which society has considered the workings of justice in its midst. Occasionally, these online forums have also provided the initial environment in which social grievances are aired, along with the mechanism by which momentum of social comment is sustained. At a minimum, they offer increased public scrutiny. There have been a significant number of cases where the justice system has been the focus of attention and, following intense public online interest, such cases have been picked up by mainstream media and led to a political reaction. In a country where the ability of the state to provide a mechanism of accountability and effective scrutiny of administrative decisions is questionable, such mobilisation of public opinion as a force is noteworthy. Does this Internet phenomenon represent a growing ability of the populace to monitor government and its actions and ultimately increase accountability of the executive? Let's consider some of the key instances of use of the Internet in connection with the legal justice system in the last few years.

Chongqing mafia trials

As of early 2010, there were ongoing anti-mafia trials in South-West China. Li Zhuang, a Beijing-based lawyer, initially inspired admiration for the way he aggressively defended his client, Gong Gangmo, one of the alleged mob bosses. As noted above, counsel for the defence is an area in which the Chinese legal profession has historically been weak. Li Zhuang claimed his client had had confessions extracted under torture and turned the spotlight on the police procedures used in the locally popular anti-mafia investigations. He was later put under police surveillance and arrested and charged with encouraging his client to give false testimony and false evidence. The police obtained the key testimony against Li Zhuang from his client Gong Gangmo, the only alleged mob boss on trial who does not now claim a forced confession. Other lawyers have suggested that the purpose of the arrest of Li Zhuang was to deflect attention away from the Chongqing authorities' conduct of the case, which has involved criticisms that defence lawyers have not been given access to case materials, or allowed to call witnesses or meet with their own clients. Many of the people put on trial in this set of cases alleged torture.

Li Zhuang entered a plea for a lesser sentence. No witness appeared in Li Zhuang's trial and there was no cross-examination of prosecution witnesses. In February 2010, when Li Zhuang's court case ended with the court reducing his sentence from 29 months to 16 months, Li managed to grab hold of a microphone and shouted to onlookers that his plea bargain had been forced. This is a chain of events in which both sides ultimately come away appearing morally compromised but in which the minutiae of the legal justice system were widely reported on the Internet and came under the microscope of public scrutiny, with each constituent element of the litigation open for comment and analysis.

Perhaps also revealing is the political background to the case. It is said the Chongqing crackdown was instigated by Bo Xilai, the Communist Party boss of Chongqing and son of Bo Yibo, one of the 'eight immortals',[27] and further, that Bo Xilai ordered the crackdown on local mafia in a bid to win popularity. It is also said that Li Zhuang's arrest could only have been ordered by Bo Xilai as Li Zhuang's law firm, Kangda, is headed by Fu Yang, the son of Peng Zhen – another member of the 'eight immortals'. On his arrest, Li Zhuang was reported as having remarked 'Do you know who my boss is?'[28]

A concern suggested here is that, to the extent the justice system is being seen to function, however inadequately, the driver is in fact an underlying political reality. The arrest of Li Zhuang is then less the workings of a robust justice system than the manifestation of a powerplay taking place between China's political elite dressed in the garb of a legal process.

BMW case

In the city of Harbin, in 2003, a tractor pulling a cartload of onions scratched the BMW of Su Xiuwen, the wife of a wealthy businessman in Harbin. As a result of this, Su Xiuwen got into an argument with the farmer who had been driving the tractor and she was observed swearing and hitting out at him. She got back into the BMW and drove the car forward, killing the wife of the farmer and injuring several others at the scene before crashing into a tree. Su Xiuwen was not charged with manslaughter and the court hearing the case found her guilty only of the relatively minor offence of causing a traffic affray.

Following the court case, the story became the focus of attention in several chatrooms and was picked up by the media. The general sentiment expressed was that the court verdict was overly lenient and there was a suspicion that justice had been perverted due to the powerful connections of the defendant's husband. It was felt this was another case of justice failing to be done due to the fact the victim was poor and lacked the connections the other party so evidently had. The flooding of the Internet by Chinese citizens over this case led Party officials to order an investigation. The investigation subsequently upheld the original verdict.

Baodong waitress

Deng Yujiao worked as a waitress in a hotel in the city of Baodong. She had been doing some washing in the laundry room of the hotel spa a few floors below the bar in which she worked when a local party official entered and demanded sexual services. When she refused, the man, together with another official who was present, tried to force her. The first official slapped her with thick piles of banknotes and said that he would 'squash her with truckloads of money'. As the struggle escalated, Deng Yujiao was stripped from the waist down and pushed on to a sofa by the men, at which point she pulled out a pedicure knife she had about her person and stabbed the main protaganist. Directly following the stabbing, she called the police in an attempt to save the man but he subsequently died as a result of his injuries. Deng Yujiao was arrested on suspicion of murder but this was later changed to intentional assault.

The case aroused intense debate, with 'netizens' expressing their sympathy with the woman and anger at the officials. It was felt the case was in some way symbolic of the struggle of the powerless in China and the abuse of power by those – the Party officials – who should be in the moral vanguard of the nation. The court heard the case on 16 June 2009 and found Deng Yujiao guilty of assault with intent but found that she had acted in self-defence, although her actions went beyond what was reasonable. However, she was absolved on the grounds of a 'mood disorder'. The verdict was widely welcomed and felt to be just, although it was noted that, during the case, the police were said to have put pressure on the woman's mother to fire her two lawyers.

Postcard campaigns

In June 2009, claims emerged on blogging sites that Yan Xiaoling, a woman living in Fujian province in South China, had been gang-raped and murdered in February 2008 and that the perpetrators had escaped without charge owing to connections with local authorities. This story began to attract a high level of attention and led to statements by officials that the claims were untrue. The official account was that Yan had suffered a haemorrhage caused by an ectopic pregnancy. Attempts were made by the police to track down those who had been making the online statements and several bloggers were arrested. They were charged with defamation and high treason.

One Chinese blogger, Guo Baofeng, posted an interview with Yan's mother on the Internet, in which she repeated the claims that Yan Xiaoling had been gang-raped and murdered and accused local authorities of a cover-up. Subsequently, on 16 July 2009, the blogging community was alerted to the arrest of Guo Baofeng, when he posted a message that read 'I have been arrested by Mawei police, SOS' and later a second message: 'Pls help me, I grasp the phone during police sleep.' Following this arrest, a fellow netizen made an online appeal for postcards to be sent to the Fujian jail where Guo Baofeng was being held. Many hundreds of postcards were received containing the single line 'Guo Baofeng, your mother is calling you home for dinner!'. Guo Baofeng was released two weeks after his arrest but other bloggers arrested and charged over the same incident still languish in jail.

The cases set out above describe instances in which the workings of the justice system have become a focus of popular attention in recent years. The online mobilisation of citizens may perhaps be hailed as a significant means by which the Chinese population can find their feet and enter into a debate on justice. The Internet provides a level of anonymity that can encourage a broad base of people to set forth their opinions. The Internet also provides a medium through which the momentum of public opinion can be made manifest and further fuelled. It is reasonable to believe that, where public opinion is strongly manifested, individuals, albeit a lesser number, may take courage to turn this into other less anonymous forms of expression of opinion, such as demonstrations and complaints to government in the face of injustice. The case of Guo Baofeng is illustrative of how the Internet can provide the forum in which attention is drawn to an issue, momentum of public opinion is gained, and this momentum then precipitates coordinated action. The sending of hundreds of postcards to a single recipient is one example of coordinated action. What is more, following the receipt of the identically worded postcards from all over China, the local officials of Mawei changed from being the monitor of online discussions instigating occasional arrests and became the physical recipient of a mass of public opinion communicating in a single voice. The psychological effect of an amorphous assortment of online discussions becoming transformed into a finger extending and pointing to one *danwei*,[29] to a group of individuals, should perhaps not be underestimated. It is the moment in which the hunter for a moment becomes the hunted, however playfully expressed the wording may be.

This is not to say that Internet mobilisation is freely permitted in China. The government does attempt to control and monitor. There have been attempts to completely remove the anonymity of Internet users by enforcing registration so that any one session can be identified with a particular individual. However, given the fluidity of Internet interactions, the state has to tread carefully. The stern image of the state clamping down on challenges to its authority in the name of strong leadership can fairly easily shift in the public perception to that of a nepotistic elite engaged in a desperate attempt to cover up, suppress and scare.

This being said, the extent to which public opinion made manifest can bring about a more just system is limited. The limits are both in the number of cases that will attract public attention to begin with and the nature of the influence. Focusing on the latter, a state response to public opinion that takes place outside the framework of the justice system is no substitute for an independent judiciary. It should not be imagined that, because public opinion leads to a change to a judicial decision, this is therefore public opinion acting as a check and balance on the legal system. Rather, it may be another example of the influence local government exerts over the judiciary and the power it has to encourage the judiciary to reach a certain decision that from a political point of view is preferable. Indeed, the lawyers in the case of Deng Yujiao made the comment that the outcome reflected the anxiety of the authorities about the extent of popular anger rather than a sign of proper justice being served.

Conclusion

China has put in place a fairly comprehensive framework of legislation just over three decades. This is a great achievement. The legal framework has been one of the planks in the economic development that China has witnessed across this time. China is also now transforming into a country that is governed by rules. The advancement of the legal system is one aspect of the ongoing legitimisation of Party rule and the CCP is therefore committed to this path.

However, the professions of lawyer and judge are still in their infancy and are deeply affected by a history of state control and a relatively weak and compromised court system. There is also the widespread problem of corruption in Chinese society, from which the legal profession is sadly no exception.

The development of the law has also not been allowed to move forward in certain areas. These areas are the constitution, fundamental rights and judicial review. While China has a constitution which sets forth a broad spectrum of basic rights of the individual, the court system effectively self-limits and prevents these rights from being the basis of any claim. China's declared approach to the issue of human rights is that subsistence and development rights rank ahead of civil and political rights, thereby designating civil and political rights a lower position in a hierarchy of fundamental rights. While there is the legal framework for a limited judicial review, this takes place in the context of a court system that has its financing and dismissals decided by the same-level people's congress and which is therefore compromised by the reality of its administrative position of dependence.

Although recent online mobilisation of Chinese citizens has meant that the state is under increased scrutiny by a wider audience, the ability for mass action to positively impact the justice system is limited.

I believe that whether or not China can find a path to the rule of law and accept western notions of judicial review, the rule of law and fundamental human rights is a question of the extent to which there can be convergence between these concepts and the Chinese philosophical heritage. Where there can be organic cultural development, there is no reason to think such concepts cannot be accepted. It may require there to be a rejection among Chinese intellectuals of the idea that Confucianism precludes individual rights and to accept that the two may exist in parallel or become interwoven. With the growing economic status of China it seems entirely possible that there may be a Confucianist revival as Chinese heritage is used to embellish and enrich cultural life. For all China's economic progress, Party rhetoric is dry and the socialist revolution has run out of ideological steam.[30]

While cultural difference may be a fairly constant fact, the relative will to accept fundamental and rapid change by importing foreign concepts is not a cultural constant. At different times in its history, a society may be more or less conducive to promoting ideas that are capable of radically transforming that society. A society that is in the process of soul-searching and self-examination provides fertile soil. After considering if, from a developmental and cultural perspective, China can or should accept broader reform on fundamental rights, we should also consider the relative willingness of Chinese society to embrace an idea that is capable of radically transforming aspects of its society.

China currently finds itself in an age of more or less constant economic development, overseen by the CCP, which has now had an unbroken rule of more than 60 years. This economic development outpaces the majority of countries in the world. From this perspective, Chinese people can be rightly proud of the achievements of their leadership. While taking Party-controlled media reports on national progress with a pinch of salt, the visible signs of economic development are apparent for all within China to see. In the recent economic storms that have battered the region, such as the Asian Economic Crisis of 1997 and the Credit Crunch of 2007, the Chinese state has been viewed as a steady hand that has allowed the nation to weather these crises as well as could be hoped.

The current leadership is also conscious of the high-level political divisions that contributed to the 1989 Tiananmen Square incident and is careful of allowing internal political divisions to undermine state control.

The economic swell, coupled with a wary attitude towards internal division, presents a situation in which China is fairly impervious to notions that threaten to radically transform Chinese society. External suggestions for reform are viewed with a collective memory of foreign imperialism and a desire on the part of foreign powers to undermine Chinese unity. Not too distant history provides memories of the national tragedies that have accompanied uncurbed idealism and this has resulted in a general aversion to idealism. Recent events have perhaps also led China to question the high regard in which it has traditionally viewed foreign expertise. The Credit Crunch of 2007 showed that the developed countries of the world were not omniscient. In fact, China witnessed these countries approaching it for assistance. What is more, China feels itself to be on the rise and its national sense of pride is in a state of recovery. The situation today can be starkly contrasted to the one existing in the late Qing, when Chinese society felt itself to have become weak, to have fallen behind and to have lost its national grandeur. In addition, rapid reform of political and civil rights is not necessarily the most stable path of development. It would seem that today's China is not a society receptive to fundamental change.

More likely, looking beyond the CCP and perhaps beyond the next decade, is that we will have another period in the development of Chinese Confucianism where ideas already familiar in Chinese culture are extended and adapted to introduce ideas that have received less attention in traditional Chinese philosophy.

As one academic put it: 'For East Asians living in the Confucian cultural sphere . . . the burning question is the reconciliation of various western values with traditional Confucian ones in both the public and the private realms of existence . . . [W]e need to investigate under which conditions the East and the West, despite the many differences between them, can be engaged in an equal and dignified dialogue.'[31]

Policy approaches

When considering policy approaches for engagement with China, it is worth pausing to consider the value of legal reforms to China's political elite. To the CCP, economic growth and progress on issues such as rule of law are important planks in the legitimisation of state rule. Sustaining momentum is vital. As each new generation of leaders takes up its position, the founding of the PRC recedes into ever more distant history. Current leaders can point only to participation in political events that have a much more ambiguous political legacy in China than the formation of the PRC. Any political credentials must now be supplemented with demonstrable progress by the Party on key issues.

Economic growth in China is closely connected to overseas investment. Such investment is facilitated by a backdrop of legal certainty and so it is important that China can present a story of clear progress made in its implementation of legal reforms.

China is also under pressure from human rights movements to show positive steps forward in dealing with civil liberties. While the reaction of China can be defensive and generally involves a call for other countries to mind their own business, it is noticeable that a high level of international attention on an individual can offer him or her a degree of protection. That is to say, despite state reactions, overseas attention is factored into the actions of the state.

China is transforming from a country run by the Party to a rule-based system. Even if economic development can be maintained without further legal reform, it is unclear if political control can be sustained without further reform.[32] In fact, in its search to legitimise its rule, the CCP could be forgiven for agreeing with the Red Queen in *Through the Looking Glass*, when she tells Alice that, in the fast-moving world she occupies, it takes all the running you can do just to stay in the same place.

Apart from allowing the CCP to maintain legitimacy, an added benefit of further implementing rule of law reforms is that it can help the

Party remove the heavy mantle of omniscience it carries as part of its Leninist baggage. By allocating responsibilities for state activity, in the event of maladministration, the Party can apportion blame and direct popular anger towards the responsible state body rather than shoulder this burden alone.

There are doubts over whether or not Chinese state leaders will allow the rule of law to develop to an extent sufficient to impose real restraints on state power and whether or not the CCP will allow its position of pre-eminence to be threatened. However, the promotion of legal reform does not require a political agenda and can be based on the policy of promoting sustainable economic development for which a liberal democracy is not a prerequisite. It is, though, likely that a stronger rule of law will produce a stronger civil society.

As pointed out by Peerenboom, when thinking about future paths of development, it is important to view rule of law as a spectrum and its development possibilities as many and varied. By approaching rule of law reforms in an overly simplistic way, debate can become polarised and more politicised and bad policy decisions can result. For example, a blind promotion of a policy of engagement that tends to strengthen the courts may ultimately impede rule of law reforms if the result is to strengthen an institution already compromised by its dealings with the Party and in which there exists a judiciary that suffers from corruption and a lack of professional pride. A greater level of independence for a judiciary yet to develop a high standard of integrity and professional ethics could prove problematic.

A binary view can also impede the understanding of changes and developments. A more sophisticated and multi-faceted view of rule of law development will allow a better analysis of the changing system within China and allow scope for China's development to differ from the path taken by other countries. A useful analysis will do more than apply an index of similarity in which China's legal system is viewed as simply approaching or retreating from the form of rule of law familiar in the West. A useful approach will begin with a robust concept of rule of law: multi-stranded and allowing for a degree of diversity in the development trajectory.[33]

A more nuanced view of rule of law and its supportive institutions will aid in the analysis of which reform objectives are relatively achievable and which lack the institutional framework to become established.

The attempts in the 1960s to export rule of law to developing nations offers a warning to anyone who might think a crude transplanting of western models is the way to nurture sustainable rule of law development.

These efforts largely failed and it became apparent that transplantation of rule of law from developed to developing countries was a difficult task.

There is a place for engagements based on more comprehensive implementations of rule of law – so-called 'thick theories' – and based on less comprehensive and therefore more universally accepted notions of rule of law – so-called 'thin theories'. The rule of law model one uses when engaging is likely to be determined by the nature of the organisations doing the engaging. There will always be a place for debate on the more comprehensive theories that extend to democracy and human rights; these can be avenues into discussion of various issues that are internally desired and the foreign organisation can in a sense be the mechanism for displacing more difficult aspects of domestic debate. However, there is no doubt that the lighter version of the rule of law model will be more easily accepted by the organisations representing the Chinese government.

An understanding of China's current system is key. Intelligent development options and proposals are more likely to be formulated when knowledge of both cultures exists. If expertise cannot be offered on the Chinese system, foreign organisations or individuals engaging with China should recognise that, while their experiences are valid and useful, they should refrain from becoming a preacher of the virtues and superiority of their own legal system.

When deciding how to engage on legal reform, due consideration should also be given to the potential for bottom-up change. The pressure for rule of law development in China comes from many sources. Many top-level laws have developed out of local-level legislation. The reform process often proceeds from the bottom up. It may be worth identifying those localities that have instigated in legislative changes later adopted by the centre and actively engage with these localities.

Finally, it is important to recognise that, while there is a positive attitude among the Chinese general public towards progressing China's rule of law, many Chinese people do not currently seek democracy.

Notes

1. Randall Peerenboom, 'Law and development of constitutional democracy: Is China a problem case?', *Annals of the American Academy of Political and Social Science* 603, Law, Society, and Democracy: Comparative Perspectives (January 2006), 192–9.
2. Lesley Hazelton, 'Doris Lessing on feminism, communism and "space fiction"', *New York Times*, 25 July 1982, at *http://www.nytimes.com/books/99/01/10/specials/lessing-space.html*, accessed 16 April 2010.

3. The World Economy website at *http://www.theworldeconomy.org/impact/Chinese_Economic_Performance_in_the_Long_Run_960_2030.html*, accessed 20 July 2010.
4. Rana Mitter in *A Bitter Revolution: China's Struggle with the Modern World*, Oxford University Press, 2004, p. 26.
5. Citing Lawrence Sullivan in M. Ulric Killion, 'China's amended constitution: quest for liberty and independent judicial review', *Washington University Global Studies Law Review*, 4(1), 2005, 43–80.
6. It was particularly associated with the long-term leader of Singapore, Lee Kuan Yew.
7. There has been the suggestion that the modern interpretation of Confucianism has been co-opted to serve the purposes of authoritarian states. So for example, a greater emphasis will be placed on those Confucian values which encourage obedience to the state, while there will be a downplay of aspects of Confucianism that suggest an individual should be anything other than subservient and meekly obedient to the ruler of the day. A greater emphasis may also be put on the public good over individual good – where individual good is manifested as rights of the individual. In trying to disentangle this position it helps to return to the original Confucianist writings for guidance.
8. William Theodore De Bary, *Asian Values and Human Rights: a Confucian communitarian perspective*, Harvard University Press, 1998.
9. David B. Wong, 'Rights and community in Confucianism', in Kwong-loi Shun and David B. Wong (eds), *Confucian Ethics: A Comparative Study of Self, Autonomy, and Community*, edited by, Cambridge University Press 2004, p. 36.
10. Chad Hansen, 'The normative impact of comparative ethics: human rights', in Kwong-loi Shun and David B. Wong (eds), *Confucian Ethics: A Comparative Study of Self, Autonomy, and Community*, Cambridge University Press, 2004, p. 90.
11. Hansen, 'The normative impact of comparative ethics', p. 93.
12. Fung Yu-Lan, *A Short History of Chinese Philosophy*, 1948, reprinted 1997 by the Free Press, p. 61.
13. As commented by Rana Mitter in *A Bitter Revolution*, p.30: 'The Chinese had chosen the worst moment to fall behind in military technology; the late nineteenth century saw a huge scramble for empire in Asia and Africa, with European powers ranging from Britain, France, and Russia, to smaller players such as Belgium and Sweden all looking for their share of the spoils.'
14. Citing Lawrence Sullivan in Killion, 'China's amended constitution', pp. 43–80.
15. Citing Lawrence Sullivan in Killion, 'China's amended constitution', pp. 43–80.
16. Rana Mitter, *A Bitter Revolution*, p. 23.
17. Robert E. Bedeski, 'The evolution of the modern state in China: nationalist and communist continuities', *World Politics*, 27(4) (July 1975), p. 557.
18. 'Official Reply of the Supreme People's Court on Whether the Civil Liabilities Shall Be Borne for the Infringement upon a Citizen's Basic Right of Receiving Education', issued on 24 July 2001.

19. 'Decision of the Supreme People's Court on Abolishing the Relevant Judicial Interpretations (the Seventh Batch) Promulgated before the End of 2007', promulgated on 18 December 2008.
20. Randall Peerenboom, *China's Long March toward Rule of Law*, Cambridge University Press, 2002, p. ix.
21. All China Lawyers Association website at *www.acla.org.cn*, accessed 23 May 2010.
22. For more detail, see Donald Clarke, 'Lawyers and the state in China: recent developments', 7 October 2009, Testimony before the Congressional-Executive Commission on China in Washington, DC, at *http://www.cecc.gov/pages/hearings/2009/20091007/dclarke100709.pdf*, accessed 15 July 2010.
23. There is approximately one lawyer for every 500 citizens in England and Wales as of July 2010.
24. Li Keqiang is the only law graduate in the current Chinese Politburo.
25. The delineation between particular and abstract administrative actions has been criticised for being both ambiguous and arbitrary but the basic concept is that a 'particular administrative action' is one in which the administrative body makes a determination or takes measures directed towards a particular person or matter and that has an impact on the other party's rights and obligations. 'Abstract administrative actions', on the other hand, are administrative rules not directed towards any particular person or matter, that have general binding force going forwards and that are capable of being applied repeatedly.
26. Pitman B. Potter, 'Selective adaptation and institutional capacity: perspectives on human rights in China', *International Journal*, 61(2), Global China (Spring 2006), pp. 389–407.
27. A group of Chinese revolutionaries who managed to stamp their mark on China's reform era history and still maintain great sway.
28. John Garnaut, 'Children of the revolution', *Sydney Morning Herald*, 13 February 2010.
29. A Chinese work unit.
30. See the OECD, '*China in the World Economy: The Domestic Policy Challenges*, 10 (2002) which states 'the engines that have driven China's growth in the past are losing their dynamism'.
31. Song Jinhan as cited in M. Ulric Killion, 'Confucianism, Asian values and particularism', *Houston Journal of International Law*, 26(3), 2004, 512–25.
32. Peerenboom, *China's Long March*.
33. Peerenboom, *China's Long March*.

8

China's 'soft power' development by 2020

Victoria Tuke[1]

Debates over China's rise have been dominated by realist-focused analysis of the 'dragon's' economic might or military muscle. Yet in recent years mounting attention has been paid to China's attempts to become 'great' by also developing its 'soft power'.[2] This term was coined by Joseph Nye as the ability to attract and persuade others through 'the influence and attractiveness a nation acquires when others are drawn to its culture and ideas'. This contrasts with 'hard power', which is manifest through military and economic means.[3] Analysing China's soft power history, strategy and trajectory provides us, as international observers, with clues to the puzzling questions: 'What kind of power is China seeking to be?' and 'How can the international system prepare for its rise?'

As has been discussed in the other contributions to this volume, China's future short- to mid-term trajectory is far from certain. A number of potential scenarios present themselves, each with a great deal of merit. This chapter deems that, by 2020, China's political structure will not have satisfied forecasts by some optimists of a liberal democratic system modelled on the West. Nor will pessimistic warnings of China's implosion be fulfilled. Instead, the CCP will continue to develop China economically while making some minor political concessions to its grip on power.[4] China's policy is one of 'work in progress', particularly regarding soft power projections: the subject of this chapter.

China's possession of soft power cannot be disputed. A rich cultural heritage reaching back millennia, a vibrant, diverse population and impressive economic track record all have the potential to work in China's favour when seeking to attract others. The dilemma facing China's leaders, however, lies in how this soft power is utilised and the extent to which the means employed damage what is inherently present.

China's diplomatic drive for 'reputational capital'[5] has not historically been an overwhelming triumph. Much of what China has learnt has been done the hard way with an extensive profile of blunders, including the years of self-imposed closure during the Cultural Revolution from 1966 to 1976, the Tiananmen affair in 1989, management of the outbreak of SARS in 2003 and a series of product safety scandals, most recently involving tainted milk powder. To its credit, however, China has sought to learn from each of these events, through an often steep learning curve.

This chapter will look at where China's soft power strategy sits today, before making some tentative predictions as to where the CCP will direct policy in the coming decade. It will also offer some suggestions as to how the international community might seek to engage with this aspect of China's rise, or, more accurately, re-emergence onto the world stage. The chapter argues that in the future China's soft power will comprise a mixture of cultural and media diplomacy in conjunction with the traditional 'hard power' attributes at China's disposal.

The audience of soft power strategies covered below is the 'western' world, understood to include the United States as well as similarly politically minded states such as those in Europe and Australasia. Such a distinction is important since China is promoting different narratives to different regions. In Africa and South America, for example, economic assistance, investment and political distance are favoured Chinese attributes while in the United States security and economic issues take precedence. In Europe, human rights issues and trade dominate while in China's neighbouring region economic stability and security are at the forefront of minds.

The chapter is organised into five parts. First there is a discussion of China's conceptualisation of 'soft power', identifying where it differs with Nye's original definition. This is followed by an analysis of the tools currently employed by China's soft power strategists, including the hosting of mega-events – with the Beijing Olympics and 2010 World Expo as examples – and China's economic model, culture and media industry. The primacy of domestic issues will then be highlighted as Beijing's ultimate priority and likely objective for China's soft power strategy into 2020 and beyond. In the fourth section the problems associated with classifying soft power, contradictions with China's assertive behaviour and differing values from the West are assessed. The chapter closes with recommendations for both Chinese practitioners and those engaging with China in the years up to 2020.

'Soft power' in Chinese discourse

The importance of soft power in Chinese discourse has roots in antiquity. In the sixth century BCE, Confucius (551–479 BCE) argued that a ruler should win the loyalty of the people with virtue rather than force.[6] Mencius' (372–289 BCE) philosophy of the 'kingly way' (*wang dao*) rather than the 'bully's way' (*ba dao*) through leading by example is also well known in China.[7] So too is the strategy of Sun Tzu from the Warring States period (476–21 BCE), who argued, 'The expert in using the military subdues the enemy's forces without going to battle.'[8]

During the early decades of the People's Republic of China (1949–), the governments of Mao and Deng rejected much of Confucianism and ancient philosophies but continued to promote a positive image to developing countries to which China donated generous funds to support its revolutionary causes.[9]

The first use of 'soft power' in China's official party lexicon came on 15 November 15 2001, in *Guangming Daily*, a newspaper published by the Central Propaganda Department.[10] On 19 March 2004, a new Division for Public Diplomacy was established under the Information Department of the Ministry of Foreign Affairs.[11] President Hu Jintao later mentioned the term in his report to the 17th Congress of the Communist Party of China in 2007.[12] Nye's concept appealed to Beijing as the question of how to become a great power absorbed China's theorists and policymakers. In previous decades, China's soft power message centred on its economic model but in the twenty-first century, China has shown itself keen to expand its reach. The term has gained considerable traction in Chinese discourse as Figure 8.1 demonstrates. In the following discussion the author employs the term 'soft power' to denote those aspects of a country which might warrant attraction, whereas 'public diplomacy'[13] refers to the means through which soft power is projected.

China's conceptualisation of 'soft power' differs from Joseph Nye's original definition in both scope and intended audience. Similar to 'capitalism with Chinese characteristics', China has 'Sinisized' the term. As will be discussed below, Chinese soft power concentrates not only on international audiences but also the domestic one. As President Hu has stated, soft power is an 'important source for national cohesion'.[14] Promoting a favourable image of China is not only required to please foreign onlookers but also to assuage potential dissent at home. The public diplomacy department of China's Ministry of Foreign Affairs has

Figure 8.1 **Appearance by article of the term 'soft power' in mainland print publications 1998–2008.**

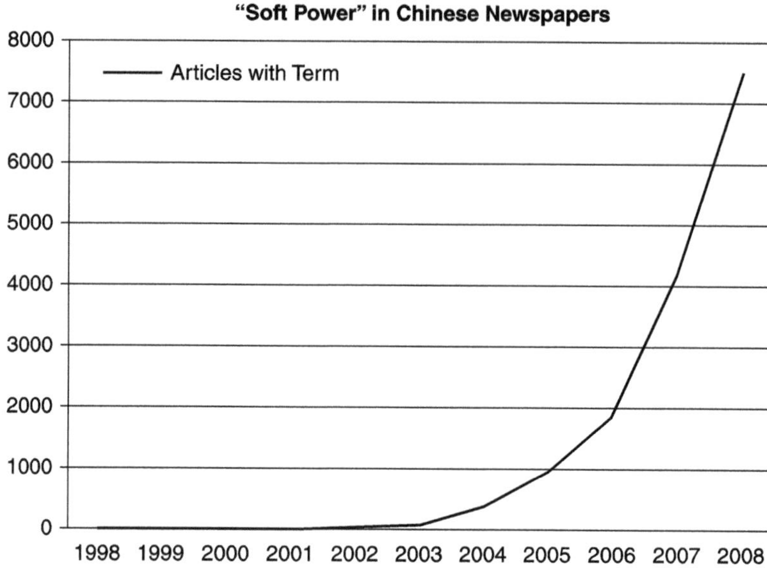

Source: Bandurski.[15]

been noted to organise activities to inform audiences on the mainland about China's diplomatic objectives far more than those abroad.[16]

Another major difference concerns what soft power is considered to include. For Nye, a country's political and social values are significant. Yet, as will be discussed below, in China this aspect is omitted since it often contrasts directly with those countries it is seeking to befriend.

China's tools of soft power

Since joining the World Trade Organisation (WTO) in 2001, China has accelerated its drive to be better understood by the broader international community and embarked on a public diplomacy campaign to this end. According to Nye, soft power 'uses a different type of currency (not force, not money) to engender cooperation'.[17] Among the methods employed by China are international humanitarian efforts, the export of culture through Confucius Institutes, promotion of their economic developmental model and staging of major events.

The 2008 Beijing Olympics

Hosting the Olympics in 2008 was a 'high-risk strategy'.[18] The CCP hoped the Games would mark the ultimate public diplomacy opportunity to reinstate China as a world power and bring 'national redemption' following a 'century of humiliation'.[19]

Instead the Olympics proved a 'double-edged sword'.[20] The international spotlight certainly showcased China's organisational capacity, economic strength and rich culture but also the government's incredible ability to control the media, its own population and even the weather.[21] The world learnt more about modern China but remained uneasy about what it knew. While 86 per cent of Chinese polled said they were happy with China's direction, the western world remained 'wary' of China's rise.[22]

China undoubtedly expected too much from the Olympics. What is more important to note, though, is that hosting the mega-event taught China's leaders several important lessons in how to conduct their soft power campaign. As the countdown to the Olympics progressed, it became clear that no single world event would change a country's image but furthermore that pleasing solely the West was not necessarily in China's best interests. As the Games approached, the Chinese government lessened its expectations and concern for western approval. Today focus has firmly shifted to the domestic audience with the purpose of stabilising political unrest and defending economic growth, even if this requires trading with unsavoury regimes.[23]

China's economic model

The economic crisis from 2008 onwards brought some unexpected relief to China in its pursuit of international respect. In some ways the banking failure and subsequent crisis diverted attention from the immediate 'success' of the Olympics but it also deflected possible criticisms of China as governments concentrated on domestic issues and sought assistance from Beijing.

Officials in Beijing were certainly not swayed into thinking that their economic system needed to change. State-led policy came into its own during the crisis with almost all countries pumping stimulus funds into their economies and intervening in the operations of financial institutions. China's confidence grew[24] as the world's developed economies looked to China to help save the global economy from downfall.[25] The speed at which China's $586 billion (over two years) stimulus[26] was implemented was initially the envy of many governments, though few of course would admit this publicly. Over time, however, scepticism over the true nature of the stimulus grew as questions were raised over how much had already been committed and whether projects identified were of genuine benefit to the economy.

Overall, similar to the political opportunity provided by the 1997 Asian Financial Crisis, the financial crisis of 2008 also hastened Beijing's ability to flex more muscle on the international stage. It is often noted in this context that one of the Chinese characters for 'crisis' also translates as 'opportunity'. The economic situation improved China's soft power in as much as respect for its economic system is greater but, as will be argued further below, such influence might in fact reflect more 'hard power' than the truly soft concept of Nye or even China's adapted model. Whilst China has been able to rescue aspects of the global system; China itself has been the major beneficiary. It would not be pragmatic for Beijing, with such a reliance on exports, to see the world trade system collapse.[27] Indeed, China's stabilising efforts have resulted in recently released growth forecasts from the World Bank of 9.5 per cent in 2010, up from a still impressive 8.7 per cent in 2009.[28] In the first quarter of 2010 it was a stratospheric 11.7 per cent.[29]

The centrality of 'culture'

While there is no national consensus behind a definition, for the majority of Chinese thinkers, China's traditional culture is considered its strongest soft power tool. Cultural diplomacy has been adopted for the understandable reason that China is widely perceived to have unique cultural traditions.[30] In order to promote Chinese culture, Confucius Institutes have flourished. Between 2004 and 2009, 282 Confucius Institutes and 241 Confucius Classrooms were established in 87 countries worldwide.[31] Whereas once Maoist rhetoric admonished the ancient philosopher, with anti-Confucius campaigns in the early 1970s, under China current's soft power strategy, Confucius is considered the ultimate ideologue of the harmonious society that China now wishes to project.[32] Perhaps in recognition of the fact that Communism has failed to appeal to foreign audiences,[33] this aspect of China's rich cultural heritage has become the emblem of Chinese attractiveness and one of the most visible aspects of China's soft power strategy.

Such an approach contrasts with the 'American-style media diplomacy approach,'[34] which has concentrated on the contemporary way of life.

The latter part of 2010 has witnessed a slight shift in this approach, however, with some attempts to integrate China's media industry into the global arena as detailed below.

The role of the media

Beijing's unwillingness to relinquish its grip on the media in the run-up to and during the Olympics was a serious blow to its soft power.[35] Lifting media restrictions was one of Beijing's most risky concessions, which ultimately demonstrated how ill prepared China's public diplomacy campaign was for the 'information age'. Traditionally information has been connected with power and China has enforced severe restrictions on the media with the understanding that 'where information is a scarce resource, those in possession of it are at an advantage'.[36] Times, however, have changed with the latest resource in short supply being attention. As Melissen noted in his analysis of the current 'paradox of plenty', information is readily available.[37] China failed to appreciate that it could not fully control the narrative of the Games.

Today, however, Beijing's latest strategy involves exactly this medium to project a 'soft' image of China. This policy did not emerge entirely as a result of criticisms during the Olympics but it is likely the West's continued demands for press freedom had some impact on Beijing's thinkers. China's leaders have long criticised western media for 'monopolising the right of voice',[38] with the protests in Tibet in March 2008 and the Olympic torch fiasco making evident to many the prevalence of 'China bashing' in western media.[39] President Hu has since voiced his intentions to redress the balance.[40] Today and in the coming decade, China intends to make its media more internationally visible.

The Chinese government plans to spend US$6.6 billion on extending China's international media outreach.[41] Among the Party's ambitions are to professionalise the party-controlled newswire Xinhua to rival Reuters or the Associated Press and challenge the television channel CNN with the unfortunately rather 'sinister sounding' CCTV 9.[42] From 1 July 2010, Xinhua is producing a global English TV service 24 hours a day.[43] As *The Economist* has also reported, *China Daily* has recently undergone a major makeover to include more foreign correspondents, investigative articles and, ultimately, 'set the news agenda instead of just follow[ing] it.'[44]

Improving China's media industry could well improve China's soft power. The proposals put forward by Baowei Zheng from Renmin University certainly address several of the current problems. Professor

Zheng echoes President Hu's calls to 'coordinate national interest on both domestic and international fronts' for the digital age, symbolised with the yin and yang symbol.[45] The image of Xinhua and CCTV has also been identified as requiring reform in addition to the need to 'grasp the mood and demands of overseas audiences' with a 'people-orientated' approach and provide information which is 'timely, thorough, transparent and effective'.[46] China's former ambassador to the UK, Fu Ying, has summed this up as 'Speak early, speak a lot, and speak clearly'.[47]

The international response to China's reforms thus far is as yet unclear but judging solely by the headline chosen by *The Economist* when reporting the revamp – 'The Chinese are coming' – Beijing faces an uphill struggle.

The Internet

The Internet has long provided China's leaders with one of their strongest 'hard power' tools in the form of cyber-patrols of potential dissent. Within the current media policy, however, Beijing hopes to capitalise on this resource in order to project its positive image. Should China's strategy be a success, global audiences will become ever more aware of China's cyber-presence, but whether this will produce a 'soft power' supply is less certain. Since the control of China's government over the Internet is well documented, web-users will remain sceptical of information which can be sourced to China. Reports in May 2010 that Wang Chen, head of the government's information office, was considering removing blogger anonymity frightened defenders of Internet freedom and only reconfirmed the unlikelihood of the Internet providing China with a 'soft power' platform.[48] China has demonstrated an impressive ability to monitor the cyber world but as the technological ability of dissenters as well as international support for Internet freedom advances, China will be unable to fully manipulate the traffic of information sent across the web. To truly utilise the Internet to project a soft image of China, barriers of entry would need to be torn down; an outcome unlikely to be seen by 2020.

Brand China

A further area where China is seeking to extend its soft power image is through its company brands. McDonald's, Microsoft and Google are but three of the numerous American brands that consistently top brand league tables.[49] The implications for the country of origin's (COO) government has been watched closely by Beijing as both Japan and South Korea, through brands such as Sony, Toyota and Samsung, have gained worldwide recognition and respect as a result of their private-sector successes. Learning from the example of these countries, China too is seeking to augment its global influence and leverage through the appeal of its products and services.[50]

In 'hard power' branding, China has already made significant gains. The strength of the Chinese economy and ability to mass-produce has attracted consumers worldwide. The 'softer' aspects of a company's image, however, through such indicators as associated aspirations of the product as well as the company's record on customer service and corporate responsibility both socially and environmentally, have been limited.[51] The major reason for this lies in China's political system, which, as recognised above, causes unease in several markets.

Fundamentally, the association of Chinese companies with the Chinese Communist Party as state-owned enterprises damages their ability to attract. In contrast to cases such as Apple, where Steve Jobs has represented the innovation his company exhibits, CEOs behind Chinese companies remain unknowns. One notable exception, however, is Huang Guangyu, founder of Gome, who in May 2010 was sentenced to fourteen years for corruption. Transparency in business has proven essential to wield corporate soft power, as the admission of failures and subsequent recovery of sales following reports of faulty Toyota cars in spring 2010 demonstrated.

Lenovo and Acer have already shown themselves able to successfully penetrate European and US markets.[52] The process will be slow but onlookers can expect greater efforts to disassociate China from the 'Made in China' label towards the 'Made by China' slogan. Certainly in the medium term, associations with poor quality, piracy and counterfeit goods will persist. In the coming decade China will continue to seek a balance between 'going global' with an image palatable to the international community while retaining its tight grip on the business practices of state-owned companies.

Diplomatic style

Nye's original conception of soft power included culture, values and policies. As has been discussed above, cultural diplomacy has represented a central pillar of China's strategy, while values have often been omitted. The third aspect of the term, 'policies', also requires further development.

As the *People's Daily* stated in 2005, 'We should build a harmonious world by aiming at performing great deeds.'[53] In foreign relations, actions certainly speak louder than words. In order to improve its attractiveness, China needs to make full use of the multilateral stage, particularly the United Nations, to present its voice and the image of itself as a 'responsible power'. By displaying its 'benignity', defined by Alexander Vuving as a key aspect of soft power,[54] China can further assuage fears of a China threat. China's actions (or lack of action in the cases of Iran and Sudan), for example, influence international opinion far more than the presence of any language-teaching facilities in foreign universities.

China needs assistance from the global community. China's more assertive diplomatic behaviour has, according to some, been attributed to over-confidence as a result of the economic crisis and holding of $2.5 trillion in foreign-exchange reserves. This reality, however, demonstrates the interdependence of China's situation far more than China's predominance. As Nye recently stated, 'when interdependence is balanced, it does not constitute a source of power'.[55] The attendance of President Hu at US President Obama's nuclear-security summit in Washington in April 2010 suggested that China does appreciate the importance of working with, rather than against international organisations and the current world order.[56] A possible deal with the United States against Iran's suspected nuclear programme and impressive donations to the Haiti Earthquake appeal are but two contemporary examples of this realisation in Beijing. This contrasts with the situation in 2002 when a $6 billion package offered to Angola was widely viewed as the reason why the government rejected a deal from the IMF, which included a number of tough provisions over where aid was directed.[57]

By 2020, China can be expected to continue to improve its diplomatic style at international forums such as the United Nations and G20 gatherings. There are nonetheless likely to be times when domestic considerations compel China to take a firmer stance than might benefit its harmonious image.

Beijing's objectives

China's government has a number of objectives. The first is to build a 'harmonious society'.[58] China's leaders realise that impressive growth rates have not led to an equal distribution of the associated dividends throughout society. Rural communities in particular have witnessed often strikingly little change in the past two decades compared to urban areas. According to the World Bank there are still almost 500 million Chinese living on less than $2 a day, with 200 million of those without access to safe water.[59] In response, Prime Minister Wen had pledged to 'resolutely reverse the widening income gap',[60] recognising the potentially destabilising effect. Harmony, and thus the absence of protests, relates strongly with the central goal of the leadership, which is to secure the legitimacy of the CCP in the eyes of the people. The idea of one 'Kingdom under Heaven' and the need for unity and stability holds immense influence in China, where the memory of the years of weakness and instability in the Republic Period from 1912 to 1949 is still strong.

Placating the rising nationalist aspirations of some parts of the public, as well as the PLA, is also required, so gaining international respect for its political system is key. China cannot be viewed domestically as a 'walkover' in international circles so must demand the leverage it believes it deserves, to contribute to, and, to some extent, shape the future world system. Sustained economic growth is another essential means to securing Communist power, hence China is working hard to portray itself as a reliable economic partner. China does not want to be feared, but trusted.

It is within this context that China's soft power strategy should be viewed. The so-called 'Beijing Consensus',[61] which threatened to overtake the Washington model, has primarily been the subject of western debates while China has largely maintained its policy of non-interference abroad. Beijing officials are intensely aware of the responsibilities such a model would require and are not looking to compete directly with the United States in a 'soft power' Cold War. Beijing is not attempting to export its ideology abroad but rather consolidate it at home.

The domestic priority

As the Beijing Games demonstrated, domestic concerns stand at the forefront of China's soft power strategy. China's membership of the WTO did not cause China to 'split apart and then dissolve', as Gordon Chang, a fierce critic of China, predicted in 2002.[62] Neither is China now 'a land of a million mutinies' as *The Economist* once suggested, even though reports of mass incidents have risen sharply in the last decade.[63] Chang was correct, however, in recognising that 'the disaffected are beginning to find their voice' in modern China.[64] The string of knife attacks on Chinese schools in the spring of 2010 demonstrated the lengths to which some Chinese will go to vent their alleged frustrations with society. Interestingly, in this case, Prime Minister Wen attempted to claim that social problems were the cause.[65] For the time being, however, Beijing has been able to transfer blame to local officials while top leaders are revered. This faith in central leadership, however, may well not last for ever. In August 2009 for example, *Xiaotang* magazine reported that government credibility had fallen, with more than 91 per cent of those polled admitting that they do not fully trust government data.[66] The five most trustworthy groups in Chinese society were instead reported as farmers, religious workers, sex workers, soldiers and students.

China has weathered the economic storm comparatively well but still faces several challenges at home. In order to successfully navigate around China's soft power strategy in 2020, the international community will need to take full account of China's domestic distractions. Legitimacy, whether supported by a ballot-directed mandate or not, remains a vital element in any government's formulation of external strategy. It is often assumed that democratic states where the population directly elects its officials are more in tune with domestic factors when formulating foreign policy than undemocratic, authoritarian regimes.[67] For China, however, while decisions on soft power strategy originate from the centre, their eyes are constantly facing behind them, ensuring that policies complement the 'smooth implementation of various key domestic programs'.[68] Practitioners of China's soft power are no longer guided by ideology but rather by pragmatism. The dominance of trained engineers and other 'problem-solving' professions within China's establishment manifests itself on this point, particularly in contrast to the dominance of lawyers and 'thinkers' in other political systems.

Challenges ahead

Demographics will prove a significant influence. China's population is ageing, a problem compounded by the effects of the 'one child' policy on providing care for the elderly. China's working-age population is also expected to reach 955 million by 2020, up from 732 million in 1995.[69] The rate of urbanisation is projected to rise from 39 per cent in 2002 to 60 per cent by 2020.[70] Furthermore, despite China's impressive stimulus package, millions of migrant workers have lost their jobs due to the global downturn. China's rapid growth has generated a widening wealth gap between the country's urban and rural residents, stoking social unrest. According to recent reports, China's budget for domestic public security already almost equals its budget for defence, demonstrating the unease felt in Beijing.[71]

The environmental consequences of growth are likely to be severe, with estimates of 20 to 30 million environmental refugees every year from 2020.[72] Such movement from rural to urban areas will also inevitably bloat the number of Chinese logging onto the Internet, further fuelling the leadership's fears of unrest and challenging the Chinese Internet 'Firewall' to its limits.[73] According to additional estimates, one billion Chinese people (70 per cent of the population) will use mobile phones, exceeding usage in the United States, Europe and Japan combined.[74] The desire among China's leaders for stricter supervision of web activity is therefore likely to increase rather than fall in the coming decade.

Already, China is facing a substantial challenge in the overheated housing market as average prices have soared. Official statistics show a rise of 10.7 per cent in February 2010 with Beijing reporting increases of almost 20 per cent.[75] China's monopoly on land is widely blamed for the situation where young first-time buyers are particularly affected.[76] China's leaders are particularly keen to please this demographic, who have grown up without the ideology which dominated the PRC's early years and are increasingly 'apolitical' and above all keen on securing their economic interests. By the end of the decade such issues will be ever more central to China's soft power strategy.

The persistence of 'hard power'

A further indication of how China's soft power priorities are directed inward rather than out can be seen in Beijing's recent diplomatic behaviour. China's 'harmonious' soft power efforts have yet to be complemented with more traditional political practices. During 2009 and 2010 in particular, China has shown itself prepared to flex its political and economic might despite the impact on its 'soft power' image.

Despite a cordial start to the Obama administration, relations with the United States began to falter following the ill-advised decision in September 2009 to impose a tariff on Chinese tyres. In addition, the issue of the treatment of the Dalai Lama and Tibet by foreign governments proved unresolved and continues to be an issue where China's soft power ambitions and domestic concerns collide. As was the case during the run-up to the Beijing Olympics, when China stood firm on Tibet to please the domestic population in the face of international criticism, meetings between both presidents Obama and Sarkozy and the Dalai Lama brought strong condemnation from Beijing.[77] On the issue of Taiwan, following a period of calm in cross-strait relations with the election of Ma Ying-Jeou in 2008, the confirmation by the US of arms sales totalling $6.3 billion in early 2010 threatened the progress made.[78] Most recently, the stand-off between the US, UK and Australian press in particular regarding China's refusal to allow the yuan to appreciate is yet another example of soft power giving way to harder methods.

At the Copenhagen Climate Change Conference in 2009, China's influence on international events and on issues around climate change in particular was evident. By sending junior officials to meet President Obama at one key meeting instead of Prime Minister Wen Jiabao, who was the main Chinese government attendee, China was portrayed as a 'public-relations disaster'[79] as far as western audiences were concerned. But it also sent the message home that China was not prepared to compromise its own interests in this key area (see Chapter 5 on the Chinese environment by Jonathan Watts in this volume).[80] Here again, China prioritised domestic industrial development over international responsibility and reputation.

As China enters the next decade we can expect ever greater activity from Beijing on the international stage. The economic crisis has hastened China's development from Deng's keeping a 'cool head and . . . low profile strategy', catapulting relations with China to the forefront of other governments' priorities.

China's military, still modernising

Gary Li's chapter in this volume shows the resources and attention given to China's military strength. To some extent, China recognises that there is a contradiction in promoting a 'harmonious world' while building up an army of 2.3 million.[81] China has made recent efforts to reduce the rate of growth in spending to only 7.5 per cent in contrast to over 17.8 per cent in 2008.[82] America, for many years an example of soft power projection, has long held the world's largest military, demonstrating that the two are not mutually exclusive. Transparency is, however, still lacking from Beijing, fuelling fears from America and China's neighbouring countries in particular.[83] Since Beijing's figures do not include the costs of new and foreign weapons purchases, it is estimated that spending has far exceeded official statements.[84] In 2008 for example, China's actual military spending has been put at between $105 and $150 billion, compared with the declared budget of $60 billion.[85] China is still the world's second largest military spender, with reported plans to develop its first aircraft carrier (see Gary Li's chapter). With such a capability, China would be projecting openly its ability to cast its influence beyond just its own land area.

The announcement of more modest defence spending was likely not directed towards the outside world. Indeed, while policymakers and China-watchers noted the news, the image of tanks and troops parading on 1 October 2009, China's National Day, lingers in mainstream public memory.[86] What is more probable is that the CCP was seeking domestic political gain by demonstrating that, as the Chinese economy was adjusting to the economic crisis with rising unemployment and trade imbalances, it therefore saw holding back on military spending as a benevolent as well as pragmatic decision.[87] As Pant has noted, it was noteworthy that during the 2010 National People's Congress, spending on affordable housing, education and health and improving the quality of life of Chinese citizens were emphasised as priorities.[88]

Weaknesses in China's soft power currency

Soft power is inherently impossible to measure. Opinion polls, media analysis, tourism and student figures are among the favoured methods but none can truly account for the success or failure of a policy. Promoting soft power is a long-term strategy, which needs to accept the impact of outside influences. Events shape opinion, which for China has had positive and negative results. The opening ceremony of the Olympic Games, response to the financial crisis and even the Sichuan and Yushu Earthquakes placed China in a more favourable light. The riots in Tibet, torch relay scuffles and the tainted milk powder scandal, however, reversed or at least weakened some of this progress. Distractions abroad, for example Russia's 2008 invasion of Georgia, have been noted by d'Hooghe as shifting fears from China's rise, as have negative feelings towards the United States for its interventions in the Middle East.[89]

A further complication arises from the difference between soft power and a positive image of China. While soft power can be a means through which to improve perceptions of China, traditional 'hard power' is often more influential. China's approach to the financial crisis, as noted above, while enhancing China's appearance in some quarters was not due to any cultural or value-driven influence but rather the importance of China as a global trading partner. As d'Hooghe has argued, in certain cases it is 'more appropriate to speak of the soft aspects of China's hard power rather than of soft power as defined by Joseph Nye'.[90]

The flexibility of the Chinese leadership should not be underestimated. On several occasions they have shown themselves adept at recognising where aspects of China's public diplomacy campaign can be improved.

Nevertheless, in the coming decade, by 2020 and beyond, China's soft power strategy will face limitations and obstacles, some out of its control, which will prove a considerable challenge to overcome.

Soft power can only complement a nation's other outward policies. As discussed above, when soft and hard power conflict, the latter holds greater influence. As America has learnt, the abundance of McDonalds across the globe does not equate to understanding or support for the US system or its foreign policies. When China announces the imprisonment for 11 years in December 2009 of a political dissenter like Liu Xiaobo for 'state subversion'[91] it can almost immediately reverse much of the good work and billions spent on soft power projects.[92]

While the importance of media access to western audiences was, it seems, taken on board by China's leadership, the value of human rights has proven a stumbling block. China's promises to improve its record when applying to host the 2008 Games[93] were unfulfilled as control was in fact tightened. As d'Hooghe has argued, reports of the girl lip-synching and computer-generated fireworks at the opening ceremony bemused Europeans, who could not understand China's 'pursuit of total perfection', while leaving the international audience feeling 'betrayed'.[94]

Western audiences have always been 'less-willing receivers of China's projected soft power'.[95] Nevertheless, should China really hope to reach out to such audiences, its policy towards political dissenters in particular deserves re-examination. According to some scholars, the Chinese side believes the EU and China share many common approaches to international issues, for example an aversion to military confrontation and support for multipolarity.[96] There is in fact a significant gap between perceptions, as China believes in a state-centric model while Europeans believe in sharing sovereignty while fiercely defending human rights and media freedom.[97] Differences of opinion regarding the execution of the British man Akmal Shaikh in December 2009 clearly demonstrate this disparity.[98]

The recipient of any expression of soft power can play as important a role as the provider in determining its success. The Obama administration has seen, in its relations with Iran, the limitations of reaching out if the other party is unwilling to listen. The international community certainly has a function here. Stereotypes cannot be overcome overnight but greater efforts should be made by western media as well to present an objective view of China.

The World Expo 2010

China's most recent crowd-pleasing attempt was the Shanghai World Exposition 2010. At an official cost of an estimated $4.2 billion[99] (twice that spent on the Olympics in 2008) Beijing hoped to attract 70 million visitors over a six-month period. China was rightly proud to be the first developing country to stage the event, choosing to emphasise Chinese tradition and culture in its Pavilion in line with Beijing's current soft power promotion.

Comparisons with other grand events, however, should be made with caution. Unlike the pioneer Great Exhibition held in London 1951, World Expos have failed in recent years to attract international applause. While officials labelled the event the 'economic Olympics', substantial deal-brokering is rare and continues to be done behind closed doors. Despite reports of some disappointing visitor numbers, China always intended the majority of tickets to be sold to Chinese, as can be inferred from the fact that the majority of commentary was in Chinese.[100]

World Expos, despite their titles, are not expected to draw in huge crowds from abroad. Only 5 per cent of visitors to the Nagoya Expo in 2005 were foreigners.[101] As China hoped, they rather intend to showcase an image domestically and abroad of modernity and hospitality. As one observer stated, the Olympics were a party thrown by China for the world, the Expo was a party for the Chinese.

Unlike the Grand Prix and Olympics, the Expo has resulted in some significant infrastructure development, which no doubt pleases many Shanghai residents who have long been keen to demonstrate their development commensurate with their capital. Stories of the estimated 55 000 people relocated to make room for the 5.3 square kilometre site and tight security did not dominate headlines in the western media on a similar scale to the summer of 2008.

Chinese leaders will be assessing both the tangible and intangible outcomes of its recent party-hosting splurge but is likely to resist further bids in the future. Indeed, once China has built its own Disneyland theme park there are few attractions China has yet to host. Furthermore, during the Expo the persistence of hard power overshadowed the 'soft' implications of China's rise. As tensions on the Korean Peninsula following the sinking of the *Cheonan* warship in April 2010 heightened pressure on China to join the United Nations in condemnation, few foreign governments were concerned with China's soft power.

China's soft power in 2020

Given current trends, by 2020 China's leaders are likely to be ever more skilled at deploying soft power to achieve their wider domestic and international goals. Yet there will remain several limitations on China's soft power projection. In addition to those listed above, China will continue to be challenged by the source of its soft power initiatives. While there is potential for reform, in the coming decade it is unlikely that China's strategists will embark on such a project, as domestic concerns continue to top their list of priorities.

Problems likely to persist

The effectiveness of soft power is dependent on the political culture it accompanies. Attempts by Chinese practitioners to separate China's political values from their soft power strategy have thus fallen short as the centralisation of soft power has proved a significant limitation. Credibility is vital in public diplomacy; an asset China will continue to battle until soft power is channelled more through individuals, universities and businessmen and not the government. As Professor Gong Wenxiang states, 'If the medium lacks credibility, it is unthinkable that it will improve the country's image.'[102] The spread of Confucius Institutes has gone some way in the right direction but government control remains. Without a pluralistic, open appearance, misperceptions and stereotypes of China are likely to persist.[103]

China's attempts to reform its media industry are welcome. Their ability to substantially improve China's 'soft power' projection, however, neglects to address the fact that the messengers of China are accountable to Beijing. As d'Hooghe has noted, media is only credible when it is 'independent and adheres to journalistic ethics'.[104] As the furore over Google's operations in China has demonstrated, media and Internet freedom remain important values to the international community, with the potential to undermine China's image abroad. China eventually blocked access for the over 400 million online users to Google. In response, at the end of March 2010, Google redirected traffic through its Hong Kong site, which is not subject to Beijing's tough censorship rules.[105]

To develop China's soft power, efforts need to be made to improve its reputation in governance. Bill Emmott notes that 'governments give most attention to their country's strengths' in public diplomacy campaigns. However, to truly advance their position in global opinion, greater attention should be given to the state's weaknesses.[106] To Emmott and many other scholars, 'China's greatest weakness is its authoritarian, unaccountable and sometimes brutal political system.'[107] The 'Anholt Index of Nation Brands' supports Emmott's argument. While China's culture and heritage boost China's ranking, for most other aspects, China is ranked in the bottom third. 'With low scores in governance, people may purchase products made in a particular country, but will likely not engage it in other ways.'[108]

Greater access to the party elite should also be permitted. A Gallup Poll in 2006 indicated that China's leadership 'remains a great unknown to many of the world's citizens'.[109] For as long as so little is known, particularly of the powerful nine-member standing committee of the Politburo, a mood of perhaps unjustified suspicion is likely to remain. The current Standing Committee, for instance, contains no one in its nine members who has studied or lived abroad, or is able to speak a foreign language. Those most likely to lead China in the next decade are mostly people who were born and brought up in the Cultural Revolution decade, when China was particularly isolated. They have very limited international experience and this inevitably impacts on their world view. They are, in all senses, very Sino-centric and not easy to understand for the outside world. Current President Hu Jintao, for instance, has given no one-to-one interviews with members of the western media. Leaders who will be rising in the coming decade, however, will be largely from a generation where many studied abroad. It will be interesting to see the impact of their international experience on how they speak and interact with the wider world.

Leading on from the above, addressing the source of China's soft power will be an essential function of China's future strategy. In an era when reputation is of paramount importance to international relations, China's message lacks credibility due to its origins. Public diplomacy, the art of getting others on your side, differs fundamentally from traditional forms of diplomacy due to the actors involved. By definition, hard power is operated by the government but for soft power, states cannot be in 'control as they would like to be'.[110] Rather than communication stemming from governments, private citizens are 'assertive participants in international politics'.[111] The indirect authority of the Ministry of Education in the operations of Confucius Institutes, for example, has occasionally damaged their ability to present China's soft power objectively. Unfortunately for China's leadership, in order to fully exploit its soft power, it must release some of its grip on both the population and the media. In the United States, institutions like the Supreme Court, the free press and free speech act as a check on government behaviour. China's 'meta soft-power', termed by Nye as this capacity to be self-critical, is still lacking in the Chinese system and particularly among policymaking circles.[112]

China's leaders have recognised the importance of the media, particularly in the digital age, in their practice of public diplomacy. The government's recent campaign to broaden its audience is to be welcomed. Public diplomacy is not a monologue; it is a conversation in which the perspective of the listeners must be considered. More, however, is needed to provide a genuine picture of China, its people, and its priorities and policies to the outside world. This can only be done, however, by credible members of the Chinese elite.

A policy China's leaders would do well to appreciate and ameliorate is the state's relationship with foreign journalists. Correspondents hold enormous power and influence over audiences abroad. One of China's biggest public diplomacy mistakes has been irritating foreign correspondents with restrictions on access, encouraging journalists to further seek those willing to speak out against China. As Bourdieu observed, the media has the ability to re-arrange reality 'like a magnet to a pile of iron fillings'.[113]

The leadership remains deeply suspicious of motives and continues to peddle the line, echoed by millions of bloggers, that the western media indulges in 'China-bashing'. Rather than setting up 'anti-CNN' sites to monitor anti-Chinese bias, the government should encourage foreign correspondents to report on China. They are a vital gateway in the complex public diplomacy practice and would add greatly to the successful dissemination of China's soft power. Audiences tend to believe news from their own domestic sources rather than those from abroad so China would be wise to tap into this important resource. Rather than simply expanding operations, for example in the media industry, the source needs to be reformed. It is unlikely the CCP will take what would be an extremely brave move by stepping back from information control in the near future. In the short term the effects may well prove destabilising, but to truly improve China's soft power root-and-branch reform of media access would be a welcome start. By 2020, however, this development is unlikely. It is more probable that, due to domestic concerns, China will continue to demonstrate its abhorrence of international media.

China's strategy might, however, engage in greater cooperation with foreign media outlets rather than initially in direct competition. China's media faces several challenges, among which the 'hegemony of discourse' enjoyed by western, English-language media and the often problematic translation of the Chinese language are but two. As Rumi noted in 2004, 'it will be some time before the Chinese mass media, with its lack of competitiveness caused by strict government restrictions on the media, can start winning large audiences abroad'.[114] It is no longer truly the case, however, that as Rawnsley commented in 2007, 'The recent SARS and Avian Flu epidemics reveal that public diplomacy is essentially reactive rather than pro-active; defensive; secretive; potentially dishonest; and, for purely political expediency, too cautious and slow in responding to crises that have increasingly already been reported in the foreign media.'[115] China's media strategy has evolved and will make further improvements by 2020.

There are also signs that China's leaders are more willing to capitalise on their vast population to project a positive international image. While governments have ultimate control over their hard power resources, the same cannot be said for soft power. The world is interested in China, a fact the Chinese government should welcome not fear. The response to the Sichuan Earthquake both in China and across the global Chinese diaspora showed the true face of modern China. Indeed opinion polls continue to confirm the world's admiration for the Chinese people in contrast to unease with governmental control. By deploying thousands of teachers and cultural ambassadors to Confucius Institutes across the world, people-to-people contacts, while intangible, are efficient transmitters of soft power.

Civil society groups and non-governmental organisations (NGOs) are also fortunately no longer banned. In 2005 there were some 280 000 registered NGOs in the country, including some 6 000 foreign NGOs, according to statistics from the Ministry of Public Affairs.[116] Should China become increasingly hospitable to these actors in the next decade, China's 'harmonious' image will spread further. It has been noted in Brussels that China has begun to make concerted efforts to improve relations with think-tanks and contribute to constructive debate.[117] Overall, however, where China's reputation has improved it could be said this has not been due to any Beijing-directed policy but rather the grassroots or world events; despite, rather than because of a central policy.

Conclusion

Looking forward, culture is likely to continue to be promoted as a key element of China's public diplomacy technique. China's recent efforts to expand its media presence, however, demonstrate an appreciation of the limits of solely cultural diplomacy. Whilst advertising China's past and traditions does promote understanding, this is a weak source of soft power. China needs to engage with the international community so will continue to advertise its strengths and seek positive reports. The difference, however, is that this will only occur in tandem with an awareness of domestic developments.

China's cultural attractiveness has witnessed some successes. Chinese art has witnessed a recent boom and the number of Chinese restaurants in the United States already surpasses that of McDonald's, Burger King and Wendy's combined. According to the Pew Research Centre survey on views of China in 2009, favourable views of China in the United States grew from 39 per cent to a more respectful 50 per cent.[118] Yet despite these positive steps, as Nye recently commented, China still lacks the industries to compete with Hollywood or Bollywood.[119] Furthermore, Chinese universities, which through the exchange of students can provide an invaluable long-term soft power currency, have yet to attract similar numbers compared to American and European institutions. In the culture market, China will continue to be outdone by the United States.

The recent economic crisis demonstrated that China's positive image is most evident when employing the 'softer' aspects of China's 'hard power': economic strength and international contributions. China's ears pricked when President Obama and Secretary of State Clinton began to talk of 'smart power': the modification of Nye to combine hard and soft aspects of a country's power to guarantee national interests. Such an arrangement will in all probability characterise China's future trajectory. As Nye himself noted, the term 'soft power' has been 'stretched and twisted',[120] nowhere less so than in China.

To improve its soft power in the eyes of many westerners, China needs to sharpen its message and complement its rhetoric of harmony with actions both domestically and in the international community. The China 'brand' has yet to be defined, with the often-competing images of poverty and wealth in areas like Pudong in Shanghai. Expressions of a 'harmonious world' have failed to convince many who look rather to military defence spending and behaviour at the United Nations to judge a state's objectives.

As the 'Soft Power in Asia' survey also noted, only small minorities (9 per cent to 25 per cent) of respondents outside China have heard at least 'somewhat' of China's concept of a 'harmonious world'.[121] To cultivate soft power, China must address not just the quantity of initiatives launched but also their quality.

Yet as China faces yet another era of transitions, economically, socially and politically, particularly with the succession of leadership in 2012, domestic issues will continue to figure at the forefront of minds. Following the experience of the Beijing Olympics, it is unlikely that China will seek again to stage mega-events on a similar scale or at least with the same objective of winning over the respect of the world. Should the government successfully land a lunar rover or even astronauts on the moon in the next decade,[122] China's leaders will seek to publicise such an achievement as much, if not more, at home than internationally.

Some comfort for those fearing China's rise should be found in Beijing's impressive ability over the past decade to learn quickly and effectively from previous errors in the projection of its soft power. China's leaders appreciate the inherent limitations in soft power projection and have adjusted their objectives somewhat to account for this. The Beijing Olympics taught China's practitioners of soft power that losing the respect of their own people far outweighed the cost of a similar response from the international community. As a result of the efforts expended, China not only realised that perceived negative aspects of their system could not be 'fixed' simply through public diplomacy[123] but also that pleasing the international community was not ultimately where they should focus. Soft power cannot be directly altered by a government but the means through which it is publicised can. In China this will continue to be the case. China's assumptions as to the rules of 'the game' of soft power diplomacy which Nye identifies are evolving from an approach that follows Western norms or 'rules'[124] to one where China is confident enough to create its own boundaries.

The reception of China's strategy in other areas of the world requires further attention. Suffice it to say nonetheless that, according to the Chicago Council on Global Affairs/EAI survey in 2008 on 'Soft Power in Asia', China ranks a respectable third.[125] According to the Pew Survey, Beijing has made some significant gains, with favourability up in Nigeria from 79 per cent in 2008 to 85 per cent.[126] As Joseph Kurlantzick noted in his book *Charm Offensive*, influence in South-east Asia remains stronger than elsewhere[127] but overall economic and military strength has not yet been translated into soft power in line with Beijing's aspirations, with divergences in values being a major area of scepticism.[128]

Those interacting with China, should they be western governments, businesses, NGOs or individuals, should be aware that their concerns factor little into China's grand governing strategy. As a result, interactions should take account of China's specific understanding of the role of soft power in their diplomacy and recognise the centrality of domestic issues. Nevertheless, by 2020 and beyond, China will continue to work to improve its record as a responsible power and project the 'softer' aspects of its identity through cultural diplomacy and sustained, impressive economic growth.

Notes

1. The author would like to thank the participants of the China Postgraduate Network Conference in Oxford, April 2010 for their insightful comments and suggestions, in addition to two anonymous reviewers.
2. For the first use of the concept, refer to Joseph Nye, 'The misleading metaphor of decline,' *The Atlantic*, March 1990.
3. Joseph Nye, cited in Ingrid d'Hooghe, *The Rise of China's Public Diplomacy*, Clingendael Diplomacy Paper 12, July 2007, p. 8.
4. Such assumptions are based on reports like that from the US Intelligence Council, 'Global Trends 2025: A Transformed World', Department for National Intelligence, November 2008, at *http://www.dni.gov/nic/PDF_2025/2025_Global_Trends_Final_Report.pdf*, accessed 8 October 2010.
5. Joshua C. Ramo, *Brand China*, Foreign Policy Centre, London, 2007, p. 27.
6. Ying Fan, 'Soft power: Power of attraction or confusion', in Simon Anholt (ed.) *Place Branding and Public Diplomacy*, 4(2), Palgrave Macmillan, Singapore, May 2008, p. 151.
7. Sheng Ding, 'To build a "harmonious world": China's soft power wielding in the global south', *Journal of Chinese Political Science*, 13(2), Springer, Netherlands, August 2008, p. 196.
8. Hongying Wang and Yeh-Chung Lu, 'The conception of soft power and its policy implications: a comparative study of China and Taiwan', *Journal of Contemporary China*, 17(56), 2008, p. 427.
9. In 1971 China donated 6 per cent of its GDP to supporting the revolutionary struggle in developing countries. Kerry Brown, 'China's soft power diplomacy in the 21st century' in Shaun Breslin (ed.), *A Handbook of China's International Relations*, Routledge, London, 2010.
10. David Bandurski, 'Is China's new communications worldview coming of age'?', *China Media Project*, University of Hong Kong, 12 November 2009, at *http://cmp.hku.hk/2009/11/12/2926/*, accessed 8 October 2010.
11. Chinese Assistant Foreign Minister Shen Guofang at the launch of the Department defined public diplomacy as 'a very important field in diplomatic work'. He continued, 'The basic goal of public diplomacy is to enhance

the exchanges and interaction with the public in order to guide and win the understanding and support of the public for foreign policies' (Ministry of Foreign Affairs of the People's Republic of China, 2004). Foreign Minister Li Zhaoxing added, 'We have actively conducted public diplomacy by publicising China's foreign policies and activities to the Chinese public, thus winning their understanding and support', cited in Yiwei Wang, 'Public diplomacy and the rise of Chinese soft power', *The Annals of the American Academy of Political and Social Science,* 616(257), 2008, p. 260.

12. Hu Jintao's report to the 17th Party Congress of the CCP, 15 October 2007, Part VII cited in Ingrid d'Hooghe, *The Limits of China's Soft Power in Europe: Beijing's Public Diplomacy Puzzle*, Clingendael Diplomacy Paper 25, January 2010, p. 3.
13. Public diplomacy is a 'foreign concept' in China where 'propaganda', which does not hold the same negative connotations as it does in the West, is more commonly used. Wang, 'Public diplomacy and the rise of Chinese soft power', p. 259.
14. Ibid.
15. David Bandurski, 'Is China's new communications worldview coming of age?' *China Media Project*, at *http://cmp.hku.hk/2009/11/12/2926/*, accessed 10 October 2010.
16. d'Hooghe, *The Limits of China's Soft Power in Europe*, p. 4.
17. Joseph Nye, 'Soft power: the means to success in world politics', *Public Affairs*, New York, 2004, 6–7, cited in Alexander L. Vuving, 'How soft power works', paper presented at the panel 'Soft Power and Smart Power,' American Political Science Association annual meeting, Toronto, 3 September 2009, p. 18.
18. Nicholas J. Cull, 'The public diplomacy of the modern Olympic Games and China's soft power diplomacy' in Monroe E. Price and Daniel Dayan (eds), *Owning the Olympics: Narratives of the New China*, University of Michigan Press, Ann Arbor, 2008, p. 143.
19. In Jiang Zemin's 2002 New Year's address, Jiang ranked winning the right to host the Olympics alongside China's WTO entry as the preceding year's key milestones in China's pursuit of prosperity. Jacques DeLisle, 'One world, different dreams: The contest to define the Beijing Olympics', in Price and Dayan, *Owning the Olympics*, p. 19.
20. David Barboza, 'Western Olympic ads cheerlead for China', *New York Times*, 20 July 2008, at *http://www.nytimes.com/2008/07/20/sports/olympics/20ads.htm*, accessed 8 October 2010.
21. According to a BBC World Service Poll conducted by Globescan and PIPA, 'Views of China and Russia decline in global poll', 6 February 2009, cited by d'Hooghe, *The Limits of China's Soft Power in Europe*.
22. BBC, 'World still wary of modern China', BBC News Online, 4 August 2008, at *http://news.bbc.co.uk/1/hi/world/asia-pacific/7540871.stm*, accessed 8 October 2010.
23. Strong economic growth of course also improves China's trade interests in the region and beyond.
24. Kenneth Lieberthal cited in Richard Pascoe, 'Year of the tiger a test for China's soft power', China Policy Institute, University of Nottingham, 2 February

2010, at *http://www.nottingham.ac.uk/cpi/publications/commentaries-reports/2010/year-of-tiger-rp-10-02-2010.aspx*, accessed 8 October 2010.

25. According to d'Hooghe, Beijing clearly exploited this position during Chinese Premier Wen Jiaboa's European 'Tour of Confidence' in January and February 2009, *The Limits of China's Soft Power in Europe*, p. 18.
26. 'China's stimulus package', *The Economist*, 12 November 2008, at *http://www.economist.com/blogs/theworldin2009/2008/11/chinas_stimulus_package*, accessed 8 October 2010.
27. There have of course, also been huge costs to China as a result of the financial crisis as argued by Leong H. Liew, 'Dealing with the inharmonious world: China and the global financial crisis', Lowy Institute for International Policy, February 2009, at *http://www.lowyinstitute.org/Publication.asp?pid=976*, accessed 8 October 2010. The temporary nature of people's opinions was also witnessed during the financial crisis with predictions in the US in 2008 that China would soon surpass America economically toned down in 2009 according to a Gallup Poll. Lydia Saad, 'U.S. surpasses China in forecast for economic powerhouse', Gallup, 16 February 2009, at *http://www.gallup.com/poll/114658/surpasses-china-forecast-economic-powerhouse.aspx*, accessed 8 October 2010.
28. 'China growth forecast raised to 9.5% by World Bank', BBC News Online, 17 March 2010, at *http://news.bbc.co.uk/1/hi/business/8571647.stm*, accessed 8 October 2010.
29. Bloomberg, 'China may post 11.7% growth, adding pressure on Yuan', *Business Week*, 13 April 2010, at *http://www.businessweek.com/news/2010-04-13/china-may-post-11-7-growth-adding-pressure-on-rates-yuan-peg.html*, accessed 8 October 2010.
30. Hongyi Lai, 'China's cultural diplomacy: going for soft power', EAI Background Brief, No. 308, 2006, p. 5.
31. Confucius Institutes are under the authority of Hanban, the Chinese Ministry of Education.
32. 'How to improve China's soft power?' *People's Daily*, 11 March 2010, at *http://english.peopledaily.com.cn/90001/90776/90785/6916487.html*, accessed 8 October 2010.
33. This was especially the case after the collapse of the Soviet Union and the failure of subsequent attempts to build socialist/communist states.
34. Wang, 'Public diplomacy and the Rise of chinese soft power', p. 259.
35. While the government agreed to relax Internet censorship for the Olympics, several of China's most sensitive sites remained blocked. Pressure from foreign journalists and the IOC forced the opening of the BBC's China website and, somewhat oddly, *Playboy*, but the sites of *Amnesty, Wikipedia* and the quasi religious sect banned in China, *Falun Gong*, could not be accessed.
36. Biljana Scott, 'Whose story wins? Public Diplomacy and Relevance Theory', paper presented at the 47th Annual ISA Convention, Terrorism, IR and Communication, San Diego, March 2006.
37. Melissen, 'Reflections on Public Diplomacy Today', speech delivered at the Conference 'Public Diplomacy', Ministry of Foreign Affairs of Republic of Turkey, Ankara, 6 February 2006.

38. 'How to improve China's soft power?'
39. Susan Brownell, '"China Bashing" at yhe Olympic Games: why the cold war continues in sports journalism', in *Beijing's Games: What the Olympics Mean to China*, Rowman & Littlefield, Lanham, MD and Plymouth, UK, 2008, pp. 149–76.
40. Banyan, 'The Chinese are coming', *The Economist*, 4 March 2010, at *http://www.economist.com/world/asia/displaystory.cfm?story_id=15607496*, accessed 8 October 2010.
41. Ibid.
42. Mark Leonard, *What Does China Think?* Fourth Estate, London, 2008, p. 83.
43. Jason Dean, 'China's Xinhua to launch english-language station', *Wall Street Journal*, 30 April 2010, at *http://online.wsj.com/article/SB10001424052748703871904575216020649004914.html?mod=WSJ_latestheadlines*, accessed 8 October 2010.
44. Banyan, 'The Chinese are coming'.
45. Boawei Zheng is a professor at the School of Journalism and Communication at Renmin University of China and director of the university's Research Center of Journalism and Social Development, Zheng, 'Enhance the use of soft power, "the cleverest strength" – the current strategy of China's foreign news media Thinking', *China Journalist*, 30 October 2009 (in Chinese), at *http://www.baoye.net/News.aspx?ID=294568*, accessed 8 October 2010.
46. Zheng, 'Enhance the use of soft power'.
47. Ambassador Fu Ying cited in ibid.
48. Michael Bristow, 'China targets online commentator anonymity', BBC News Online, 11 May 2010, at *http://news.bbc.co.uk/2/hi/8671856.stm*, accessed 8 October 2010.
49. 'Acer, Lenovo outpace US PC rivals in market share', 3 December 2009, *Electronista*, at *http://www.electronista.com/articles/09/12/03/isuppli.confirms.acer.overtook.dell/*, accessed 8 October 2010.
50. Edward Tse and Andrew Cainey, *Attracting Global Interest: How Chinese Companies Can Leverage 'Soft Power' in the International Marketplace*, Booz Allen, Hamilton, 2007, p. 1
51. Ibid.
52. 'The BrandFinance® Global 500 2010', at *http://www.brandirectory.com/league_tables/table/global_500*, accessed 8 October 2010.
53. 'China's diplomacy: pursuing balance to reach harmony', *People's Daily*, 28 December 2005, cited in Ding, 'To build a "harmonious world"', p. 197
54. Vuving, 'How soft power works', p. 8.
55. Joseph Nye, 'China's bad bet against America', *East Asia Forum*, 28 March 2010, at *http://www.eastasiaforum.org/2010/03/28/chinas-bad-bet-against-america*, accessed 8 October 2010.
56. Banyan, 'Bottoming out', *The Economist*, 15 April 2010, at *http://www.economist.com/world/asia/displaystory.cfm?story_id=15908304*, accessed 8 October 2010.
57. Jason Miks, 'Welcome the dragon?' *The Diplomat*, 18 March 2010, at *http://the-diplomat.com/china-power/2010/03/18/welcome-the-dragon*, accessed 8 October 2010.

58. Jiang Zemin's speech in Cambridge, 22 October 1999; see 'President Jiang spells out Chinese values', *People's Daily Online*, 23 October, 1999 cited in d'Hooghe, *The Limits of China's Soft Power in Europe*, p. 8.
59. Mukul Devichand, 'Millions "left behind in rural China"', BBC News Online, 12 May 2010, at *http://news.bbc.co.uk/2/hi/8668086.stm*, accessed 8 October 2010.
60. Wen Jiabao cited in article published in *Qiushi*, the official magazine of the Communist Party of China (CCP) Central Committee in 'Wen vows to deepen China's income reform', Xinhua, 1 April 2010, at *http://www.chinadaily.com.cn/china/2010-04/01/content_9677782.htm*, accessed 8 October 2010.
61. Ramo, 'Brand China'.
62. Gordon C. Chang, *The Coming Collapse of China*, Arrow, London, 2002, p. 274.
63. It should also be remembered on this point that true figures for the number of protests in China is near impossible to locate and that unofficial estimates predict an increase in social unrest in recent months. 'Angry China', *The Economist*, 1 May 2008, at *http://www.economist.com/opinion/displaystory.cfm?story_id=11293645*, accessed 8 October 2010.
64. Chang, *The Coming Collapse of China*, p. 284.
65. 'China's Wen says social tensions behind school killings', Reuters, 14 May 2010, at *http://uk.reuters.com/article/idUKTRE64D0CH20100514*, accessed 8 October 2010.
66. 'Drain of credibility', *China Daily*, 4 August 2009, at *http://www.chinadaily.com.cn/opinion/2009-08/04/content_8515596.htm*, accessed 8 October 2010.
67. Essentially this revolves around a debate over the extent to which domestic factors impact the external behaviour of a state. This belief that systemic factors dominated was thrown into debate by Putnam's 'two-level game' theory. See Robert Putnam, 'Diplomacy and domestic politics: the logic of two-level games,' *International Organization* 42, (Summer 1988), pp. 427–601.
68. Wang Jisi cited in Li Mingjiang, 'Domestic sources of China's soft power approach', *China Security*, 5(2), 2009, p. 39.
69. Michel Andrieu, 'China, a demographic time bomb,' *OECD Observer* 217–8, Summer 1999, at *http://www.oecdobserver.org/news/fullstory.php?aid=40* (accessed 8 October 2010), cited in Cheng Li, 'China in the year 2020: three political scenarios', *Asia Policy*, 4 (July 2007), p. 26.
70. Xinhua News Agency, 'China's urbanization rate to grow to 60 percent in 20 years', May 21, 2001, at *http://www.hartford-hwp.com/archives/55/360.html* (accessed 8 October 2010), cited in Cheng Li, 'China in the year 2020', p. 20.
71. Interview with Yiyi Lu, 'No China's not arrogant', *The Diplomat*, 31 March 2010, at *http://the-diplomat.com/2010/03/31/no-china%e2%80%99s-not-being-arrogant/*, accessed 8 October 2010.
72. Elizabeth C. Economy, 'China's Environmental Challenges,' Testimony to the Subcommittee on Asia and the Pacific, House International Affairs Committee, 22 September 2004, at *http://www.cfr.org/publication.html?id=7391* (accessed 8 October 2010), cited in Li, C. 'China in the year 2020', p. 26.

73. The rate of ascent for Internet use is quite astounding. According to UN statistics, while in 2000 1.8 per hundred inhabitants used the Internet, by 2005 this was 8.4 and jumped to 15.8 in 2007. See *http://data.un.org/CountryProfile.aspx?crName=CHINA*, accessed 11 October 2010.
74. 'Year 2020 to see one billion mobile subscribers in China,' RNCOS weblog, 22 November 2006, at *http://www.rncos.com/Blog/2007/04/Year-2020-to-See-One-Billion-Mobile-Subscribers-in-China.html*, accessed 11 October 2010, cited in Li Weitao, 'Telecom industry on a roll', *China Daily*, 12 April 2006, at *http://www.chinadaily.com.cn/bizchina/2006-12/04/content_749312_2.htm*, accessed 19 October 2010.
75. Takatoshi Ito, 'China's property bubble worse than it appears', *East Asia Forum*, 23 March 2010, at *http://www.eastasiaforum.org/2010/03/23/chinas-property-bubble-worse-than-it-appears/*, accessed 11 October 2010.
76. Peter Yuan Cai, 'China's housing crisis', *East Asia Forum*, 18 January 2010, at *http://www.eastasiaforum.org/2010/01/18/chinas-housing-crisis-2/*, accessed 11 October 2010.
77. 'China protest at EU-Dalai meeting', *BBC News Online*, 7 December 2008, at *http://news.bbc.co.uk/1/hi/world/europe/7769123.stm*; 'China "hurt" by Dalai Lama visit', *BBC News Online*, 19 February 2010, at *http://news.bbc.co.uk/1/hi/world/asia-pacific/8524724.stm*, both accessed 11 October 2010.
78. 'China hits back at US over Taiwan weapons sale', *BBC News Online*, 30 January 2010, at *http://news.bbc.co.uk/1/hi/8488765.stm*, accessed 11 October 2010.
79. Banyan, 'From the charm to the offensive: China's smile diplomacy shows its teeth', *The Economist*, 7 January, 2010, at *http://www.economist.com/world/asia/displaystory.cfm?story_id=15211534*, accessed 11 October 2010.
80. China also sent a low-ranking official to a meeting of the P5 (plus Germany) at the United National Security Council to discuss sanctions against Iran. Nye, 'China's bad bet against America'
81. Harsh V. Pant, 'Tamer-looking defense budget may mask China's real build-up', *Japan Times*, 15 March, 2010, *http://search.japantimes.co.jp/cgi-bin/eo20100315a1.html*, accessed 11 October 2010.
82. 'Flowering friendliness? China's prime minister, Wen Jiabao, offers some gestures of conciliation', *The Economist*, 5 March 2010, at *http://www.economist.com/world/asia/displaystory.cfm?story_id=15640891*, accessed 11 October 2010.
83. One recent example was the corruption charges against four Rio Tinto executives in March 2010. Australian Prime Minister Kevin Rudd said following the ruling, 'In holding this part of the trial in secret, China I believe has missed an opportunity to demonstrate to the world at large transparency that would be consistent with its emerging global role.' 'China and Australia swap criticism over Rio Tinto case', *BBC News Online*, 30 March 2010, at *http://news.bbc.co.uk/1/hi/world/asia-pacific/8594609.stm*, accessed 11 October 2010.
84. Pant, 'Tamer-looking defense budget may mask China's real build-up'.
85. 'Overkill: China is piling up more weapons than it appears to need', *The Economist*, 22 October 2009, at *http://www.economist.com/specialreports/displaystory.cfm?story_id=E1_TQGSRQJJ*, accessed 11 October 2010.

86. 'Flowering friendliness?'
87. Pant, 'Tamer-looking defense budget may mask China's real build-up'.
88. Ibid.; Jonathan Holslag, 'The limits of China's global charm offensive', *Japan Times*, 24 April 2010.
89. Cited in Peter Ford, 'Beijing launching a "Chinese CNN" to burnish image abroad', *Christian Science Monitor*, 5 February 2009, cited in d'Hooghe, *The Limits of China's Soft Power in Europe*, p. 30.
90. Ibid., p. 32.
91. 'Chinese dissident Liu Xiaobo jailed for subversion', *BBC News Online*, 25 December 2009, at *http://news.bbc.co.uk/1/hi/world/asia-pacific/8430409.stm*, accessed 11 October 2010.
92. In October 2010 Liu Xiaobo was awarded the Nobel Peace Prize for his efforts to highlight China's human rights violations. The response from Beijing was expectedly fierce, labelling Liu a criminal, threatening a souring of relations between China and Norway (despite the Nobel Foundation's independence) as a result. Several states including the United States and Japan supported the choice of Liu. China's international image thus suffered a further setback.
93. 'We are confident that the games coming to China not only promote our economy, but also enhance all social conditions, including education, health and human rights', Wang Wei, Secretary General of the Beijing Olympic Bid Committee, 2001.
94. d'Hooghe, *The Limits of China's Soft Power in Europe*, p. 30.
95. Ibid., p. 32.
96. Ibid., p. 8.
97. Ibid. According to the 2009 Freedom House report on press freedom, whilst access for foreign journalists has improved, the level of harassment towards Chinese colleagues has increased. Once again, the domestic Chinese are where the government is concentrating its efforts. International media watchdogs have also reported that at least 30 journalists, mostly freelancers, and 68 cyber-dissidents were in prison in China at the year's end. Jason Miks, '(Little) Press Freedom', *The Diplomat*, 30 April 2010, *http://the-diplomat.com/china-power/2010/04/30/little-press-freedom-in-china/*, accessed 11 October 2010. See also Freedo House, 'Freedom in the World 2009 survey release', at *http://www.freedomhouse.org/template.cfm?page=445*, accessed 11 October 2010.
98. China has accused Britain of putting on a political show after a UK review of human rights around the world was highly critical of Beijing. Damian Grammaticas, 'China hits out at UK human rights report', *BBC News Online*, 18 March 2010, at *http://news.bbc.co.uk/1/hi/world/asia-pacific/8574845.stm*, accessed 11 October 2010.
99. This still places the Shanghai Expo at the most expensive to date but local media have reported the actual cost to be $58 billion, 'Key facts about the Shanghai World Expo', Reuters, 30 April 2010, at *http://www.alertnet.org/thenews/newsdesk/TOE63T03O.htm*, accessed 11 October 2010.
100. Reports from the Expo, however spoke of especially long queues for the British and American pavilions.
101. John D. Van Fleet, 'The greatest show on Earth', *The Diplomat*, 23 April 2010, *at http://the-diplomat.com/2010/04/23/the-greatest-show-on-earth/*, accessed 11 October 2010.

102. Cited in d'Hooghe, *The Limits of China's Soft Power in Europe*, p. 33.
103. Pascoe, 'Year of the tiger a test for China's soft power'.
104. d'Hooghe, *The Limits of China's Soft Power in Europe*, p. 31.
105. Miguel Helft and David Barboza, 'Google shuts China site in dispute over censorship, *New York Times*, 22 March 2010, at *http://www.nytimes.com/2010/03/23/technology/23google.html*, accessed 19 October 2010.
106. Bill Emmott, *Rivals: How the Power Struggle Between China, India and Japan Will Shape Our Next Decade*, Allen Lane, York, 2008, p. 169.
107. Ibid., p. 268.
108. Pere Berkowitz et al., 'Brand China: Using the 2008 Olympic Games to enhance China's image', in Simon Anholt (ed.), *Place Branding and Public Diplomacy,* 3(2), Palgrave Macmillan, Singapore, April 2007, p. 171.
109. Julie Ray, 'China's Leadership Better Regarded Outside the West', Gallup, 29 April 2008, at *http://www.gallup.com/poll/106858/Chinas-Leadership-Better-Regarded-Outside-West.aspx*, accessed 11 October 2010.
110. Melissen, *Wielding Soft Power: the new public diplomacy*, Clingendael Diplomacy Papers, No. 2, May 2005, p. 33.
111. Melissen, *Wielding Soft Power*, p. 32.
112. d'Hooghe, *The Limits of China's Soft Power in Europe*, p. 36.
113. French sociologist Pierre Bourdieu cited in Tom Plate, 'A viewing guide for the "third" Beijing Olympics', *Jakarta Post*, 1 August 2008, at *http://www.thejakartapost.com/news/2008/08/01/a-viewing-guide-039third039-beijing-olympics.html*, accessed 11 October 2010.
114. Aoyama Rumi, 'Chinese diplomacy in the multimedia age: public diplomacy and civil diplomacy', December 2004, pp. 1–60, at *http://dspace.wul.waseda.ac.jp/dspace/bitstream/2065/800/1/20050307_aoyama_eng1.pdf*, accessed 11 October 2010.
115. Rawnsley, cited in Wang, 'Public diplomacy and the Rise of chinese soft power', p. 266.
116. Paul Mooney, 'How to Deal with NGOs – Part I, China: mindful about political unrest, China Keeps a close watch on its NGOs', *Yale Global*, 1 August 2006, at *http://yaleglobal.yale.edu/content/how-deal-ngos-%E2%80%93-part-i-china*, accessed 11 October 2010, cited in Li, C. 'China in the year 2020: three political scenarios', p. 22.
117. Holslag, 'The limits of China's global charm offensive'.
118. 'The China model: The Beijing consensus is to keep quiet', *The Economist*, 6 May 2010, at *http://www.economist.com/world/asia/displaystory.cfm?story_id=16059990*, accessed 11 October 2010.
119. Joseph Nye, 'Hemmed in by a lack of clarity', *Caixin Online*, 4 May 2010, at *http://english.caing.com/2010-05-04/100140779.html*, accessed 11 October 2010.
120. Joseph Nye, 'Think again: soft power', *Foreign Policy*, February 2006, web exclusive at *http://www.foreignpolicy.com/story/cms.php?story_id=3393*, accessed 11 October 2010, cited in Vuving, 'How soft power works', p. 3.
121. Christopher B. Whitney, David Shambaugh et al., *Soft Power in Asia: Results of a 2008 Multinational Survey of Public Opinion*, Chicago Council on Foreign Affairs, 2008, p. 5.
122. Li, C. 'China in the Year 2020: three political scenarios', p. 28.

123. d'Hooghe, *The Limits of China's Soft Power in Europe*, p. 36.
124. Nye, *Soft Power*, Chapter 1.
125. Whitney, Shambaugh et al., *Soft Power in Asia*, p. 3.
126. 'The China model: The Beijing consensus is to keep quiet'.
127. Joseph, Kurlantzick, *Charm Offensive: How China's Soft Power Is Transforming the World*, Yale University Press, New Haven, CT, 2007.
128. 'With the notable exception of Vietnam and to a lesser extent South Korea, majorities in the United States (68%), Japan (55%), and Indonesia (63%) all believe that their values converge either "a little" or to "no extent" with China.' Whitney, Shambaugh et al., *Soft Power in Asia*, p. 5.

Index

www.ingramcontent.com/pod-product-compliance
Ingram Content Group UK Ltd.
Pitfield, Milton Keynes, MK11 3LW, UK
UKHW020137290926
15471UKWH00003B/545

9 780081 017401